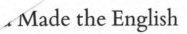
Made the English

How England Made the English

From Hedgerows to Heathrow

HARRY MOUNT

VIKING

an imprint of

PENGUIN BOOKS

VIKING

Published by the Penguin Group
Penguin Books Ltd, 80 Strand, London wc2r orl, England
Penguin Group (USA) Inc., 375 Hudson Street, New York, New York 10014, USA
Penguin Group (Canada), 90 Eglinton Avenue East, Suite 700, Toronto, Ontario, Canada m4p 2y3
(a division of Pearson Penguin Canada Inc.)
Penguin Ireland, 25 St Stephen's Green, Dublin 2, Ireland (a division of Penguin Books Ltd)
Penguin Group (Australia), 250 Camberwell Road, Camberwell, Victoria 3124, Australia
(a division of Pearson Australia Group Pty Ltd)
Penguin Books India Pvt Ltd, 11 Community Centre, Panchsheel Park, New Delhi – 110 017, India
Penguin Group (NZ), 67 Apollo Drive, Rosedale, Auckland 0632, New Zealand
(a division of Pearson New Zealand Ltd)
Penguin Books (South Africa) (Pty) Ltd, Block D, Rosebank Office Park,
181 Jan Smuts Avenue, Parktown North, Gauteng 2193, South Africa

Penguin Books Ltd, Registered Offices: 80 Strand, London wc2r orl, England

www.penguin.com

First published 2012

001

Copyright © Harry Mount, 2012

Typeset by Palimpsest Book Production Limited, Falkirk, Stirlingshire
Printed in Great Britain by Clays Ltd, St Ives plc

A CIP catalogue record for this book is available from the British Library

isbn: 978–0–670–91913–0

www.greenpenguin.co.uk

ALWAYS LEARNING   **PEARSON**

Sobered by excitement, Dick danced. He found in the girl a suggestion of all the pleasanter English things; the story of safe gardens ringed around by the sea was implicit in her bright voice and, as he leaned back to look at her, he meant what he said to her so sincerely that his voice trembled.

F. Scott Fitzgerald, *Tender is the Night* (1934)

To Tristram and Virginia Powell

Contents

Illustrations

Illustrations in the text

title page '1890' from Osbert Lancaster, *Progress at Pelvis Bay*, John Murray, 1936 (by permission of Clare Hastings).

page xxiv Rydal Water and Grasmere, the Lake District, 1835 (G. Pickering/W. J. Cooke).

page 5 'The British Character. Absence of the Gift of Conversation', by Pont, *Punch*, 18 September 1935 (copyright © The Cartoon Museum).

page 22 Cartoon by Nicolas Bentley, from George Mikes, *How to be an Alien*, 1946. Copyright © Bella Jones and the Estate of Nicolas Bentley.

page 29 Geological map of England (copyright © Arthur Banks).

page 71 Stonehenge, 1850 (C. Reiss).

page 80 Cartoon from Ronald Searle's *Merry England, etc.*, Perpetua Books, 1956 (copyright © the Estate of Ronald Searle). Reproduced with kind permission of the Estate of Ronald Searle and the Sayle Literary Agency.

page 102 The principal landowners' estates of west and north-west London.

page 112 Whitehaven, Cumbria, 1839 (G. Pickering and T. Jeavons).

page 125 The English countryside before enclosure – Laxton, Nottinghamshire, in 1635, from J. V. Beckett, *A History of Laxton – England's Last Open-Field Village*, Blackwell, 1989 (copyright © J. V. Beckett).

page 133 County varieties of field gates (copyright © Richard Allen).

Inset illustrations

Black and white inset

Colour inset

Great Britain, Phoenix House, 1953–4.

2. *Mr and Mrs Andrews* by Thomas Gainsborough, 1750 (copyright © National Gallery, London).

3. Hampton Court's ornamental chimneys (copyright © Historic Royal Palaces; photo: Robin Foster).

4. Durham (copyright © David C. Tomlinson/Getty Images).

5. *The Garden of Hampton House, with Mr and Mrs David Garrick Taking Tea* by Johan Zoffany, 1762 (copyright © The Garrick Club, London).

6. *A Gentleman and a Miner with a Specimen of Copper Ore* by John Opie (1761–1807) (copyright © The Royal Cornwall Museum/ Bridgeman Art Library).

7. *Stockwell Garden, South London, Spring 2004* by Virginia Powell (copyright © Virginia Powell).

8. *Canning Town* by Henry Lamb, 1947 (copyright © The Estate of Henry Lamb, Private Collection).

9. St Mary's, Cavendish, Suffolk (copyright © Country Life).

10. Arlington Row, Bibury, Gloucestershire (copyright © Country Life).

11. High Street, Puckeridge, Hertfordshire (copyright © Pictures of Britain: Peter Etteridge).

12. 'The Descriptive Map of London Poverty' by Charles Booth, 1889 (copyright © Museum of London).

13. *Train Landscape* by Eric Ravilious, 1939 (copyright © The Estate of Eric Ravilious/DACS).

14. 'Ermine Street/A15', Shell poster by David Gentleman, 1964 (copyright © Shell Brands International, image courtesy of Shell Art Collection).

15. 'Letchworth – the First Garden City', poster (copyright © First Garden City Heritage Museum).

16. 'Bridlington', LNER poster by Henry George Cawthorn, 1930 (copyright © SSPL/Getty Images).

17. Sir John Soane's monument to his wife, 1815 (copyright © Harry Mount).

18. Sir Giles Gilbert Scott's K6 phone box, designed in 1935 (copyright © Harry Mount).

19. 'Your Britain – Fight for it now', poster by Frank Newbould, 1942 (copyright © Imperial War Museum).

20. Still from *Withnail and I* (copyright © Handmade/BFI).

21. *The Road Across the Wolds* by David Hockney, 1997 (copyright © David Hockney).

Introduction

A friend of mine, who lives abroad, says there is one thing he really misses about London.

It's what he calls 'the unnoticed background'; things like the precise consistency, smell and look of the dead leaves we kick up on walks on Hampstead Heath on his holidays back in London.

Or the petrichor – the smell from the oils exuded by plants when it rains – and the light film of rainwater on Camden pavements.

He even misses what those pavements are made out of: the faint pink Aberdeen granite of hefty, pitted London kerbstones, flanked by smooth, dark-grey Caithness flagstones.

On his last trip back, my nostalgic friend got particularly distressed in a west London mews, when he saw that the Victorian granite setts had been replaced with asphalt.

We might not notice that background from day to day as acutely as my friend does – it's often people from abroad who have the best eye for the peculiar Englishness of England. But, inadvertently, that background has a huge effect on the sights and sounds of everyday life. And we certainly miss it when it changes or is removed altogether.

The change in that background is particularly noticeable on the Caribbean island of St Martin – or St Maarten, as the Dutch call it. St Martin is split into French and Dutch colonial halves; the smallest island in the world to be divided between two countries.

There is no physical border between the two territories. But you can hear it whenever you cross the invisible border, because the sound of the tyres on the roads is different – each territory has followed the different tarmac composition of its colonial motherland.

Soon you'll start noticing a similar effect in England – old-fashioned English asphalt, which melts in high temperatures, is gradually being replaced with French asphalt, which has a higher melting temperature.

A really sensitive driver would also notice the difference in sound between the average London road – which gets a fresh tarmac coat every thirty-seven years – and the average main road in Wales, resurfaced once every ninety-five years (and every 108 years for minor roads).

A tiny difference perhaps, but pile enough of those tiny differences on top of each other, and they end up affecting the lie of the land in a big way. Taken together, they produce the Englishness of England. And you don't have to be a feverish jingoist to spot that Englishness, wherever you are in the country.

If you took a flight from Newcastle to Rome, fell asleep and woke up, disorientated, not knowing how long you'd been dead to the world, a glimpse out of the cabin porthole would tell you in a second whether you'd passed over the Channel. Dover may only be a three-minute trip from Calais in a plane but the differences between the look of the English and French landscapes are still enormous.

Whether your view is of a field in County Durham or a bypass in Norfolk, there are a thousand things that signal to your brain, 'I am over England' – and not France, Switzerland or Italy – even if you'd be hard-pressed to separate each element and identify it.

These are the basic questions that this book tries to answer. If you look out of an English window – or a window flying over England – how do you know that you're in, or over, England?

And, what's more, how did our national characteristics create the lie of the land, and how did the lie of the land dictate our national characteristics?

The connection between landscape and character is so great that it affects most aspects of our behaviour, not least our diet.

In 2009, Professor Andy Taylor of Nottingham University carried out a study of distinct 'taste dialects' in different parts of Britain. Professor Taylor, who interviewed 13,000 people for the study, discovered that, in the same way that accents vary in different regions, so do regional tastes for certain foods.

According to Professor Taylor's findings, the Welsh, with their industrial past, like strong-tasting foods – such as onions, leeks and Worcestershire sauce – that cut through dirt and grime after a day's work in the mines.

In north-west England, they apparently go for moist comfort food while, across the Pennines, crunchy snacks are more popular. In chip shops in the north-east, you get chips and bits – all the burnt, crispy batter left over after frying. A hundred miles down the M62, in Lancashire, local taste veers towards chips and wet – the pure green liquid from mushy peas.

And so it goes on. Sweet, soft foods that are tasted on the front of the tongue and can be eaten with the hands – like naan bread – are popular in the Midlands. The Balti curry, cooked and served in a thin steel pan, with naan bread on the side, was invented in the so-called Balti Triangle, between Sparkhill and Moseley in Birmingham, in the early 1980s.

The Scots like soft, creamy food – ice cream is popular – and the south-west apparently goes for sweet flavours; thus the apples in Cornish pasties.

A similar geographical pattern crops up in British obesity maps. In December 2010, it was reported that the West Midlands, Britain's former industrial heartland, was the fattest place in Europe. Almost a third of the adults living in and around Birmingham were obese; a figure twice as high as the EU average.

In England's industrial heartland, extremely demanding physical jobs had been replaced by deskbound ones – fat-rich meals remained part of the culture, but they were no longer burnt off by industrial labour.

Diet and obesity have, in turn, had a distinct effect on life expectancy. In the south-east, men can expect to die, on average, at 79.7; in the north-west at 77.[1]

We are defined by our diet and surroundings in life; and in death, too. When the police were trying to identify 'Adam' (whose name was later identified as Ikpomwosa) – the torso of a black boy spotted floating in the Thames near the Tower of London in September 2001 – his diet was the best clue.

The amount of British food in his stomach and pollen in his lungs showed that he had only been in the country for a few days. His stomach also contained an unusual mix of plant extracts, traces of the toxic calabar bean, clay particles flecked with gold, and levels of strontium, copper and lead that were two and a half times normal levels. There were also traces of a potion with ingredients used in African magic; implying he'd been murdered in a ritual killing.

Further analysis of the minerals in his bones – again a result of diet and the soils where his food was grown – suggested that he was brought up somewhere around Benin City in Nigeria; where indeed he did turn out to come from.

None of this is an exact science. There's another more straightforward reason why curry and naan bread are popular in the Midlands – the car-making region provided work for Asian immigrants in the 1950s and 1960s. Still, the reason why so many cars were made in the Midlands is because the area was at the heart of the Industrial Revolution – a reflection of Britain's coal-rich geology.

The line between geography, geology, diet and national character still holds true. Britain – an island built of coal, surrounded by fish – can never get really cold or starve.

That theory has been tested by cheaper foreign coal, over-fishing and overseas snatching of our fish stocks. But the point remains broadly true – we rarely do starve or freeze to death. Our lives and deaths – and characters – are, to a great extent, produced by our surroundings.

On a wider scale, the whole northern hemisphere – its history and the character of its people – is greatly influenced by a serendipitous combination of shallow minerals, easily harvested hard timber, fertile soil, plenty of water sources, and few droughts, parasites, natural disasters, predators or endemic diseases. This beneficial combination further suited the growth of stable, property-owning democracies. Areas that aren't so blessed with natural benefits like this – such as Africa – inevitably find it harder to develop and progress politically.[2]

Any attempt to relate this two-way traffic between the look of England and the English character – and how each affected the other – is mined with difficulties.

There are thousands of factors behind a national character, presuming you accept such a thing exists in the first place; thousands more that create the way a country looks.

I have concentrated on four factors: England's geography, geology, history and weather.

You can point to pretty strong basic effects of our geographical position on our character. At its simplest interpretation, cold weather requires thicker clothes, more time spent indoors and more fuel. An island nation is not only relatively easy to defend; islanders will also see less of neighbours who live across, say, a 21-mile channel of water, than those who live in countries divided only by terrestrial borders.

It works the other way, too – our surroundings are produced

by our character. This is a harder route to track. You can definitively say that, in a cold place, people wrap themselves up in warm clothes. It's harder to show that a particular country's inhabitants are perhaps unusually sensitive, and so in turn produce a particularly pretty national landscape.

But you can draw general conclusions along these lines. Nikolaus Pevsner, the German émigré architectural historian, connected the decent English home, the temperate climate and the moderate politics, to disappointing English art – and our failure to produce a Bach, Beethoven, Brahms, Michelangelo, Titian or Rembrandt.[3]

The English may not be romantic, passionate or imaginative, but they are objective, pragmatic and good at close observation; that's why, Pevsner thought, English artists like Gainsborough and Reynolds were so good at honest portraits. In the absence of great art, the English distinguished themselves instead with irrepressible humour, architectural quirkiness, and a love of the pastoral and the domestic. It's telling that Gainsborough's most popular picture – Mr and Mrs Andrews – is half double portrait, half rural landscape, in a landscape-shaped frame.

Pevsner was particularly impressed with the quiet, sedate, understated English terraced house – dependent on proportions rather than ornament, on refined decoration rather than inventiveness.

George Orwell went further than Pevsner, saying that the English completely lack artistic ability except when it comes to literature – the only art that can't cross frontiers. Apart from Shakespeare, said Orwell, the best English poets were barely known on the Continent.[4]

Orson Welles, playing Harry Lime, made a similar generalization about national character in *The Third Man* (1949) in an improvised speech to Holly Martins, played by Joseph Cotten, on the Prater wheel in Vienna.

'In Italy, for thirty years under the Borgias, they had warfare, terror, murder and bloodshed, but they produced Michelangelo, Leonardo da Vinci and the Renaissance,' said Welles, 'In Switzerland, they had brotherly love, they had 500 years of democracy and peace – and what did that produce? The cuckoo clock.'

(Welles later admitted, 'When the picture came out, the Swiss very nicely pointed out to me that they've never made any cuckoo clocks.')

I don't completely agree with Pevsner. There are English artists and architects who come close to the best Continental Europeans. But both Pevsner and Welles ring true when it comes to their broad generalizations about a national look shared by buildings, art and – I would add – landscape.

Another generalization to consider is the question of English versus British. There has been endless discussion about what we mean by English as opposed to British, but this book is focused primarily on English rural and urban landscapes, and on the English character. There are differences between England and Northern Ireland, Wales and Scotland, and their inhabitants, which could fill a book of their own. I didn't want to get bogged down in those relatively small, if compelling, differences. Instead, I wanted to talk about the differences that separate England from the rest of the world (the vast majority of which, in fact, England shares with Northern Ireland, Wales and Scotland).

Many things I say about England apply elsewhere – the clouds that drift over Cardiff often cross the Welsh border, too. And I will still occasionally refer to Northern Ireland, Wales and Scotland for comparison. I will also sometimes refer to Britain as opposed to England, when the relevant statistic is only available for the larger area.

Before picking out what the English look is, we must distinguish between the two most powerful forces behind it: natural force and manmade force.

Natural forces created the first layer of modern England – the mountains, hills, rivers, lakes, forests and coastline.

And then came the second layer – the manmade one. Most of England – rural and urban – has been occupied by man for over a thousand years. A stroll through any part of it shows man's handprint in practically every century; a handprint usually made for a practical purpose – to enclose a field with hedges, say, or to carve a railway line through a hill.

Even landscapes that look untouched by man have often been sculpted by him. The smooth fells of the Lake District have been grazed by Herdwick sheep for more than a thousand years; its fields are divided by drystone walls laid by farmers in the eighteenth century; even the water level of its lakes is determined by the demands of Manchester's half a million residents for fresh water.

Sculpted by man and sheep – Rydal Water and Grasmere, the Lake District, 1835.

Man's handprint can be mammoth, if concealed by great age – like the first removal of the forests and woods, with much of them cut down before the Romans turned up; or the late-eighth-century Offa's Dyke, running from the coast at Prestatyn, Flintshire, down to the Severn at Sedbury, Gloucestershire.

The Fens were transformed from swampy marsh into a fertile spot by Dutch engineers who drained the land in the seventeenth century, leaving behind half of the best agricultural land in England; its fertility provided by marine silt, ancient fen vegetation and fen peat.

In fact, all four distinct areas of Norfolk, including the Fens, were sculpted by man. The Breckland was once thick forest, which, cleared in the Iron Age, led to the erosion of sands to produce heathland. The Wash, created by glaciation, used to stretch much further inland, until seventeenth-century drainage schemes produced more fertile land around Downham Market.

And the Broads are the only Anglo-Saxon archaeological site that has become a huge modern holiday camp. Originally, they consisted of around fifty peat pits, dug out from the tenth to the thirteenth centuries, with the removal of around 900 million cubic feet of peat.[5] After the decline in peat-burning, thanks to increased coal imports, the pits were flooded. They were further concealed by higher sea levels that came with a warmer climate after 1250. Then, after a big flood in 1287, the Broads were actively flooded to produce fisheries. Man and nature had accidentally co-operated in producing a landscape that now looks utterly natural.

Human modifications are often hidden deep beneath this apparently natural disguise. The moors of northern England, and the Scottish Highlands, have more heather than anywhere else in Europe, in order to boost the numbers of grouse, the much valued game birds. The heather is intensively cultivated and burnt back in rectangular strips – producing what look like miniature fields. The burning is done in rotation, to produce a variety of age and height in the heather: grouse use the taller patches for shelter, while they eat the fresh, young shoots.

Before this manicured cultivation was introduced, the moors had patches of wild heather – but not in the same abundance, or with the same regularity of appearance. Long, long before, much of the moorland was part of the ancient wildwood.

Those seemingly ancient grouse moor landscapes were in fact created as recently as the nineteenth century, when the sport grew increasingly popular, for several reasons: the invention of the breech-loading shotgun in the early nineteenth century; Queen Victoria's acquisition of Balmoral in 1854; and the introduction of trains to carry the sporting rich overnight from London to the north.

The grouse moor look took off across Britain, and the world. Surrey heathland became fashionable in the nineteenth century because it reminded Victorians of the Scottish Highlands. It's no accident, either, that parts of New Zealand look like Scotland; Scottish immigrants planted the hills with heather in the nineteenth century, to bring back memories of the old country.

This similarity between landscapes – on opposite sides of the world – depends on a precise combination of geology, soil, flora and fauna, as well as the human will to shape the land in a certain way.

Look at New Zealand on a globe, and it shares plenty of characteristics with Britain: as an archipelago not too far from a pole, close to a big land mass, largely populated by English-speaking, white humans of Western European extraction.

With the best will in the world towards New Zealand, the British archipelago got a slightly better deal. It's that much closer to the neighbouring land mass, and that land mass – Europe – has for the last 2,500 years been a hotbed of intellectual, commercial, religious and scientific innovation.

Examine Britain on a globe, and it is serendipitously situated. Not only does it look east towards Europe, but also south to Africa and west to North America. All those places are made that much more accessible from Britain because of our island nature. The logistics of the British Empire would have been hard to arrange from anywhere else.

Even if you rarely leave Britain's shores, it is still unusually blessed, in its geology, geography, history and in the element that has done more than any other to mould England – and the English. And that is the weather.

1. Weather Report

He had a horror of showing white hairy shin between sock-top and trouser cuff when sitting down, legs crossed – it was in some ways the besetting and prototypical English sartorial sin.

William Boyd, *Ordinary Thunderstorms* (2010)

Our weather has stayed much the same for centuries, global warming notwithstanding. It shouldn't be surprising that related national stereotypes have remained consistent, too.

In letters sent home from the Vindolanda fort at Hexham, Northumberland, near Hadrian's Wall, in around AD 100, Roman legionaries long for fine Italian Massic wine, garlic, fish, lentils, olives and olive oil. And they complain about the food the Picts eat – pork fat, cereal, spices and venison. Today's Geordie diet is still some distance from the Mediterranean one.

What's more, these Mediterranean legionaries, marooned at the northern edge of the Roman Empire, were freezing cold the whole time.

One letter from southern Gaul – the blissfully hot south of France – is addressed to a poor shivering legionary at Vindolanda, listing the contents of the accompanying package: 'Paria udonum ab Sattua solearum duo et subligariorum duo' – socks, two pairs of sandals and two pairs of underpants.

Just like the rest of us, Roman soldiers needed underpants and thick socks in the frozen north, particularly if they were sun-kissed, olive-skinned Italians and Frenchmen; not robust, barely clothed Geordies, cheerfully exposing their stark white, goose-fleshed torsos to the easterly winds that whip straight from Scandinavia into Northumberland across the North Sea.

Nothing changes very much, as a quick survey of outfits in Newcastle's Bigg Market on a gloomy Saturday night in February – compared with those worn by Italians for a sunlit winter stroll around the Colosseum – will tell you.

In AD 98, the Roman historian Tacitus said of England, 'Caelum crebris imbribus ac nebulis foedum; asperitas frigorum abest' – 'The sky is obscured by constant rain and cold, but it never gets bitterly cold.'

Tacitus was right – our climate is a temperate, rainy one. While London only gets 1,500 hours of sunshine a year (and Glasgow and Belfast, 1,250 hours), Rome basks in 2,500 hours of annual sun. Northumberland – where those shivering legionaries were stationed – gets just 1,350 hours.

It's even worse in winter, when our northern daylight hours are that much shorter – in the whole of January, London gets forty-five hours of sunshine; Rome 130.

Our national character is dictated by figures like this. They also dictate the way the country looks – and the way we look, the way we dress, the shade of our complexion. Some linguistics experts have even suggested that the differences between the American and English accent were produced by the differing climates.[1]

Brightly coloured parrots and tigers live in tropical climates; brown, black, white and grey animals – sheep, cows, rabbits – are better off further north.[2] And so it is with humans – we look different as we go north.

Exposed white shins aren't a problem for natives of southern countries; southern skins never go lobster red. The strange English taste for being toasted to an uneven shade of scarlet on their summer holidays is a direct product of not getting much sun at home.

'You get used to eating caviar and, at some point, it begins to taste as ordinary as anything else,' Boris Becker said in 2011.

The same goes for sunshine – when you're abroad, you don't go in frantic search of what you already have at home; you seek out what you don't get enough of.

Generous supplies of southern heat mean southern Europeans don't rush to grab every second in the sun; or fling open the windows on cold winter days when a watery sun reveals itself for a moment or two, and you can see your breath indoors. Nor do they dress quite so badly – or go topless, as many Englishmen do – when the sun comes out.

In Mediterranean countries, the heat is so stitched into their souls that, in summer, they think, 'I'll wear my normal June/July/August clothes,' which means light trousers, long-sleeved cotton shirts and loafers. Those used to hotter climates realize that covering up in light cotton makes you cooler, in both senses, than exposing raw flesh to the sun.

Meanwhile, the English think, 'God, it's hot. Let's wear something special/ludicrous to celebrate, something that exposes as much skin as possible.'

The odd thing is that the English invented elegant, cool summerwear: linen shirts, trousers and suits. But that was when they spent a long time – often whole lifetimes – living in hotter countries. Dealing with a blistering sun on a daily basis means you're wary of it, rather than hungrily chasing it, mad dogs and Englishmen apart. Victorian Englishmen learnt to absorb the prospect of heat into their everyday dressing routine, and do their best to avoid it.

Our poor modern fashion sense isn't helped either by our northern puritanical streak: a fear of showing off that bleeds into a fear of dressing well, even in cold weather.

The climate also explains the relative lack of shutters in England as opposed to the Mediterranean – who needs to keep the sun out over here? That's why our shutters are on the inside, if and when we have them – they're used for security at night, not for providing shade during the day.

In hot southern countries, you open the inner windows and leave the outer shutters closed; in colder northern countries, you open the inner shutters in the morning, and leave the outer windows closed for most of the year.

The English awkwardness in company is also related to our climate. We simply don't get out as much as southern Europeans: their warmer climates and longer winter days induce a chattier, more outdoors existence.

Our weather means we've never really embraced the Continental café society, envisaged by Tony Blair with the relaxation of licensing hours in 2005. The French and Spanish sip wine gently through the warm night, punctuating the evening with a leisurely passeggiata; we drink beer heavily, furiously and statically, huddled up indoors against the cold, desperately using drink to fuel our stilted conversations.

Bad weather explains our constitutional gloom, our tendency to play things down, and our inability to work up much excitement over anything. All human beings are sub-tropical in origin: we only left the warmth of Africa several hundred thousand years ago. With our sun-kissed, atavistic DNA, we're still not too pleased with the grey, damp life and the short winter days that come with living more than 50 degrees north of the equator.

Because of our gloomy, northern climate, we just can't do piazza life. Although we've had pedestrianized streets for almost four centuries – the Pantiles in Tunbridge Wells was the first in England, dating from 1638 – we're not well-practised at staying calm in large open spaces after dark.

'The British Character. Absence of the Gift of Conversation', by Pont in
Punch, 18 September 1935.

Come closing time, and pedestrianized streets across the country – like Carfax, in Oxford – become pedestrianized fighting
areas. (To be fair, despite our extreme public drunkenness, we're
much less drunk in our cars than people in most other countries
in the world, thanks to Draconian drink-driving laws; there are
many fewer scratched cars on the street here than abroad.)

Our fevered drinking habits are also related to our relationship with the opposite sex: the English male is particularly bad
at talking to the English female. That awkwardness has grown
out of a long history of English gender segregation. And that
has a great deal to do with early industrialization, itself related
to England's geology.

In 1985, a newspaper compared the daily lives of manual

workers from Liverpool and Turin, in the light of the Heysel
Stadium disaster that year. Thirty-nine Juventus fans were killed
when Liverpool fans rushed towards them before the European
Cup Final, causing a dilapidated retaining wall to collapse on
top of the Italians.

The Liverpool manual worker lived off meat, battered fish,
chips, crisps and beer; he spent all day at work, and most of the
evening at the pub with his male friends. He didn't, though,
drink at lunchtime – as is the case with all English classes when
at work, except on special occasions. On sunny days in St James's
Square, central London, where I often have lunch, along with
hundreds of office workers, not a single one has an alcoholic
drink with their sandwich.

Meanwhile, the Turin worker went home at lunchtime for
pasta and veal, washed down with a carafe of red wine shared
with his wife, and then spent the evening with his family.

With work days like this, Italians end up talking much more
to their wives, and their children, than the English do – not just
because they are generally chattier, but also because they physi-
cally spend more time in the same room as them.

In England, the Industrial Revolution – the earliest in the
world – dictated the bad diet of that Liverpool manual worker;
as it still does the inability to get fresh, local food in our supermarkets; and our inability, too, to set up good, cheap restaurants.

It's been like this for a while. In 1808, the Romantic poet
Robert Southey – writing under the pseudonym of Don
Manuel Alvarez Espriella, a supposed Spanish tourist in England – said, 'Everywhere you find both meat and vegetables in
the same insipid state . . . Nothing is so detestable as an Englishman's coffee.'[3]

Rural peasant economies on the Continent – concentrated in
those areas and countries which, unlike the north of England,
weren't rich in fossil fuels and metal ores, or hadn't yet been

industrialized – were based around smallholdings farmed by families.

Families breakfasted, lunched and dined together, either at home, like the modern Turin worker, or in the field, helped by a climate that was more conducive to al fresco living.

To break out of this peasant economy so early, as England did, was exceptional. Sir Michael Postan, the Russian-born professor, was staggered when he first came to England after the Russian Revolution, and saw the countryside: where were all the peasants with their square-faced bottles, he wondered.[4]

While Russian farmworkers were still working the fields, alongside their families, a century ago, the English worker was leaving home at dawn to go off to the factory, mine, mill or, increasingly, to the office, seeing less and less of his wife and children.

A peasant life is dictated by the seasons, too – with long periods of winter inactivity, and the working day brought to an end by dusk. Industrialization – together with gaslight and electric light – meant the working day could stretch beyond dusk and carry on regardless of the seasons.

As the English agricultural economy turned industrial in the late eighteenth century, and common land and smallholdings were increasingly enclosed for commercial agriculture, the direct family connection with the food-producing land broke down.

Food was increasingly canned and mass-produced over here, while peasant smallholdings continued across the Continent. And eating straight from the land meant eating freshly.

English factory workers not only didn't come home until the evening, but also, after tea, they promptly packed off to the pub with their male colleagues until closing time.

Drinking-induced segregation increased after 1830, when the Beer Act – introduced by the Prime Minister, the Duke of

Wellington – removed all tax on beer, in order to divert people from the horrors of Gin Lane. Within a year, 31,000 new pubs were built. And those pubs remained almost exclusively male for over a century; right up until the 1960s, 'nice' women wouldn't go near a pub.

There are now 60,000 pubs left in Britain, although that number is rapidly falling, at the rate of forty a week. Still, though, we largely remain beer-drinkers, even if wine is catching up: the average Briton drinks more than 13 litres of pure alcohol a year, the sixteenth-highest figure in the world rankings.[5] Of that figure, 43 per cent comes from beer – what you'd expect in a hop-growing, northern country, as opposed to a vine-growing, southern one. Only 30 per cent of our alcohol intake comes from wine, 21 per cent from spirits.

Gender segregation deepened with the Second World War and its aftermath. Men were necessarily separated from their wives and families during the fighting. Once they got home, six years' absence had its effect. After the war, sales of garden sheds soared, as returning servicemen desperately sought a refuge from the shock of domestic life.

Plenty of us have stayed in the shed ever since – there are 11.5 million sheds in Britain, more per head than anywhere else in the world; and we spend £8.5bn on DIY every year, far more proportionally than other European countries.

Throw in schools that were largely segregated until the twentieth century – and the cult English taste for sending children away to single-sex boarding schools – and you begin to see how entrenched gender segregation is; or at least used to be. Even if schools are largely desegregated now, as are the pub and the workplace, you don't wipe out the sociological effects of several centuries of enforced segregation that easily.

Generations of boys and girls sitting in different classrooms, of men drinking in all-male pubs and working in all-male offices, mines and factories, have a powerful effect on Homo Britannicus: he can only really socialize comfortably in the company of Femina Britannica when drunk.

We have the same awkwardness with anyone exotic or foreign, thanks to our long periods of isolation, shut away on our cold island, with its empty streets during working hours, its long working days and its grim, gauche approach to social life.

The attitude was spotted a long time ago. 'The locals are not very social to strangers,' Robert Southey wrote of the English in 1808.[6]

Only now, though, is this more honest picture of the awkward, aggressive, drunken English – as opposed to the polite, tea-drinking obsessive queuers of legend – beginning to feed into the foreign picture of us.

'Liverpool and Manchester are as depressing places as you're likely to find anywhere,' reported Road Junky Travel, an American website, in 2010, 'Whilst the locals can be entertaining on a good day, the weather is shit, heroin is epidemic (but meth is catching on) and you've got a better chance of thugs putting you in hospital for no apparent reason than in any other part of England – and that's saying something.'

The weather also dictates our clumsy approach to sex. In an appropriately titled study of the English – *La Vie en gris*, or 'The Grey Life' – the philosopher Jacques Derrida compared 'the Englishman's inability to escape from the straitjacket of his inhibitions' with the 'skipping Frenchman's inability to understand that the sex act is more satisfying if accompanied by a dark edge of shame'.

That attitude might explain why most public statues in France are by male sculptors, of women. In England, they're mostly by men, of men. Nothing homosexual there – just a greater comfort taken by one Englishman in the company of another; while Frenchmen are happier in the company of women.

Italian men – brought up by extremely affectionate mothers
– are that much more comfortable among women, too. Encouraged by their mothers to think they are the most wonderful men
in the world, they don't suffer from a lack of confidence in talking to the opposite sex.

Add in the English awkwardness with children; plus the phenomenon that the further north you go, the more all nationalities
drink; and it all makes for a group of people who reach for the
bottle to take the edge off the awkwardness.

English weather may not be extreme, but that doesn't stop it
being unique; and uniquely accommodating to plants, animals
and humans.

Within the gentle extremes of our temperate climate, there is
extreme variety in weather conditions. It helps that Britain is a
longish, thinnish island, stretching roughly north–south across
several different climate zones.

That long, thin shape means you get varying extremes of
temperature across the country, whether you move east or west
towards the coast, or north towards cooler weather. Spring
warms up the country at different times, too, moving north at
roughly walking pace.

Differences in climate across England are also produced by
tiny, precise, geological idiosyncrasies. Torquay's seafront palm
trees can only survive because they're protected by the vast
expanse of Dartmoor and Exmoor to the north. Eastbourne is
less windswept than neighbouring areas of Sussex, because it
lies in the shelter of the 600ft hills of Beachy Head. Tennyson
said of his house at Farringford, Freshwater, Isle of Wight, that
it was 'Something betwixt a pasture and a park / Saved from sea
breezes by a hump of down.'

England's urban garden squares benefit from an idiosyncratic microclimate, too. Terraced houses on all sides shelter

the squares in winter; and the squares enjoy early warmth at the beginning of summer because of the greater heat of city centres. Eccleston Square, central London – nurtured for thirty years by a particularly talented plantsman, Roger Phillips, and his team – can accommodate 200 camellias, 200 climbing roses, 150 shrub roses and 30 peonies.

And the reverse is true, too: some parts of England are decidedly unsheltered. Centrepoint, the tower block at the east end of Oxford Street, in London, has its own bleak microclimate. A near-constant wind swirls round the building, even when there's just a gentle breeze a few yards away.

Across the country there are pockets of extreme cold – frost hollows – where dense cold air sinks into natural basins, producing very low, localized temperatures in winter. You can spot these frost hollows in early autumn – leaves fall earlier in them than higher up the valley. There are notable frost hollows in Redhill, Surrey, and Rickmansworth, Hertfordshire, which, despite being only fifteen miles from central London, can have temperatures that are 15°C lower.[7] Rickmansworth's frost pocket is produced by a railway embankment which stops cold air draining from the valley.

But these are rare cold spots in a country with an unusually benevolent climate. And the most powerful factor in producing that climate and the Englishness of English weather – and much of the Englishness of the English – is the Gulf Stream.

London is on much the same latitude (51°30'28"N) as Calgary in Canada, Kiev in the Ukraine and Irkutsk in Siberia. It could never have become the greatest, most famous city on earth if it had shared the weather conditions of those places – which aren't warmed by the Gulf Stream. Calgary was cold enough to hold the Winter Olympics in 1988; Irkutsk, on the shores of frozen Lake Baikal, has a sub-Arctic climate, with temperatures settling at around −19°C in January.

The Gulf Stream is one of a series of wind-driven sea currents dictated by so-called thermohaline circulation, which distributes warm water from the Gulf of Mexico. In the Gulf, the air gets so hot and moist that it cooks up the hurricanes which smash into the Gulf Coast, as Hurricane Katrina did in 2005, obliterating New Orleans.

Our weather system comes from the same source, but it's been tamed by the time it hits our shores; between August and November, the remnants of a Gulf hurricane occasionally give Britain a light battering, courtesy of the Gulf Stream, as Hurricane Katia did in September 2011. A month later, Katia carried a tree trunk all the way from the Florida Everglades to Bude, Cornwall, along Gulf Stream currents. Occasional coconuts and turtles, too, bob up and down all the way from the Gulf and end up in the Outer Hebrides, transported by those thermohaline sea currents.

It's because of the Gulf Stream that daffodils bloom in Cornwall in spring before all other counties; it's why parts of Cornwall don't get their first frost until December, while other bits of the country get hit in early October. For the same reason, azaleas, rhododendrons and camellias do well in the county.

The Gulf Stream is the reason, too, why swallows fly from Africa as far north as Britain, in late spring. It explains why we have such a wide range of bird life across the country: our climate accommodates wintering birds from the north and summering birds from the south. Of the 14 million seabirds in Europe, 7 million of them – over twenty-five species – breed on the British coast.

Those warm Gulf Stream currents move up the eastern seaboard of America, to become the Atlantic Drift, the wellspring of our prevailing south-westerly wind. South-westerly winds often bring wind and rain but, still, they are warmer than the rarer east winds – which come straight from freezing Russia, with not much in the way to stop them. Wormleighton in Warwickshire – perched 500 feet above sea level, the first high ground west of the Urals – is blasted by a good deal of that cold air.

The south-westerly wind has had an enormous, if subtle, effect on how England looks, and how the English behave.

It's because of the south-westerlies that Staines and Runny-mede, south-west of Heathrow, are blighted by aircraft noise. Planes take off into the wind – on runways pointing south-west – to create greater lift.

That prevailing south-westerly wind across London used to mean that polluted air was spread east across the poorer half of the city. The phenomenon can be seen in Charles Booth's 1889 poverty maps.[8] The blackened areas on the map, denominating 'Lowest class. Vicious, semi-criminal', are prevalent in east London; the yellow areas – 'Upper-middle and Upper classes. Wealthy' – are concentrated in the west around Kensington.

When the police first published the details of crimes committed in different areas of Britain in February 2011, the pattern remained much the same in London – with deeper poverty and more crime in the east.

Immigrants have always tended to arrive in the poorer eastern parts of London – first the Huguenots in the seventeenth century, then the Jews in the late nineteenth century and, more recently, the Bangladeshis. Thistlewaite Road, in Hackney, where Harold Pinter grew up in the 1930s in a largely Jewish area, is now mostly populated by Bangladeshis.

In London's case, the effect is exacerbated by the Thames: east is downstream, and downstream is always the gritty, maritime, dockside end of any city; upstream tends to be up in the hills, more deeply embedded in the countryside, and richer.

From the late Middle Ages onwards, the Thames-side palaces and country houses of London spread in a westerly direction away from the city; they included Hampton Court, Richmond

Palace, Osterley Park and Syon House. The western suburbs – in Surrey, Berkshire and Buckinghamshire, in particular – were valued in the nineteenth century for their fresh air, purified by the south-westerlies; ever since, they have been the heartland of rich suburbia.

For decades, Essex and Suffolk, to the east of London, have been less fashionable than Oxfordshire and Wiltshire – there aren't many Wessex Girl jokes. That's partly because of the prevailing winds; partly because the eastern counties lead to nowhere but the sea. Counties to the north and west of London open up the great expanses of the north, Scotland, Wales and the West Country. As a result, modern transport links out of London are better to the north and west than to the east.

Oxfordshire grew prosperous in the Middle Ages because it was en route from wool-rich Gloucestershire to the port of London. Rutland, with more grand churches per square mile than any other county, benefited from drovers' roads running to all four points of the compass.

The east–west division goes for other cities, too. If you want to head for the smarter part of any British city, you're usually best off walking into the wind. Towards the end of the eighteenth century, the eastern side of Leeds was filled with factories, while the western edge was upmarket and residential.

South-westerlies mean that harbour walls, quays and breakwaters – like the Cobb at Lyme Regis – are placed at right-angles to the prevailing wind. Sea walls run from north-west to south-east to protect boats from the wind that comes tearing in from the Atlantic. For much the same reason, the spa town of Malvern was settled on the north-eastern side of the Malvern Hills, to shelter it from the south-westerlies.

It was because of prevailing south-westerlies, too, that 2012 Olympics planners messed up their PR campaign in Portland, Dorset, home to the British sailing team. Olympic flags on the edge of the town, welcoming visitors to Portland, were almost always blown in the wrong direction by the south-westerlies. New arrivals had to read the writing on the flags backwards; it only read the right way to people leaving town.[9]

South-westerlies meant the British Navy has always been stationed at the western end of the Channel – in Falmouth and Plymouth – to get the benefit of the prevailing wind. The British Western Squadron was stationed off the western approaches to the English Channel in the eighteenth and nineteenth centuries, too. With the wind behind the fleet, it could control the whole Channel. Any German or Dutch ship coming in the other direction had to fight against the wind.

A Spanish or French fleet coming up the west coast of the Continent was also at the mercy of the Western Squadron. When the Spanish Armada attacked in 1588, it was wrecked on the coast of Ireland and Scotland by the south-west wind – which destroyed five times more ships than Elizabeth I's navy did. As a result, it was called 'the Protestant Wind', and a commemorative medal was struck, stamped with the words, 'He blew with His winds, and they were scattered.'

Rain carried by those south-westerlies collides with the mountains and hills of highland Britain, leaving lowland Britain with much less rain. While the south-east coast gets 1,800 hours of sun a year, the Western Highlands get 1,000 hours. The moist air is forced higher and becomes less dense as the barometric pressure drops. The less dense the air, the cooler the temperature, the less moisture it can support, and the excess moisture condenses into rain.

Once the air hits the lee of the mountains, this process works in reverse: the air sinks, gets warmer and can carry more moisture. A rain shadow is formed – meaning it's wet to the west, dry to the east. That's why Manchester's annual rainfall, in the north-west, is 33.67 inches; and London's, 23.3 inches.

The effect is heightened if the descending air sucks in drier air from above the rain clouds. This is the föhn effect – named after the *Föhn* wind which produces oddly warm weather in the northern Alps. The föhn effect means the warmest place in Britain in January is Llandudno – seven of the last eight warmest January days in the last century have happened here. It also explains why parts of north Northumberland, the Somerset and Devon coast north of Exmoor, and the North Yorkshire coast near Whitby can be unusually warm in winter.

That pattern – of a gloomy north-west and a sunny south-east – can change in May, when the prevailing wind often turns into a north-easterly: then London gets 200 hours of sun over the month, and Tiree, in the Inner Hebrides, gets 235 hours. The north-easterlies bring cloud to eastern England and Scotland, while western Scotland is sheltered by the Highlands.

It's only because of the Gulf Stream's warming effect that, despite being so far north, we can have such northerly, extreme changes in season and daylight hours, and yet survive comfortably.

In 2003, David Hockney moved to Bridlington, in his native Yorkshire, after spending the previous twenty-five years in Los Angeles. There are only minor seasonal differences in daylight hours in California; and minor differences in the light effects on the landscape. But, in the north of our northerly island, those differences are enormous. Bridlington gets extremely short days in winter and 3.30 a.m. dawns in summer; the time when Hockney gets up, having gone to bed at dusk, in order to maximize his painting hours.

'If you're in my kind of business you'd be a fool to sleep through that, especially if you live right on the east coast, where there are no mountains or buildings to block the sun,' says Hockney, 'Artists can't work office hours, can they? I go to bed when the sun goes down and wake when it starts getting light, because I leave the curtains open.'[10]

The variety of English weather conditions dictates which

parts of England are heavily settled, which parts better suited to agriculture, which best left to semi-wilderness.

Despite that variety, a uniquely temperate combination of geographical, geological and meteorological factors makes every corner of the British Isles habitable by man.

Few places in England have such hostile climates that you couldn't spend the night or build a house there. You might not want to live on the slopes of Scafell Pike, England's tallest mountain, 3,209 feet above Cumbria – but it's habitable all the same. You simply couldn't live on Mount Everest; almost ten times higher, at 29,029 feet.

Some places, like the forests of the Weald (derived from *Wald*, German for forest) in Sussex and Kent, or the marshy Somerset Levels, were once a lot more inhospitable than they are now. But even these more impenetrable places were eventually settled in the Middle Ages, long after the Romans had colonized more habitable spots.

Broadly speaking, hospitable weather conditions, easily fordable rivers, and a shortage of marshes and unconquerable mountains made England the rich, advanced country it just about remains today; and one filled with settlements stretching back thousands of years.

That's largely why England is now the sixth most densely populated major country in the world, with 401 people per square kilometre. England, with fewer wild places than Wales or Scotland, is particularly packed. Taken as a whole, the United Kingdom drops to the seventeenth most overcrowded country in the world, with 255 people per square kilometre. Only Bangladesh, Taiwan, South Korea, Lebanon and Rwanda are more crowded than England.[11]

One of the reasons we can all squeeze in together without too much trouble is our kind, forgiving climate – we just don't do big weather.

Yes, we might get 'Fen Twisters' – in June 2010, two 80ft-high, 100 mph tornadoes tore across ten miles of Norfolk. Trees were cut down and a trampoline was flicked into power lines, sparking a blackout for 300 homes. There are about thirty tornadoes a year across Britain – more per square mile than anywhere else in the world; and there are more tornadoes in Norfolk than anywhere else in Britain. But, still, it's hardly on the level of the death and destruction of the American Midwest.

Our extremes of temperature aren't really that extreme, either. The hottest British temperature recorded was 101.3°F in Brogdale, Kent, on 10 August 2003. The lowest was −16.96°F, on 11 February 1895, and 30 December 1995, both in Braemar, Aberdeenshire, and 30 December 1995, in Altnaharra, in the Highlands. The strongest gust of wind was 142 mph, in Fraserburgh, Kent, on 13 February 1989.

Compare these figures with the hottest place on earth, Al 'Aziziyah, Libya, which hit 136°F in September 1922; or the coldest known temperature, −128.6°F in Vostok Station, Antarctica, in 1983; or the windiest, 253 mph on Barrow Island, Australia, during Cyclone Olivia in 1996.

The wettest day in English history was recorded during the Cumbrian floods of November 2009, when 12.3 inches of rain fell on the Met Office's gauging station at Seathwaite in a single day. On 16 June 1995, in the wettest place on earth, Cherrapunjee, in the north-eastern Indian state of Meghalaya, it rained 61.53 inches in a day.

In 2008, the biggest earthquake in Britain in twenty-five years hit Market Rasen in Lincolnshire. Measuring 5.3 on the Richter Scale, it caused damage costing £10m. England has 300–400 earthquakes a year but, because we're so far from the major tectonic shifts around the mid-Atlantic Ridge, the seismic effect is minimal.

Not very nice for those who have to pay for it, but still nothing compared to, say, the effects of Hurricane Katrina, which killed 1,836 people and caused damage worth £60bn; or the earthquake that struck Japan in March 2011, which killed more than 10,000 people, and measured 8.9 on the Richter Scale.

It's the gentleness of English weather, combined with its unpredictability, that makes it such a popular subject for conversation.

A Croatian friend of mine, who has lived in Oxford for a decade, still doesn't take her coat with her on unusually warm spring days. She is so used to the constant weather in her home town, Split, that she still thinks that, if it's warm in the morning here, it'll be warm in the afternoon. She's often disappointed.

In Croatia – and other countries where the weather functions like clockwork – there isn't much point in discussing the utterly predictable. The Croatian equivalent of the *Daily Telegraph* wouldn't sell many copies if it splashed its front page with the headline, 'It's Blooming Marvellous', in a warm summer. Croatian summers are always warm, and rarely warm in a surprising way.

British newspapers are full of stories about the weather because it is so unreliable, if undramatic. Even the south-westerly wind – our prevailing wind – is never a dead cert: around 35 per cent of our winds are south-westerlies; with south-easterlies and north-westerlies each accounting for 20 per cent of the total; and north-easterlies taking up the remaining 25 per cent.

It's because of that unpredictability, too, that we talk so appreciatively of sudden warm snaps, that we strip off and dive into the sea the moment the sun comes out – we know it's not going to last. If you're in Croatia, you can take your time undressing – you know it's going to be sunny, not only in half an hour, but also tomorrow and the day after that, throughout the summer.

The gentleness and unpredictability of our climate make us that much more interested in it, and appreciative of it, too. If nature has a pack of deadly hurricanes and tsunamis up its sleeve, it's something to be tamed, feared and guarded against. If it's full of soft showers and surprising glimpses of gentle sunshine, it is a thing to be treasured, and recorded.

No other country has done so much to record its weather, and for so long. The first weather journal in the world was kept by the Reverend William Merle, a Fellow of Merton College, Oxford, 670 years ago.

The paraphernalia of weather recording were mostly invented by the British, too: including the domestic barometer, the tipping rain gauge, invented by Christopher Wren in 1662, the anemometer, dreamt up after the Tay Bridge disaster in 1879, the Campbell-Stokes sunshine recorder, the storm warning, the forecast, the isobar, and the Stevenson screen – those white louvred boxes on stilts that shelter measuring instruments from direct heat and sunlight, while allowing the free circulation of air.

Our temperate climate also makes the English obsessive walkers. People don't really go for a walk in America. They go for a hike – in such a vast country, with such dramatic terrain and weather patterns, the outdoors is a rugged place to be tackled only through rugged activities like hiking, mountaineering and mountain-biking; not by something so unathletic or low-key as walking.

When I lived in New York and went for a walk upstate at the weekend, American friends were surprised that I wore the same shoes I wore to the office. They put on hiking boots, even for a half-hour potter along the dry, flat paths along the Hudson River.

They took much the same approach to bicycling. New Yorkers went for fifty-mile bike treks on Saturday, kitted out in luminous body socks and space-age, Mekon helmets. The idea of bicycling a few miles across town, in a suit, to go to work, seemed outlandish. Bicycling was an out-of-town, leisure and fitness pursuit; not a means of transport to be absorbed into your immaculate, sweat-free, urban professional life.

Because the English weather is so temperate, and the landscape so accommodating, there's no need for walking clothes, luminous body socks or special shoes; except perhaps for the all-purpose wellie – a boot that strikes Americans as being tremendously odd. Why would you need wellies in town, where there's no mud, they ask; and surely you need something more professional for vigorous country hiking?

The English walk long distances because nowhere really seems very far from anywhere else, and you'll never get fatally caught out by the weather or the terrain. Epping Forest, the biggest forest in Essex, is a mere 5,500 acres – you can walk across it in one direction in an hour; in the other, in just over three hours. It hardly compares with the vast forests of South America or Russia.

One evening in 1811, the poet Shelley, after dinner with friends in London, realized he didn't have enough money for the stagecoach to Oxford; and so he decided to walk. It's true that dinner finished earlier in the early nineteenth century, and that Shelley had finished his last goblet of port by 6 p.m.; but, still, Oxford was no closer to London than it is today.

Setting off along the route of today's M40 – the old sheep-droving road from Herefordshire and the Cotswolds to London, dating from the Middle Ages, when wool was England's main commercial crop – the poet completed the fifty-five miles at a brisk 4½ miles an hour trot, arriving twelve hours later, in time for a kipper breakfast.

In August 2009, Rory Stewart, the MP and writer, had a free day and so walked from London to Oxford at almost exactly

Shelley's pace; getting up at 4.30 a.m. and arriving in the town for tea. If bad weather had interrupted his walk, it would never have been bad enough for him to stop it. And, however bad the weather might have got, he would have played it down. Playing down bad weather has been an integral part of the English walk for several centuries.

> 'A walk before breakfast does me good.'
> 'Not a walk in the rain, I should imagine.'
> 'No, but it did not absolutely rain when I set out.'
>
> Jane Austen, *Emma* (1815)

'*Good afternoon!*'

Cartoon by Nicolas Bentley, from George Mikes, *How to be an Alien*, 1946.

Walking has always been our thing – from the *Canterbury Tales*, through to the Jarrow March and the charity walks of recent years; and walking in all weathers, too, because we know the weather's not going to be that bad.

Or not that bad, as far as we're concerned, anyway. Those from abroad think differently. In a 1958 guide to English life, *Customs on the Other Side of the Channel*, the Italian writer Guido Puccio included these two essential English phrases in his glossary: 'To cover long distances on foot – *percorrere grandi distanze a piedi*'; 'Takes his walk, no matter what the weather – *fa la sua passeggiata con qualsiasi tempo.*'

Staying in Northern Ireland in early spring, in a rural spot between Belfast and Bangor, I went for a walk around a thickly wooded lake. As I set out, there was the faintest drizzle and, because it was warm, I didn't bother with a raincoat, but made do with a cotton shirt and sunhat. About a third of the way round the lake, it began to pour – with all the rain sweeping in from the Atlantic that, a couple of hours later, would thud into Manchester.

I could have turned back, but it was pleasant enough, and I kept on going. By the time I got back to the house, I was soaking, water dripping off the floppy fringes of my sunhat. At the French windows stood – appropriately enough – a Frenchman.

'Oh, that is so marvellous,' he said, 'A Frenchman would never go for a walk in this weather, and certainly not dressed like that.'

Like the Americans, the French – living in a country that's part of a much bigger land mass, spreading beyond Western Europe into Asia – don't share the English concept of going for a walk. The greater extremes of weather on the Continent, too – and the greater the care for the right sort of clothes – mean they don't have the same approach to going for a walk in bad weather, or in everyday clothes. The practice has been going on for quite a while. In 1808, Robert Southey wrote that the English dress inadequately in the 'dark and overclouded, quite English weather'.[12]

There are great stretches of the world where going for a walk in the wrong clothes just isn't an option: if I'd gone out in the rain in early spring in northern Norway, say, with just a shirt and a hat, I'd have come home coated in a thin layer of ice.

In places with reliable supplies of sun, the inhabitants don't see the point of walking in the rain either. If you live in Florence, and know it's going to be sunny day after day, why choose to go for a walk on a rainy one?

Even if it rains a lot in England, it rarely rains so violently that it would stop you taking a walk in it, as James Bond observes at the end of *Dr No*. He is in Jamaica, his arch-enemy dead, his knockout girlfriend, Honey Rider, about to leap into their double sleeping bag. And yet, despite being in tropical paradise, Bond longs for 'the douce weather of England – the soft airs, the "heat" waves, the cold spells – the only country where you can take a walk every day of the year.'[13]

Charles II agreed. Though brought up in France, he said that 'he lik'd . . . that Country best, which might be enjoy'd the most Hours of the Day, and the most Days in the Year, which he was sure was to be done in England more than in any country whatsoever . . . It invited men abroad more days in the year and more hours in the day than another country.'[14]

James Bond and Charles II were right – England is too warm to stay indoors, too cold to sit around and do nothing once you get outdoors.

For all our obsession with the rain, there isn't really that much of it. It only rains, on average, once every three days in Britain – and then only for brief spells. London is dry 94 per cent of the time; the reason Boris Johnson, the city's mayor, said there was no need for a roof in the Olympic Stadium for most spectators in the 2012 Olympics. The city is drier than Istanbul; south-east England has less water available per person than Sudan or Syria.[15]

From this love of the temperate outdoors, the English developed their taste for open-air portraits and sporting pictures, an obsessive love of gardening, and a talent for inventing, and playing, sports. Love of the outdoors also fed into the English taste for keeping the central heating off – or for having no central heating at all – and the bedroom window open, until December.

That love was allied to a deep faith in the magical, health-giving properties of sea and country air, and, by extension, the English taste for picnics in bad weather.

As early as 1762, David Garrick was painted by Johan Zoffany, taking tea on the banks of the Thames with his wife. Four years later, Oliver Goldsmith's *The Vicar of Wakefield* contained the first description of a picnic in English literature. Already the crucial ingredient of an English picnic – discomfort – was present. Goldsmith writes about eating dinner in a freshly scythed field, where 'we sat, or rather, reclined, round a temperate repast, our cloth spread upon the hay'.

This indifference to bad weather bleeds into the pleasingly unself-indulgent side of the English, along with its more extreme Spartan edges: including a positively masochistic taste for discomfort and rain, and the ideal combination of the two – the camping holiday.

Cunningham Camp, on the Isle of Man, the first ever English campsite, was founded in 1894. It was teetotal, too.

2. The Lie of the Land: The Geology of England

Know most of the rooms of thy native country before thou goest over the threshold thereof. Especially seeing England presents thee with so many observables.

Thomas Fuller (1608–61), English clergyman and historian, *The Holy State and the Profane State* (1642)

It was on a train to Newcastle from King's Cross, to write an article about Britain's oldest Marks and Spencer, in the city's Grainger Market, that I first thought of writing this book.

About a quarter of an hour before we pulled into Durham, I headed for the buffet. When I got back to my window seat, at a table in the quiet carriage, a middle-aged man in a tweed jacket in the row of seats behind me leant over and said, in a polite but jaunty way, 'I'm very sorry to disturb you, but are you a geographer?'

An odd question, I thought, forgetting that I had left a copy of L. Dudley Stamp's *Britain's Structure and Scenery* open on the table when I went to the buffet.

'We're both geographers,' he said, gesturing to a smartly dressed man of about the same age, sitting next to him, 'and Stamp is the absolute classic. We all read it at university.'

The two men turned out to be the Reverend Ian Browne, a geography graduate and chaplain at Oundle School, Northamptonshire, and his common room colleague, Gary Phillips, the school registrar. They were off to Edinburgh to give a sermon and a lecture respectively.

We chatted a bit about the late Sir Laurence Dudley Stamp, Professor of Geography at Rangoon and London, and one of the leading British geographers of the twentieth century.

'And so,' I asked, as the train headed towards Durham, 'can you look at any view in Britain and see why it looks like it does?'

'Just about,' said the chaplain. 'So that,' he said, pointing to a bulging green ridge running along the top of a hill next to the train, 'is the typical sort of landscape you get with sandstones from Coal Measures.'

'It's the same sandstone they used to build the cathedral,' said Gary Phillips, as we pulled into Durham, with that tremendous view of the cathedral to our right. 'It's usually a dull buff colour but, in the chapel of Durham Castle, it's a lovely golden brown with a terrific watermark on it,' he added, pointing towards the castle.

I swapped addresses with them and returned to my seat to read my book. How lovely, like Sir Laurence Stamp, and my two new geographer friends, to know how the wind, rain, frost, snow, ice, streams, rivers and sea have sculpted the earth's crust for millions of years.

The extreme variety of the English landscape was largely created by chunks of raised sea bed and fragments of land mass that began life south of the equator 600 million years ago, and gradually migrated north. Britain is a random collection of soils and stones, flipped over by tectonic grating, frozen by ice ages, sculpted by volcanoes, fried by the sun, sometimes swamped by the sea, sometimes lifted above it.

Across the country, you can see various vivid stages in these processes. Off the Norfolk coast, there are 5,000-year-old tree trunks, survivors of the dense forest that covered much of the country before the land bridge to Europe was inundated with melted ice. Several of those trunks are still scored with the teeth marks of Mesolithic beavers. Stones on the Isle of Wight are still stamped with dinosaur footprints.

No other country in Europe packs so many different stones into such a small area as Britain does. In a thirty-mile journey, you'll come across as many different landscapes as you might cover in 300 miles in a blander, more geologically uniform country like, say, Canada, Australia or America.

To identify those different geological landscapes, it's useful to remember that the different layers of stone tend to dip downwards along a line running across England from north-west to south-east. Up in the north-west, the lowest stones in the sandwich – the oldest ones – are pushed towards the surface; while, in the south-east, those lowest stones are tipped deeper down, leaving newer stone at the top.

Northamptonshire's layers of stone have been compared to a deck of playing cards splayed on a table, with the oldest strata exposed at one end, the newest at the other. Where rivers cut through these layers – as the Rivers Nene, Tove, Ouse and Ise do, in Northamptonshire – the oldest strata are exposed at the bottom, the newer ones revealed further up the sides of the valley. River valleys also expose the chalk underbed of Suffolk, otherwise concealed by clay, sand, gravels and glacial sands.

The tectonic plate on which England sits is still dipping south-eastwards, tipping us, very slowly, into the Channel: the coast around the Thames estuary is sinking at around a foot a century, while Scotland is slowly rising.

England is still moving on the surface, too. After the floods that devastated Cockermouth in the Lake District in 2009, millions of tons of gravel were scattered across the fields on the valley floor, either side of the River Cocker. The rivers hopped out of their normal course and meandered down the middle of the valley.

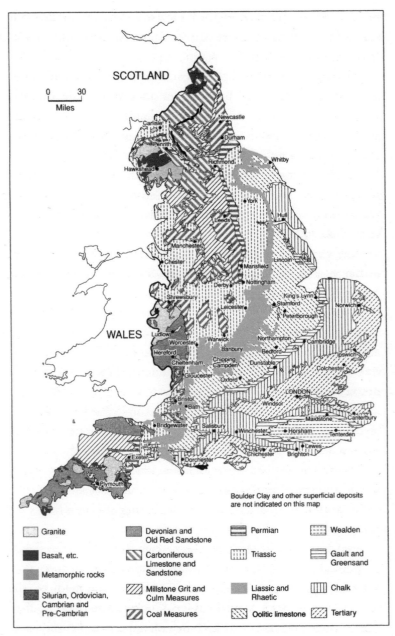

Astonishingly varied – the stones of England.

You tend to find better stone in the west – in the central lime-stones, the West Midlands sandstones, and the ancient granites, slates and sandstones of the West Country.

As you move east, the stones not only get younger, but their quality also lessens. The Jurassic sandstone of Dorset, topped with limestone, gives way a few miles east to rock with a later sandwich of inferior materials above it – shales (rock made from clay mud, spotted with minerals), marls (a sort of chalky clay), clays and ironstones. East Anglia, the south-east and the south are largely made of clays, sand, shales and chalk.

This eastward, reverse-ageing process continues until you reach the south-eastern coast at Dover. The White Cliffs are made of chalk – a much younger material than all those rocks further west. A soft, porous, white limestone, chalk is responsible for more quintessential English landscapes than any other single rock.

As well as forming the White Cliffs of Dover and the outcrop on which Windsor Castle perches, chalk produced the landscapes of the North and South Downs and Salisbury Plain, the biggest stretch of unploughed chalk downland in the country. Mineral-rich chalk soil deepens the gaudily streaked colours of autumn leaves in Sussex – just as dramatic as New England in the fall. Old man's beard, too, thrives on hedges grown in chalk soil.

The quality of agricultural land produced by chalk varies: from fertile arable land to fescue downland with short grass and unploughable, thin soils, to steep hills that develop into hanging beech woods.

High Wycombe's chair-makers were well-placed for the hanging beech woods of the Chilterns – ideal for making the back spindles, legs and stretchers of Windsor chairs. Beech trees, found in England for 8,000 years, originally grew only in the south – Burnham Beeches, Buckinghamshire, now has the big-gest collection of pollarded beeches in the world. But they have spread north over the millennia: a great stand of them now acts as a shelter belt in the Pennines.

Chalk provides the best foundation for typical English sporting pursuits, too. Cricket was supposedly first played on the short, downland grass of the chalk downs of southern England, with balls made from woollen rags. In this rather romanticized view – which puts sheep, the motor of England's economy for centuries, at the heart of the narrative – shepherds used the wicket gate of the sheepfold as the wicket, and their crooks for bats.

Downland is ideal racing and training country, notably at Epsom, Surrey, and on the Berkshire Downs. The chalk of the Berkshire Downs, around the racing Mecca of Lambourn, produces springy grass and a softish falling surface, unlike bone-rattling clay. The chalk wolds in Yorkshire, around Malton, are similarly accommodating.

Leicestershire is hunting country, too – the Quorn is England's most famous hunt, in part because of the zinginess of the light soil, compared with the heavy clay soil of southern vales; taking a fence on the Laughton Hills near Market Harborough is like jumping off springs.

Chalk streams produce the best fishing in England; and there are more chalk streams in England – 161 of them – than in any other country. It is chalk that makes the fishing rivers of Wiltshire and the Hampshire Downs: the Avon, the Itchen, the Meon and the Test. Fed by underground aquifers, chalk streams are rich in the calcium which feeds crayfish, water snails and shrimps; the streams are also filled with plant nutrients, like nitrates, phosphates and potassium, ideal for the mayfly.

The effect of a chalk bed on the landscape varies. Much of the foundation of Norfolk is chalk, but the county barely resembles the North and South Downs – equipped as they are with the smooth, rolling chalk landscape of legend, with gentle curves cut into the hillside and broad, spreading humps swelling across the horizon, as if moulded by some celestial, shallow-bladed ice cream scoop.

That archetypal chalk landscape look is so distinctive that William 'Strata' Smith (1769–1839) – called the Father of British Geology – could see, on his first visit, that the Yorkshire Wolds were made of chalk from twenty miles away. He sensed chalk in the broad outline of the land and the smooth, rolling, waterless valleys, quickly drained by chalk's porousness.

More often than not, war artists, in search of a tender, rural, threatened view of England, picked chalk downland for a backdrop. On the eve of the Second World War, Eric Ravilious kept returning to the ancient hillside chalk figures carved into the soft contours of classic English downland, among them the Wilmington Giant, near Eastbourne, the Uffington White Horse, Oxfordshire, and the Cerne Abbas Giant, Dorset.

There are two notable Raviliouses of the Westbury Horse, Wiltshire – one from a train, one with a train chuffing along in the background. By the 1930s, the railway – originally considered an interloper into the landscape – could be seamlessly absorbed into an archetypal image of the English countryside.

The Uffington White Horse is raised up high on the north side of the Ridgeway. The 5,000-year-old road – the oldest in Europe – is dictated by geology, as it runs along a 700ft-thick band of chalk stretching for eighty-seven miles from Ivinghoe Beacon in the Chilterns, near Tring, Hertfordshire, down to Overton Hill, near Marlborough, Wiltshire.

That band of chalk slips under the Thames and the River Kennet, before cutting through the New Forest. It dips under the Channel beneath the Solent and Spithead, and then raises its head above the water at the western end of the Isle of Wight. There, at Alum Bay, the chalk reappears in candy-coloured stripes.

The connection between chalk downland and quintessential England is made explicit in the morale-boosting Second World War poster painted by the War Office artist Frank Newbould. Above the caption, 'Your Britain, Fight for it now', the poster has a chalk landscape for its backdrop, with a shepherd and his dog leading sheep towards a farm nestling in a fold of the South Downs.

Other posters in the 'Your Britain' series showed Salisbury Cathedral and a country fairground in the shadow of a medieval village church, with a Gothic broach spire. Most British troops fighting on the Continent came from our industrial towns and cities, but the propaganda link identifying England with rural England – and the patriotic images do tend to be English, rather than British – still went unquestioned.

Of all the geological factors that have shaped England and the English, the most powerful is the fact that we live on an island off the edge of a vast land mass, moored between the Atlantic and the North Sea.

Our island nature is at the heart of our character. It doesn't take much of a leap to connect a small, overpopulated island to a reserved, private population obsessed with class and horrified by intrusion.[1]

The English Channel – used as a highway and a barrier – made England. Our island status looms large in our view of ourselves – thus the affection for Shakespeare's lines in *Richard II*: 'This precious stone set in the silver sea, Which serves it in the office of a wall, Or as a moat defensive to a house, Against the envy of less happier lands, This blessed plot, this earth, this realm, this England'.

Foreigners, too, are struck by our island status. Britain was made 'that fortunate day when a wave of the German Ocean burst the old isthmus which joined Kent and Cornwall to

France,' said the American writer Ralph Waldo Emerson in the middle of the nineteenth century.

Emerson's romantic line is pretty much true. England was once connected to the Continent by a band of chalk that let the first immigrants stroll into England at the end of the Ice Age; only for rising sea levels to cut off the land bridge.

The island is still changing shape – tens of thousands of acres have been added to the English land mass in the last 1,500 years, particularly in the saltmarshes around Essex and the Wash.[2] Further north, the English land mass is shrinking: the forty-mile stretch of Holderness coast, in the East Riding of Yorkshire, has the highest rate of erosion in Europe, with the coast retreating at around two metres a year.

Thirty per cent of the English live within six miles of the coast. And no one in England is more than seventy miles – or two hours' drive – from the sea. But that doesn't mean we're forever taking day trips to the coast. We may be an island race but we're now an island race that largely turns its back on the sea.

One reason why London has become the residence of choice for the global rich in the last decade is its geographical position – a civilized, democratic stopping-off point for Muscovite oligarchs on their way to New York; a temperate refuge from Arabian summer heat for Saudi billionaires. But you're unlikely to find either group making their way to the coast.

For all our closeness to the sea, most major English cities tend to be some way from it – unlike major coastline cities like, say, Hong Kong or Los Angeles, or, for that matter, Cardiff, Belfast or Dublin. English cities are more likely to be on a major river, at a spot where the river has narrowed enough to be forded.

Over the last two centuries, the Industrial Revolution, rather than the sea, has dictated the size and importance of English cities. Of the top ten most populated English cities, only Liverpool,

the sixth biggest, and Bristol, the eighth biggest, are maritime cities.

Even international maritime cities turn from the sea now. New Yorkers look inwards towards the raised spine of Manhattan, away from the Atlantic, and the Hudson and East Rivers; even though the island is only 2.3 miles at its widest. Until very recently, both the east and west shorelines of New York were pretty much inaccessible, cut off by highways and piers.

The British coast isn't quite as inaccessible as that – although Londoners have largely lost touch with the Thames, since the construction of the Embankment in the 1870s. Sir Joseph Bazalgette's engineering solved London's sanitation problems – the new Embankment helped to conceal 1,300 miles of new sewers – but it also meant Londoners couldn't wander down to the river so easily.

Like New Yorkers, the modern English remain for the most part landlubbers, seaside holidays apart. The Industrial Revolution – together with the invention of planes, trains and cars – means we have turned increasingly to the land, not only for our transport, but also for our livelihoods.

We now have very little of the reverence for – or fear of – the sea once shared by most inhabitants of this island: Anglo-Saxon poets treated England as the quintessential harbour; with rural England a haven from the wild sea. It's true that 95 per cent of British imports still arrive by sea, but how many of us ever see them turn up? In 2009, only 26,700 Britons worked on water. These days, most of us only use the sea as a holiday site and our main drain.[3]

For all the talk about us being an island race, the island we're on is in fact a pretty big one – the ninth biggest in the world, the biggest in Europe, and the third most populated in the world, after Java, Indonesia, and Honshu, Japan.

Bill Bryson should really have called his book *Notes from a*

Pretty Big Island Surrounded by Lots of Smaller Ones – the British Isles are made up of 1,374 islands. The vast majority of us live on the big one in the middle – and most of us rarely see the sea from day to day.

Still, however little we might see the sea or earn our livelihood from it, the very fact of our being an island race deeply affects other countries' opinion of us, and our opinion of ourselves; and those opinions are enough in themselves to make us different.

Our island nature doesn't make us exactly xenophobic. The English have on the whole been pretty good at absorbing incomers from the Romans, via the Vikings, Normans, Huguenots, through to Jews, West Indians, Asians and Eastern Europeans.

But, still, the English remain fundamentally awkward with strangers – whether they're foreign or English – not least because of their island isolation. It's no coincidence that 'insular' comes from the Latin for island.

The English may complain about foreigners; yet, when they live next door to them, they're perfectly polite, as long as they don't have to cross each other's thresholds. The cramped conditions that come from sharing a heavily populated island mean that, while the English bemoan the general morals of the nation, on the whole they accept their next-door neighbours' shortcomings. They can't escape them; so they put up with them.

If you've never had to live cheek by jowl with your neighbours, in small, terraced houses with postage-stamp-sized gardens, then you react more aggressively to the tiniest imposition on your rights.

American militia groups of freedom fighters take against state intervention in their private lives that much more ferociously, because they live in the wide-open backwoods of the vast, thinly populated Midwest, West and the South. They just aren't so used to being imposed upon.

The cramped quality of island life also means that, for all the tolerance shown by the English, they like putting up barriers against any real interference in their private lives. The desire for privacy extends to a lack of interest in anything beyond their small world; a lack of interest intensified by the English happening to speak the world's most popular language; not much need, then, to learn another.

For all the English absorption of waves of immigrants, there still have been very few invaders in the past 2,000 years, principally because of that island status. Napoleon may have thought the Channel a 'ditch to be jumped' but he never did jump it; neither did the Spanish Armada or Hitler. Watery borders are harder to cross than terrestrial ones.

Island status has tended to make England a strong, independent country; one that hasn't embraced European integration – or the euro – with the enthusiasm of neighbours across the Channel who share a land mass.

But it also makes for a relatively unsophisticated people – afraid of foreign food and languages; happier to speak English and eat fish and chips on Spanish package tours, rather than risk embarrassment, and an upset stomach, by striking out on their own abroad.

Too much emphasis on the uniformity of a single island race risks ignoring the geological differences between different counties.

That connection – between English counties and their supposed idiosyncratic landscapes – struck me on a recent visit to north Holland.

Travelling by train through the flat fields, I was intrigued by how similar those fields were to seventeenth-century Dutch landscapes by Aelbert Cuyp: the fields were carved into rectangles by arrow-straight dykes, with Friesian cows sprawling on their banks.

My train journey took three hours, from Schiphol Airport to Groningen, and the landscape barely seemed to change all the way there – it appeared uniformly Cuyp-like, and stereotypically, almost ludicrously, Dutch.

On the return trip, this time with a Dutchman, he pointed out tiny distinctions between the various landscapes that I hadn't noticed on the outward leg – differences between the ways the small clumps of willows had been pollarded; how the dykes varied in length and breadth.

People from abroad have said the same of England as I initially said of the Dutch landscape: that it all looks pretty much the same; that the differences between, say, the craggy, bony, mountainous horizons of Cumbria and Kent's soft, low-slung landscape, with its orchards and oast houses, don't amount to much. To them, it all looks much-of-a-muchness, in a uniformly English way.

However little we might happen to know about oast houses or the mountains of the Lake District, that strikes us as ridiculous. Most of us have innate attachments to different counties, springing from what strikes us as extreme dissimilarities between them.

We might prefer, say, Dorset's exposed rural roads to the lanes of Devon, deeply carved into the field margins, diving into clefted combes; we might have robust views of the merits of hilly Gloucestershire over very flat Norfolk.

Perhaps we exaggerate those county differences a little because of our affection for them. It's not as if individual counties were originally planned according to their geological features; when the Anglo-Saxons carved England up into Northumbria, Mercia, Wessex, East Anglia and Kent, they hardly did it on the basis of what each region looked like.

But, still, there are strong historical, literary and sociological reasons why some counties began to look different over the

centuries and developed certain idiosyncratic characteristics, whether you're an Englishman or a Dutchman. And, in fact, there often happen to be extreme geological differences between the counties. Certain geological features naturally cross county borders but, still, they are more marked in some counties than others.

When it comes to dividing Britain into similar-looking chunks, Sir Halford Mackinder, a leading British geologist in the first half of the twentieth century, made a good general rule.

Draw a line from the mouth of the Tees, in the north-east, down to the mouth of the Exe, in the south-west, and all the main hills and mountains – Highland Britain – will be on the north-west side of the line. The Caledonian earth movements built up the Highlands around 470–430 million years ago.[4]

To the south-east of Sir Halford Mackinder's line lies Lowland Britain – the most fertile, and most heavily settled, part of the country, smoothed out during the Ice Age by glaciers, which deposited a rich layer of silt and clay as they melted.

You can trace the beginnings of a north–south divide to those differences in landscape either side of Mackinder's line. Certainly the Romans tended to build most of their villas on the well-drained, light, lowland soils, on the south-eastern side of the line.

Glacial action levelled the Midlands – ice sheets smoothed away soil and loose rocks, leaving behind a gently undulating rock surface ridged with outcrops of harder stone. The heart of England is really a plain – more grassland than arable – divided by hawthorn and oak hedges. The rolling fields of the West Midlands are formed by sandstone embedded with Upper Carboniferous Coal Measures.

Within that flattish Midlands plain, there are still some geological differences – the plain straddles the soft rocks of the south and east, and the hard rocks of the north and west. So it's not all flat: in Birmingham, from Selly Oak to Sutton Park, the Bunter Pebble Bed of shales and red sandstones – with layers of cobbles and pebbles deposited by rivers 200 million years ago – produces a varied landscape of steep-sided, thickly wooded valleys, punctuated with heath and gravel.

The Midlands are hemmed in by more dramatic geology. To the north lie the Pennines. To the west, the plain furls up into the Malvern and Abberley Hills and the Wyre Forest. The Armorican movements – so called because they created the rocks of Brittany, also known as Armorica – pushed up the Malverns, the Pennines and the Mendips. They also bent the Coal Measures – Britain's coal-bearing seams, built up around 360 million years ago – into basins, with a powerful effect on which parts of England would turn industrial in the eighteenth and nineteenth centuries (see Chapter 10). Armorican granite masses include Land's End, Bodmin Moor and Dartmoor.

Glaciers carved out much of the Lake District – the scooped-out valleys they formed were scattered with a rough scree of angular stones, melded together to make so-called breccia. The Skiddaw Slates were laid down first, followed by the volcanic rocks that produced the mountains of Langdale Pikes and Helvellyn.

In the later Ice Age, an ice cap developed over the Lake District – the ice spread through the valleys, widening and deepening them. As the ice retreated, it left behind moraines – piles of glacial debris – that blocked the mouths of the valleys and produced the lakes.

Where rivers seeped from under the glaciers, they carried gravel and sand with them, leaving a trail of long ridges and irregular mounds made of these materials – called kettle moraine, it can be seen in Brampton, Cumbria, and the Till Valley, Northumberland.

Outside the Lake District and the Pennines, England may be

short on mountains, but it's long on escarpments – steep-faced hills, formed by differing levels of erosion in sedimentary rocks or faults in the earth's crust.

Hadrian's Wall was built on top of a cliff formed by one of these faults: the Whin Sill, a line across the neck of Britain, where magma poured between a pair of tectonic plates to form a 70ft-high sill, on top of which the 20ft wall was built.

Escarpments provide natural ancient roads – like the Ridgeway – and boundaries. Oxfordshire's border runs along the escarpment of the lower Cotswolds, from Edgehill to Chipping Norton.

They also make for dramatic inland cliffs. If you head south on the A46, from Stroud to Bath, to your left it's all 170-million-year-old Middle Jurassic limestone, producing a high, stone cliff. To your right, you'll see a low, flat valley, formed 20 million years earlier by easily eroded Lower Jurassic clay.

This fault line runs from Gloucestershire to Lincolnshire, via Warwickshire, Rutland, Leicestershire and Nottinghamshire. The escarpment dictates the use of the land all the way.

Heading north on the A15 through Lincolnshire, to the right there are high, limestone plains, grassy enough to produce good grazing for sheep, and flat enough for RAF airfields during the war. On the left, in the Lower Jurassic valley, the sheltered land is farmed more intensively.

When these beds of rock, gently slanting in the usual south-easterly direction, break or slide, you end up with steep faces – or scarps – facing west, with gentle slopes to the east. These are prominent in the so-called Scarplands of England – stretching from southern Dorset, through the Vale of the White Horse, Northamptonshire, Lincolnshire and up into Yorkshire; like the flat vertical face of Lincoln Cliff, the ridge that runs north–south through central Lincolnshire. The Scarplands include the scarps of the Hambleton and Cleveland Hills, the

North Yorkshire Moors and the Cotswolds escarpments formed by Jurassic limestones and sandstones.

The angle of these hills and scarps changes according to the angle at which the beds of stone were laid. If the beds are vertical, with the central, tallest bed aligned with the crest of the hill, then the hill will be fairly symmetrical, with even slopes on either side – like the Hog's Back in Surrey or the central ridge of the Isle of Wight.

These escarpments lack the high drama of the Alps; English mountains are foothills compared to the Himalayas. The intense settlement and cultivation of most of England for several thousand years has also taken the edge off any surviving drama in the landscape, lending the country a rich, fertile coat that some have called dull, particularly in the south.

'England – southern England, probably the sleekest landscape in the world,' George Orwell wrote at the end of *Homage to Catalonia* (1938), 'It is difficult when you pass that way, especially when you are peacefully recovering from sea-sickness with the plush cushions of a boat-train carriage under your bum, to believe that anything is really happening anywhere.'

England – particularly southern England – is certainly sleek and comfortable, built on that undramatic, small scale. But it is those qualities that make the effect of our landscape so exceptionally moving. There is a calmness, a lack of flashiness, a restrained look that loses out in grand spectacle terms to the swaggering giant landscapes of the world; but it gains in subtlety, in the pleasure derived from closely observed, understated beauty.

Cheddar Gorge demonstrates the point. In the heart of limestone-rich gorge country – Somerset limestone was easily carved by the meltwaters that came with the end of the Ice Age – the gorge is called England's Grand Canyon.

It is indeed Britain's deepest canyon, at 371 feet. But it still has some way to catch up with the real Grand Canyon, in Arizona;

277 miles long, it ranges from four to eighteen miles wide and sinks deeper than a mile, or 6,000 feet. The whole of Britain is only 600 miles long and 200 miles wide.

If I asked you for a stroll one morning along the floor of Cheddar Gorge, following the B3135 near the village of Cheddar in the Mendips in Somerset, we could walk its three-mile length and be back in time for tea. Try walking the Grand Canyon, and you wouldn't be back for a month.

America big, England small — a crashing cliché, but true nonetheless.

'The whole conception [of carving presidents' heads into a cliff-face] really requires the vast American background of prairies and mountain chains,' said G. K. Chesterton, 'Anyone would feel, I think, that it would be rather too big for England. It would be rather alarming for the Englishman, returning by boat to Dover, to see that Shakespeare's Cliff had suddenly turned into Shakespeare.'

There's a parallel between the small-scale, undramatic English landscape and English art. Alan Ayckbourn, Philip Larkin, Barbara Pym, Kingsley Amis, Alan Bennett, Anita Brookner . . . they all concern themselves with what you might call little art, with the small things in life, happening in out of the way places.

'So little, England. Little music, little art. Timid, tasteful, nice. But one loves it, one loves it,' says Guy Burgess, the spy in exile in Moscow, in Alan Bennett's 1983 play, *An Englishman Abroad*.

These modern writers are in a long tradition of little art, related to our island nature, temperate climate, unthreatening landscape and the uneventful, small horizons of English life. Jane Austen wrote of 'the little bit (two inches wide) of ivory on which I work with so fine a brush'. Thomas Hardy said, 'It is better for a writer to know a little bit of the world remarkably well than to know a great part of the world remarkably little.'

Still, drama lurks beneath the genteel veneer of Jane Austen's

Bath or Hardy's Wessex; as it does beneath the sleek, grassy coat
of the English landscape. Contrary to what Orwell said, a huge
amount has happened here over the last several billion years and,
if you look closely, you can work out precisely what.

The best way is to look at the stone that's been extracted from
under that fertile coat, and then used for English buildings:
whether it's the oolitic limestone of Cotswold cottages, the
gingerbread-coloured ironstone of Northamptonshire, or the
delicately carved tombstones of Somerset, made of Dundry
stone, Pennant sandstone and Bath stone.

Most countries have a wide selection of building stone. But
it's the sheer quantity and variety of stones that set England
apart; along with the fact that the country is still full of buildings constructed out of local stone.

Before the arrival of the trains, cross-country transport was
so limited, and so expensive, that it was easier to quarry building materials from the ground beneath, rather than carry it great
distances. The Hospital of St John in Sherborne, Dorset, was
built in 1438, using Lias stone from Ham Hill. The quarry was
only twelve miles away but, still, the expense of transporting
the stone was greater than the cost of the stone itself.[5]

Even stained glass could be made on the spot, to save on transport costs. Medieval furnaces were built in riverside kilns in
woods, producing forest glass from river sand and beech wood
ash. In the middle of a remote forest, glaziers could create
extremely exotic colours, using metallic oxides like cobalt to
produce blue glass, and gold for pink glass.

Dependence on close-at-hand materials means you can spot
the exact moment the geology below the ground changes, by
examining the buildings above it.

Buildings in east Leicestershire change colour as you move
north, from pale limestone to golden-brown Middle Lias marl-
stone – called ironstone, because it's rich in iron oxide. In

Lincolnshire, where the Middle Jurassic limestone runs out, the drystone walls above it suddenly give way to hornbeam and blackthorn hedges, threaded through with dog roses.

Above that belt of limestone – an excellent building stone, formed when dinosaurs walked through Lincolnshire – lie the county's biggest, most beautiful buildings. Lincoln Cathedral even has its own quarry, producing Lincoln Silverbed limestone, a creamy, beige stone, still cut and carved by masons trained in medieval techniques.

In places where there isn't much building stone, but there was the money to buy and transport it, stone from other parts of the country – and foreign countries, too – was used.

Fifteenth-century Eton College, next door to Windsor, was largely built – thanks to generous endowments – with Caen stone from Normandy, Merstham stone from Surrey, Bath stone, Clipsham limestone from Rutland, Headington limestone, Magnesian limestone from Yorkshire, Kentish Ragstone from Maidstone and Jurassic Taynton stone from the Forest of Wychwood in Oxfordshire. Taynton limestone was also used for All Souls College, Oxford, and Windsor Castle; a brown, large-grained, shelly stone, around 175 million years old, ideal for fine carving.[6]

The later the building, the more likely it is to use exotic stone, as transport costs decreased over time. Salisbury Cathedral, erected in the thirteenth and fourteenth centuries, was principally built of local Chilmark limestone, quarried only twelve miles away. St Paul's Cathedral, built in the late seventeenth and early eighteenth centuries, is largely made of Portland limestone from the Isle of Portland, Dorset.

When groups of really old buildings survive, it's usually because of the quality of the local stone. Most Anglo-Saxon houses, built of timber or clay, with straw roofs, eventually rotted into the ground. The only surviving medieval timber church is in

Greensted, Essex; the oldest continuously inhabited, timber-framed house in England is Fyfield Hall, Fyfield, Essex, built in 1150. In the robust stone Norman churches that replaced less substantial Saxon churches, the only Saxon remnant will often be the crypt, concealed beneath the later superstructure.

Extensive Saxon buildings only survive in counties with easy access to durable stone – like St Laurence's Church, in Bradford on Avon, Wiltshire, built in AD 1000 from the local Jurassic Great Oolite limestone, one of the best English building stones.

If chalk creates the English landscape of legend, then another kind of limestone – Jurassic, oolitic limestone, a sedimentary calcium carbonate stone – creates the legendary English building. A scimitar-shaped sash of this wonderful limestone loops, from north-east to south-west, across England's torso, from Yorkshire through Nottinghamshire, Leicestershire, Oxfordshire, Wiltshire and Gloucestershire, down to Somerset and Dorset.

The deep brown, cream and Cheddar-yellow stone of Cotswolds villages and Oxford colleges is Jurassic, oolitic limestone, cut with limonite, an iron mineral; the more iron in it, the deeper the honey-yellows and the browns. Where that oolitic limestone peters out in the west, in a line of escarpments falling to the Severn Vale, the picturesque golden cottages – and the Japanese tourists tracking their course – begin to disappear.

Those Cotswold cottages also draw their quintessential Englishness from their mottled, lichened, crooked roofs – made from Stonesfield slate, or pendle, as they call it in the Oxfordshire quarries. Stonesfield is strictly a limestone, not a slate, but it splits naturally to give the appearance of slate. Where other slates split along geological fault lines, the pendle is split by the moisture – or quarry sap – trapped within. Medieval masons used to leave the slate stone outside over the winter and clamp it, so that, when the frost came, the stone split into slates.

A similar splitting technique was used on Collyweston stone slate – also really a limestone, not strictly a slate. Quarried in Northamptonshire, between Deene and Stamford, Collyweston slates often cover the roofs of Cambridge colleges. In Lancashire, heavy, dark Carboniferous sandstone slates, known as flagstones, were used for roofs; it helped that the sandstone was immune to disintegration from smoke and soot in the industrial north.

Part formed from animal skeletons, Collyweston stone is rich in fossilized mammals and lizards. Oolitic limestone, part formed from the shells of sea creatures, is flecked with fossilized fish scales and teeth, often visible to the naked eye. All British limestone is formed by fossilized marine organisms, apart from an Isle of Wight limestone, used for much of Winchester Cathedral; it's the only limestone formed by freshwater organisms.

Ammonites, too – those round fossils, shaped like looped snakes – are the remnants of Jurassic and Cretaceous molluscs. They're often found in Dorset, particularly on the Isle of Portland, where they are incorporated into walls.

Northamptonshire lies on a ridge of oolitic Barnack limestone, the best building stone in the country, used to finish the battlements and pinnacles of England's newest cathedral, Bury St Edmunds, Suffolk, in 2000. Some of the biggest, stone-hungry buildings of Norman England were built on the Barnack limestone ridge, near Barnack village. The pitted moonscape of the nearby quarry is now known as 'hills and holes', produced by centuries of digging. From the Saxon period onwards, Barnack stone was sent downriver to Peterborough, then on to Ely, Bury and Cambridge, to build many of the churches in East Anglia.

Limestone country tends to be spire country, too. Stone-rich Northamptonshire has 200 medieval churches and around eighty spires. It's been called the county of squires and spires; William

Camden, the late-sixteenth-century antiquarian, said it was 'passing well furnish'd with noblemen's and gentlemen's houses', and it is still largely divided into ancient estates.

Wherever you have limestone, you get limewash, too: lime slaked in water, producing a breathable whitewash layer for cottages across the country. The distinctive strawberry ice-cream pink of East Anglian cottages was made by adding a dash of oxblood to the mix. The pinkish look was often further stylized with pargeting – combing the wet plaster into decorative patterns.

Most of England's cities derived their character from local stones, bricks or timber, before the 1950s takeover by concrete, glass and steel. Bristol is principally grey, because of the Pennant sandstone quarried to the east of the city; although Pennant blushes plum and chocolate brown, too. Bath is pale gold, thanks to Bath stone, an oolitic limestone originally quarried at Combe Down, a mile and a half south of Bath city centre.

Because of the extreme variety of English stones, towns, which are otherwise very similar, feel completely different because of the stones beneath.

Cambridge, with limited medieval access to building stone, was originally largely built of clunch (a type of hard chalk) and brick, before better stone was imported. Chalk, for all its beautifying effect on the English landscape, is not a good building stone, ending up dirty and pock-marked; the chalk churches of Hertfordshire are often now pebbledashed or rendered with cement as a result.

England's other archetypal university town, Oxford, is only sixty-seven miles from Cambridge. In most sociological respects, the towns are as similar as can be. But Oxford looks, and feels, different because it happens to be on the oolitic limestone belt, and so has always been a town built of handsome stone. It's partly because of that honey-coloured stone that Oxford gets the monopoly on romantic university stories: whether they're about dreaming spires, teddy-bear-carrying sons of marquesses or opera-loving detectives investigating murder sprees in senior common rooms.

In the same way that geological characteristics cross county boundaries, a single county can encompass a huge variety of rocks.

Berkshire, for example, is a mixture of extremely different geological landscapes. Around Bagshot Heath, it's all pines and sandy heath, covered with heather and gorse. Rural Berkshire, in the west of the county, rests on the chalk landscape of the Downs. Commercial, commuters' Berkshire lies to the east, on the flat, featureless landscape near Reading, formed by the London clay of the Reading Beds.

Some counties, though, are defined by a single stone, like Cornwall, a county of granite – formed, like other igneous rocks, such as gneiss and basalt, by volcanoes. The county's granite buildings outnumber those in the other granite counties – Cumbria, Devon and Leicestershire – combined. Cornwall's rugged, robust, ancient feel has a lot to do with the ultra-hard, long-suffering stone that underpins much of the peninsula.

The coarse-grained, grey and silver-grey stone is so difficult to carve that the mouldings on Cornish churches are necessarily simple. For the same reason, Cornish church towers – like those at St Levan and St Buryan – tend to be chunky piles of enormous stone blocks; the bigger the block, the less carving is needed.

Granite is so hard-wearing – and so hard to carve – that individual, untouched stones were used for walls, cattle troughs, gate-posts and even bridges. And it's so heavy that, on some Cornish barns and cottages, no mortar is needed to hold the granite blocks together.

Much of the farmland at Land's End is divided by Bronze Age banks made up of 'grounders' – enormous granite boulders which rolled down from the moors in the glacial period. Often they're so hard to move that the banks have swerved in order to incorporate them.

Look under a Cornish hedge, and you might well see a moor-stone – a granite stone taken from the hills and moors as a foundation for the hedge. A hefty moorstone might not be as sophisticated as the drystone walls of the north, but few things are stronger or more watertight.

Pelastine granite from Penryn was used for Tower Bridge; and De Lank granite from Bodmin Moor for the wave-blasted Eddystone Lighthouse off the Devon coast.

Four previous lighthouses were built on the Eddystone Rocks before the current lighthouse was erected in 1882. The first was too small, the second destroyed by a storm, the third by fire and the fourth undermined by waves. The current incarnation has lasted 130 years, thanks to its 2,171 pale-grey, granite blocks, each block dovetailed with other blocks on five of its six faces.

Granite also produced the island of Lundy, the solid founda-tions for St Austell, Bodmin, Land's End, Carnmenellis, Camborne–Redruth and the outcrop on which Dartmoor sits. The weathered granite tors of Dartmoor were left behind when the soils and softer stones around were worn away. The same effect produced the Scilly Isles: granite chunks which remained above water once the sedimentary rock had been eroded by the waves.

The ancient standing stones of Berkshire were formed by a similar process. Berkshire sarsens – large sandstone boulders – were left lying on the earth after the surrounding earth had been weathered away. Sarsens like this were then used in building the chambered barrow at Wayland's Smithy, Ashbury, and, later, that at Windsor Castle.

By plotting the position of these barrows, you can still see where early Bronze Age settlements, from 1650 to 1400 BC, flourished in England.

The Bronze Age heartland of south Wiltshire and Dorset is rich in barrows. They're found, too, in Berkshire, the northern border of Bronze Age Wessex. Some later Bronze Age fields still survive on the Berkshire Downs; and there are still plenty of Iron Age lynchets – cultivated hillside terraces – across England, particularly on chalk downs. Plough a Berkshire field and you might cut through 4,000 years of history.

It isn't all unrelenting granite in Cornwall. The huge slate quarry at Delabole was begun before 1600 and reached a peak in the nineteenth century, producing a vast 400ft-deep hole, a mile in circumference. Cornish slate roofs – in brown and fawn, as well as grey – combine harmoniously with granite, with the largest slates at the eaves, the smallest next to the ridge, giving the illusion of greater depth. Slate-hung walls were popular in Cornwall, too, particularly in the early nineteenth century, as they were in Devon and the Lake District.

Until canals allowed the easy, cross-country transport of cheaper, lighter Welsh slate in the late eighteenth century, slate-rich counties used their own slates: like the lovely green and blue-grey Swithland slate of Leicestershire, dotted with lichen and moss. Swithland slate was also used for gravestones, door-steps, plinths, window sills, gate posts, cheese presses, chimney pieces, salting troughs and milestones.

The only problem was its weight; unlike light Welsh slate, it could slowly crush any building it covered, and so fell into disuse. Today, in Swithland Wood, the old slate quarry is a gaping crater, 190 feet deep, filled with water.

Cornwall's hard, rocky, granite profile is intensified by the absence of trees, blasted by south-westerly winds that whip in straight off the Atlantic. The higher you go in Devon and

Cornwall – climbing up to the moorlands of Dartmoor, Bodmin Moor and Exmoor – the more blasted you are by the wind, and the fewer trees there are. Above 2,000 feet, Dartmoor has probably always been treeless.[7]

Until the sixteenth century, much of England was pretty well wooded, but not Cornwall – which has always been short of trees; and so it's been short on half-timbered cottages, too.

The Cornish often built in cob, or clob, instead – two parts mud and chopped straw, one part shilf, or shards of waste slate. Cob is laid on stone or pebble plinths, painted with cream or pink limewash, and usually roofed with thatch, because cob can't support a slate or tiled roof. Different counties used different cob recipes: the clay cottages in the New Forest are strengthened with heather; Milton Abbas, Dorset, is largely built of chalk and clay cob.

Where the stone ran out, or was inaccessible, people turned to other materials. In Leicestershire, the stone is often hidden beneath 150 feet of boulder clay, meaning the inhabitants resorted to building mud houses. John Evelyn wrote of Leicestershire in 1654, 'Most of the rural parishes are but of mud, the people living as wretchedly as in the most impoverished parts of France.' Several mud houses, laid on a waterproof stone platform, survive in Leicestershire; there are hundreds in Devon.

The extreme variety of English stones gives counties a distinctive look. And the ease of carving of many of those stones, and the fertility of the soils, means much of England was settled, in substantial stone-built developments, at an early stage.

Sometimes, though, unsuitable geology made early human existence unbearably bleak, leading to a lack of ancient settlements. The great stretches of Oxford clay in Bedfordshire and Huntingdonshire were barely colonized by the Romans – the less than ideal soil was also covered with thick forest – except along the more heavily settled Ouse valleys and gravel terraces.

Charnwood Forest, Leicestershire, was largely uninhabited until the early nineteenth century, because it grew on top of a geological freak: ancient pre-Cambrian volcanic rocks – syenite and diorite – that were extremely hard to cut into. Any pre-Victorian cottages in the forest are necessarily timber-framed because of the lack of building stone. Thanks to the inhospitable geology, this barren, hedgeless wasteland wasn't enclosed until 1829.

Where easily harvested stone wasn't available, locals turned to timber for building material. Much of early medieval England was thickly wooded – thus the predominance of timber vaults in churches from York Minster to St Albans Cathedral; a legacy, too, of the English skill at ship-building. In France, stone vaults predominated.

The desperate stripping of England's woods for construction, as well as heating, started early. North Norfolk was pretty much bare by the time the Domesday Book was written in 1086. Like much of the rest of England, where there wasn't much stone or timber, Norfolk turned to bricks. By 1650, the King's Lynn Corporation was paying 14 pence a foot for oak; and only 13 shillings a thousand for bricks. King's Lynn became a brick town.

Heavy use of brick – particularly exposed brick – is a deeply English characteristic, symptomatic of our preference for the homespun, domestic look over the imposing, grand scale. It helps that brick is that much cheaper than stone. Brick is also expressly English, rather than Scottish: the long brick terraces of Manchester and Liverpool give way, over the border, to the sandstone of Glasgow and the granite of Aberdeen.

The world's biggest consumers of bricks per capita, after Britain, are Kentucky, Tennessee and Alabama – continuing the long Southern tradition of robust Anglophilia. When they build an out-of-town shopping centre in the Deep South, more likely than not, it's in neo-Georgian, brick style, recalling the Old Country.

Even our modernist buildings – like Tate Modern, formerly Bankside Power Station, the stripped-down, sleek, futurist building, built by Sir Giles Gilbert Scott from 1947 to 1963 – are made of brick. Industrial buildings also used bricks heavily. Stanley Dock, Liverpool, constructed in 1900 with 27 million bricks, is the biggest brick building in the world.

In other countries, the outer brick walls of modernist and industrial buildings are plastered, smoothed over and whitewashed – to tackle a more powerful sun, as well as to produce a cleaner, more even, minimalist, monochrome look.

Continental Europeans mocked our mass-built, modernist houses in the 1930s for the homespun use of brick, particularly when combined with our addiction to historical styles. Our interwar buildings may have been new, but they were neo-Dutch, neo-Swedish or neo-Tudor, and only rarely neo-neo: that is, utterly original, and embracing the future as opposed to the past.

The English devotion to brick is a relatively recent phenomenon. Between the departure of the Romans from Britain in AD 410 and the first surviving, home-made brick at Little Coggeshall Abbey, Essex, in around 1225, the English lost the art of brickmaking.

For 800 years, they could only reuse old Roman bricks. Since then, the English have perfected the art, although they did make some pretty hideous bricks along the way, including the screaming red bricks from Accrington, known as 'Accrington bloods', made from the local shales in the Lancashire Coal Measures.

After the Great Fire of London, the new terraces were largely built in brick – often distinctive, yellow-brown, London stock brick, made with local clay, much of it from Kent and Essex. It made sense to manufacture bricks locally; because they were so heavy, they were expensive to move. Until as late as the Second World War, bricks were rarely transported more than thirty miles from the brickfields where they were manufactured.

Brickfields – dangerous, unhealthy places to work – scarred the landscape across the country deep into the nineteenth century.

The dimensions of those bricks were price sensitive. In 1784, a Brick Tax was levied on every thousand bricks, irrespective of size; and so brick dimensions began to grow. Tudor bricks are, on average, 9 inches by 4½ inches by 2¼ inches. Georgian bricks – a ¼ inch thicker than Tudor ones before 1784 – got 3 inches thicker after the tax was introduced.

Machine production made those dimensions more precise. By the end of the nineteenth century, yellow stock brick gave way to machine-made red bricks, their edges so even that the mortar joints were reduced to less than a third of an inch thick.

Kent – handy for brick-making specialists from northern Europe – has the best brickwork in England. Those foreign specialists introduced Flemish bond – a style of laying bricks, head first ('headers'), then lengthways ('stretchers'), in a single 'course', or row. Before then, English bond – alternate rows, each entirely made up of headers or stretchers – had been popular. Flemish bond dominated English bricklaying from the 1630s until the nineteenth century.

Kent's proximity to northern Europe also meant Dutch gables were popular, particularly in Thanet, Hythe, Worth and Ash; as were big, orange Dutch roof pantiles, introduced to England as ballast on cargo ships in the seventeenth century. These were mostly replaced by local tiles in the eighteenth and nineteenth centuries. Kent tiles were made from Wealden clay, studded with Paludina limestones, largely consisting of snail and other mollusc shells.

The tiles were often laid on long, swooping roofs, called catslides, dropping down almost to the ground (catslide roofs could also be thatched). Or they were hung vertically to protect the walls. When Kent tiles were polished, they produced so-called Bethersden marble, found on elaborate tombs at Chilham and Woodchurch churches.

Thatched roofs were popular in counties where the right sort of clay for tiles was in short supply, like Suffolk, which has a higher percentage of thatched roofs than any other county. In Norfolk, wheat, field straw and Norfolk reed from the Broads were used for thatching, although plenty of thatched roofs were later replaced with tiles.

For all the English variety in building stones, we are short on marbles and exotically coloured stones. An exception is Blue John, the purple, blue and yellow crystallized fluorite found only at Treak Cliff Hill, in Castleton, Derbyshire; it's often seen in grand Derbyshire houses, including on the chimney pieces at Kedleston Hall and for a vase at Chatsworth.

Orwell's misguided point about the sleekness and dullness of the English landscape could be applied to its stones. There is a great variety of English stones, but few have the dramatic colours of the best Italian marble or the white purity of Carrara marble, used to build the Pantheon, Trajan's Column, Siena's Duomo and Marble Arch.

England's stones may not be much good at producing splashes and streaks of lurid colour; but they do produce a quiet, understated strain of beauty, in harmony with the landscape they were extracted from.

The best English buildings – particularly medieval ones, of thickly lichened limestone – may not be dazzling, polychromatic jewels, but they are no worse for that. They blend into the landscape, rather than standing wholly apart from it. They appear to grow out of the earth they're rooted in; like the fifteenth-century Knole House, Kent, the childhood home of Vita Sackville-West, who said of the house, 'It has the tone of England; it melts into the green of the garden turf, into the tawnier green of the park beyond, into the blue of the pale English sky.'

3. England's Feet of Clay: Our National Soil Collection

You must be so good as to tell me my road, and if there is
anything in my way worth stopping to see – I mean literally
to see: for I do not love guessing whether a bump in the
ground is Danish, British or Saxon.

Horace Walpole to the Reverend William Mason, 6 July 1772

In April 2009, the MPs' expenses scandal erupted across the
front page of the *Daily Telegraph*, echoing through the high
Gothic halls of the Palace of Westminster.

Most memorable of the victims were Sir Peter Viggers, Tory
MP for Gosport, who claimed £1,645 for an ornamental duck
house, and Douglas Hogg, Viscount Hailsham, MP for Sleaford
and North Hykeham, who claimed £2,115 to have the moat
cleared around his Victorian house in Lincolnshire. The idea of
a moat chimed with all the clichés about landed knights of the
shires and Tory grandees.

To devotees of the English landscape, the curious thing
about Douglas Hogg's moat was its location – in Lincolnshire.
Lincolnshire just isn't great moat territory.

Good moat country is dictated, like most landscape details of
Britain, by climate, geography and history. Or I should say
England, which has the lion's share of moats, with 5,000 of
them; Scotland has only thirty-one.

Different counties are variously equipped for moat-digging.

The Lincolnshire soil isn't suited to it; unlike England's most moat-friendly counties, Essex, with 770 moats, and Suffolk, with around 740.

East Anglia as a whole has about a quarter of all the moats in England and Wales, because it's flat, with clay soil – ideal moat conditions. That East Anglian clay was deposited by glaciers moving over the landscape, dropping stones, boulders, sand and mud as they went.

You don't get too many moats on hills; it's harder to keep the water in. And, as soon as a landscape starts to run short on water-retaining clay, the moats start to run out, too. Moats built on the edges of clay soil tend to fail – like the medieval ones in West Stow and Hengrave in Suffolk, near Bury St Edmunds. They were later filled in, because the water kept on leaking away.

Moats dug out of clay can survive where the house they once encircled no longer does; moats and fish ponds often mark the sites of long-disappeared granges, religious houses and manor houses.

Peak moat-digging time in England was from 1150 until 1325, reaching a high point in the middle of the thirteenth century.[1] Although the period was also rich in castle-building, moats weren't built for defensive purposes – they were too shallow for that. Because barns were usually built outside the moat, a besieged, moated house would be cut off from its food supply. The moat platform – the area within the moat – was also usually too small to store large livestock or enough supplies to survive a siege.

Since moats weren't used for military reasons – most of them can be waded through, even by the average, overladen knight – there were no restrictions imposed on moat size; unlike in France, where there were depth limitations to prevent owners building invulnerable fortifications.

There were no restrictions on the size of the moat platform

either. At the moat in Up End, North Crawley, Buckinghamshire (another flattish, moat-friendly county, with 170 identified examples), the platform is big enough to accommodate several fish ponds.

In medieval England, moats were really status symbols. The bigger the moat platform, the grander you were. A half-acre platform was for inferior freemen and clergy; an acre platform, like Douglas Hogg's, signified a lord of the manor. Hogg's moat, though, still isn't quite in the first division, partly because it's one of the square moats built after the first wave of round-moat building.

Moats are idiosyncratic, prominent things, but more day-to-day features in the landscape also respond to the precise soil conditions of England.

So, the majority of England's 400 vineyards like light soil over south-facing chalk. Around 10 per cent of the 1,000 English hectares under vine are at the Denbies vineyard in Surrey's North Downs – England's biggest vineyard, where the chalk structure of the soil is ideal for wine-making; the same soil as the Champagne region in France. (Chablis, incidentally, is made from grapes grown 100 miles south-east of Paris, in Kimmeridgian clay – named after Kimmeridge, the Dorset village which sits on the same belt of Upper Jurassic limestone, formed by compacted oyster shells.)

The structure of the soil sometimes works against, not with, man. In June 2009, fifteen months after its disastrous opening, Heathrow's Terminal Five faced further problems. The £4.3bn building was hit by 'heave', a kind of reverse subsidence that's gradually pushing the terminal upwards. Heave is caused by swelling of the London clay on which the terminal is built.

That clay, a marine mud deposit, is full of sulphide minerals which, when exposed to air, oxidize and expand. As a result, tiles have had to be repaired on the south side of the terminal, and the problem may continue – London clay goes on swelling for several decades.

The depth of soil over the rocks below isn't normally as volatile as that. But depth does vary extremely over the country. In the village of Cranborne, Dorset, there are only three or four inches of topsoil over the solid chalk. Thin soil like this is ideal for wildflowers, and for slow-growing grass – at Cranborne, there's only one late grass cut a year, in September.

Soil can be so deep that it masks the relief of the rocks beneath, and the landscape is almost completely defined by the earth.

The Luftwaffe bomb that just missed the west front of St Paul's Cathedral on 12 September 1940 burrowed right down through the foundations, dozens of feet into the earth below. The soldier who dug it out, Lieutenant Robert Davies (later imprisoned for thieving during the Blitz), had to dig down through the mud, sand and clay soil for three days, to get to the bomb – 'a vast hog', as he described it.

Of German bombs dropped on Britain during the war, 69 per cent penetrated less than 15 feet into the earth; 1 per cent, like the St Paul's bomb, were buried more than 30 feet below the surface. The deepest ever burrowed down 62 feet into the ground.[2]

You can have combinations of soils, too, with a fertile layer laid over an infertile one. The alluvium, a loose combination of soil and sediments, on top of the Wealden clay of Kent, produced the right growing conditions for the rich orchards of the Garden of England.

Not that the whole of Kent is such a fertile garden. While the Thanet Sands in the north-west of the county produce fertile, loamy soils for fruit-growing, the stiffer clays of Blean Woods, just outside Canterbury, are harder to cultivate; that's why they've survived as ancient woodland.

The poor soils and hilly country of the Pennines meant they became grouse moors, reservoirs and sheep pastures. The Millstone Grit rock beneath that poor soil is responsible for the fine soft waters in the reservoirs. It also produces good growing conditions for the heather fed on by the grouse.

Soil and stone work in concert. The more fertile limestone areas of the Pennines produce fescue pastures for the sheep, as well as dramatic rock formations for the tourists. The poorness of the soil and the wildness of those hills also meant the southern Pennines were undeveloped enough to form the first national park, the Peak District, in 1951.

Like the stones of England that so influence the landscape, English soils are many and varied – and are in fact often dictated by the geological make-up of the rocks beneath. Like the stones, too, soils change over short distances – another reason for the country's multicoloured, patchwork look.

Different plants – even closely related ones – will choose different soils in which to lodge their roots. The sessile oak, which thrives on sandstone and limestone soils, encourages open woodland with grassy undergrowth. The pedunculate oak does better on heavy clays, leading to a thicker, more impenetrable woodland floor.

In the light, acidic sand of Berkshire, you'll find gorse, camellias, pines and rhododendrons. Twenty miles away, across the Hampshire border, the alkaline soil is good for flowering shrubs, hazel coppices and beech trees.

Further south, in the village of Exbury, also in Hampshire, another belt of sandy acidic loam was ideal for creating the garden of Lionel Rothschild (1882–1942). By his own admission 'a banker by hobby, a gardener by profession', he developed more than a thousand new rhododendron and azalea hybrids – a feat only possible in that acidic soil.

Despite its relatively small size, England was subject to many different types of soil creation. A single county might have several different earth-creating forces at work; both glacial and geological.

East Anglia consists almost entirely of layers of material deposited by Ice Age glaciers, covering the rock and stone beneath. The first glaciers drifted across East Anglia, laying loamy, fertile soils across the north-east, around Yarmouth, Sheringham and Norwich.

Another glacier, the Great Eastern glacier, moved across south Norfolk and Suffolk, depositing a 150ft-thick layer of chalky boulder clay mixed with chunks of chalk and pebbles. The resulting lakes, with their clay and loam beds, produced the modern corn prairies of East Anglia – the bread basket of England. Where that same glacier left belts of sand and gravel, the land is that much less fertile.

A lucky combination of glacial and geological forces produced ideal pasture for the undersung sculptor of the English countryside and the English village – the sheep. The motto of John Barton, a fifteenth-century wool merchant in Holme, Nottinghamshire, was 'I thanke God and ever shall / It is the sheepe hath payed for all.'[3] His motto could stand for much of southern England.

The historian Niall Ferguson has said of the English that 'their one novel economic idea in the Middle Ages was selling wool to the Flemish'.[4] It was a powerful economic idea, all the same, and one that made for some exceptionally rich humans; and rich humans build big buildings.

Despite the modern decline of our sheep-farming, Britain remains the seventh-largest wool producer in the world, with Australia, China and New Zealand the top three. But the wool industry is nothing to what it once was.

Sheep drove the English economy from the twelfth century

until the Industrial Revolution, and opened it up to the world: in 1446, the Medicis opened their first bank in London, so that Florence could buy wool from the Cotswolds. By the end of the Middle Ages, there were three sheep for every person in the country.

In Suffolk, Norfolk and Essex, the fertile flatlands made for excellent sheep pasture in the fourteenth and fifteenth centuries. Suffolk and Norfolk also benefited from the flourishing cloth trade; Norfolk's 600 medieval churches – more than any other county – were built on the back of wool and cloth. That East Anglian sheep boom spread into Oxfordshire, Lincolnshire, Gloucestershire and Kent – where the Perpendicular churches of Cranbrook, Maidstone and Tenterden were built on the back of it.

Churches built on those wool and cloth fortunes were as big as medieval churches got – in the tall, broad-windowed, Perpendicular, late-Gothic style; called 'woolgothic' in Gloucestershire. Counties like Wiltshire – with its uplands too barren for sheep – are correspondingly short on great Gothic churches.

In wool-rich villages, the churches often remain the biggest buildings in the village. Technology and engineering may have leapt forward in the last half-millennium; but, still, there has been no impetus to build anything bigger than a Perpendicular church since the medieval agricultural boom.

The Industrial Revolution may have blighted many towns and cities, but it preserved England's villages. From the eighteenth century, industry moved from village to town. The workers followed, leaving behind them the classic English village, a frozen creation, largely of the Tudor to Georgian periods (barring, perhaps, an earlier church and patches of modern housing on the village's fringes).

When you see a huge Perpendicular stone church like Stoke by Nayland in Suffolk, looming over the half-timbered guildhall, it's hard to believe that the bigger, more sophisticated stone church is more than a hundred years older than the sixteenth-century wooden guildhall. Much more money was spent on the holy building, not least on getting the best stone for it – in a county that isn't rich in stone.

Of the legacies that built medieval churches in Suffolk, well over 90 per cent were left between 1400 and 1555, during the Perpendicular Gothic period; three quarters of them in the century after 1450. Most of the legacies came from the new rich – members of the merchant class, their fortunes built on wool and cloth. Only a minority were from the aristocracy.

Sheep could destroy villages, too, as Thomas More wrote in *Utopia*.

> The sheep that were wont to be so meek and tame and so small eaters now, as I hear say, be become so great devourers and so wild that they eat up and swallow down the very men themselves. They consume, destroy and devour whole fields, houses and cities.

One village, Wharram Percy in Yorkshire, which flourished between the twelfth and fourteenth centuries, was deserted in the fifteenth century, thanks to sheep. The landowner, realizing that sheep were more profitable than peasants, cleared the area for grazing. A lone ancient church, like Wharram Percy's, with barely any buildings alongside, is often the sign of a deserted medieval village; and any bumps in the neighbouring fields the remains of the ancient settlement.

With an eye on the bull-market periods when buildings went up in various counties, you can work out the peaks and troughs of the local economy. So, Herefordshire is rich in Norman buildings up until 1200. There's not much construction in the thirteenth century. Then, from 1300, as local fortunes improved, there was a huge amount of rebuilding, enlarging and improving. New church windows were inserted with elaborate cusped lancets and Y-shaped tracery. Colossal churches – mini-cathedrals almost – pop up in small villages like Madley, in the Golden Valley. By the mid-fourteenth century, the boom construction years were over; Madley Church has remained the biggest building in the village ever since.

Sheep-farming had a considerable effect on English trading cities, too. When Dick Whittington was appointed Mayor of London in the late fourteenth century, he also became 'the collector of the wool custom and subside in London', accumulating a huge income from what looks like a clear conflict of interest.

The Spencer family built their ancestral home, Althorp House, Northamptonshire, on the back of sheep. In the late fifteenth century – peak of the English sheep boom years – John Spencer, a rich sheep farmer from Warwickshire, first took a lease on the manor on the site of Althorp.

Sheep also built the house in *Brideshead Revisited*; as recalled by Lord Marchmain on his deathbed, when he talked of 'the fat days, the days of wool-shearing and the wide corn lands, the days of growth and building, when the marshes were drained and the waste land brought under the plough, when one built the house, his son added the dome, his son spread the wings and dammed the river.'

The infertility of certain soils has its own powerful effect on the landscape, too, and who chooses to live there.

So, the Lickey Hills, eleven miles south-west of Birmingham, have remained the city's wild playground because of the poor soil. It's not good enough for cultivation; and it's just far enough from the city centre to escape development.

It's only because of the sterile sands beneath the New Forest that it has remained forest; even if it has changed from a Norman oak forest, via beech plantations, to the Victorian stands of fir trees, surrounded by rhododendrons and gorse, that now dominate the landscape.

Because this heathland was infertile, it was sparsely inhabited through the Middle Ages. Bigger Dorset towns, like Poole, with its fishing industry and port, and Wimborne Minster, near the rich soil of Cranborne Chase, turned their faces away from the heath.

Beneath those sandy Dorset heaths, there's a bed of chalk. Whenever it collapses, the sand is sucked away, leaving behind sinkholes as deep as 40 feet. Puddletown Heath, inspiration for Egdon Heath in Hardy's *The Return of the Native*, is punctured with 370 of them.

Hardy's Dorset heaths now retain just 15 per cent of their original heathland cover; but there's still enough left to support four different types of heather, including the native Dorset Heath variety, reptiles such as the sand lizard and the smooth snake, and birds like the nightjar and Dartford warbler.

Before we weep for the loss of Hardy's broad heaths, it's worth remembering that they, too, like many English wildernesses, aren't so wild; they were manmade, produced in the Bronze Age 4,000 years ago, when inferior woods, created by the poor, acidic soil, were cleared.

Elsewhere, heathland has been turned into fertile cornfields, notably in north Norfolk – thanks to the eighteenth-century farming reforms of Thomas Coke, whose descendant, the Earl of Leicester, still farms the land on the coast around his Palladian seat, Holkham Hall.

Coke dug out fertile marl from under the barren topsoil and spread it over the fields. He also fine-tuned the art of crop rotation. By 1800, two thirds of Norfolk land was under the plough, and the county was exporting more grain to Holland than all other English counties combined. On his Holkham estate, Coke's rental income soared by 44 per cent between 1720 and 1760. This local boom explains the county's rich collection of Georgian farmhouses, with one in practically every Norfolk village.

Another eighteenth-century agricultural improvement came with the seed drill, invented by Jethro Tull in 1701. It had a regimenting effect on the landscape: in Gainsborough's portrait *Mr and Mrs Andrews*, painted in 1750 in Sudbury, Suffolk, you can clearly make out the long, straight rows of wheat planted with Tull's drill.

It was the soil – or lack of it – that decided the look of Breckland, 370 square miles of sandy, dry heaths, stripped of vegetation, on the Norfolk–Suffolk border. 'Brecks' were temporary fields planted by farmers, which turned to wilderness after the soil had been exhausted and the heavier chalk, clay and limestone particles washed out of the earth. The resulting light, sandy soil was so thin and sparse that farmers, when asked whether their land was in Norfolk or Suffolk, would say, 'It depends on which way the wind is blowing'.

In the eighteenth and nineteenth centuries, landowners planted trees to stop the soil erosion, and engineers developed irrigation systems to draw water from beneath the chalk. In time, the fields and forests round Thetford, Norfolk, in the heart of Breckland, became some of the best farming and sporting estates in England.

Where the brecks weren't re-energized, the Forestry Commission, in 1922, planted the biggest lowland coniferous forests in the country. As well as boosting red squirrel numbers, the conifers lent a strange north German feel to what is still one of the least populated areas of southern England.

Conifers aren't necessarily an alien tree. It's just that, where they're introduced en masse, they can smother the landscape with their Teutonic uniformity, particularly when contrasted with our ever-changing, deciduous woodlands.[5]

To begin with, the Forestry Commission was obsessed with conifers. Shortly after the Commission was founded, it planted 74,000 acres of them on English heaths and bogs. Now the Commission is, slowly, reversing the process: since 2002, it has only restored 5,000 of the 57,000 acres of ancient deciduous woodland planted with conifers over the last century.

You can often see where Forestry Commission land begins. Its stands of fir trees on the Lancashire moors have squared-off edges to them – commerce, unlike nature, adores a straight line. The contrast shows up sharply in Herefordshire, between neat stands of Forestry Commission conifers on the hills near Radnor and the ragbag of Arthur Rackhamesque oaks, tangled up with undergrowth, strung along the River Wye from Ross, in Herefordshire, to Monmouthshire.

At the end of the Ice Age, our native trees moved through a cycle – first came birch, then pine, followed by mixed oak trees, now held up as the quintessentially English trees. Scots pines are native to the Scottish Highlands, but were introduced into England. There are fewer pine trees in England now than at the end of the Ice Age; the Continent has many more than we do.

Our rarest native tree is now the black poplar, with only 6,750 counted in 2001 in England, half of them in the Vale of Aylesbury in Buckinghamshire. There is still, satisfyingly, an ageing black poplar hanging on in Poplar, east London, which took its name from the tree. Black poplars frame the scene in Constable's *The Hay Wain*; if the tree disappeared, it would be a tragedy to rank with the near-disappearance of another of Constable's favourite subjects – the elm.

Dutch elm disease has killed 25–30 million elms since a new strain of the disease arrived in around 1967. They live on in some disease-free outposts, like the Scilly Isles. A pair of 200-year-old elms survive in Moreton-in-Marsh, and there are more in Brighton, where a cordon sanitaire was established at the height of the outbreak. Some elms have crept back but otherwise the English landscape is utterly changed by their disappearance. Seven Sisters in Holloway, north London, was named for the seven elms that once stood there; now only the name survives.

The birches haven't gone – they're still often the first tree to move on to land that's just been opened up, by railways and in forest clearings. Their ancient presence is reflected in place names, like Birkenhead, Cheshire, 'the headland covered with birch'. Ash trees, another native species, can also be spotted in place names, such as Knotty Ash in Lancashire, Askrigg in Yorkshire and Ashby de la Launde in Lincolnshire. Water-loving alders, another native, do well in the damper parts of England, in the north and west; in the drier south and east, they crop up in marshes and on riversides. They echo through place names, too: like Aldercar, Derbyshire, and Aldershot and Alresford, Hampshire.

But, while the place names remain, the trees that inspired them have often disappeared. Woodland now covers only around 7 per cent of England. No wonder we have to import 85 per cent of our timber and wood products.

More than three quarters of our trees are less than a hundred years old; but the 5 per cent that are ancient are unusually well looked after – a reflection of the English reverence for the historical. Country house parks and patches of old royal hunting forests – such as Savernake Forest, Wiltshire, or Hatfield Forest, Essex, both rich in ancient trees – have been preserved for centuries. In the Middle Ages, a forest meant a place to keep deer rather than a place expressly for trees; so they were carefully tended as valuable game reserves.

Ancient trees are certainly better looked after here than on the Continent: you could walk from Athens to Boulogne without seeing a single tree that's more than a century old.[6] The English are often accused of preferring animals to humans; they are also indulgent of their old trees. And perhaps for a shared reason: an awkward, isolated, cold, northern race finds animals and trees easier to get along with than their fellow human beings.

When Lord Cobham created the Elysian Fields at Stowe, Buckinghamshire, in the early eighteenth century, he breezily flattened a whole medieval village, but he preserved the 500-year-old common yew that survives today. And when Capability Brown stripped country-house parks to produce his trademark 'improved' look several decades later, he removed hedgerows without compunction, but left the old trees alone.

Ancient woods are usually found in hard-to-cultivate places: on infertile land that can still accommodate trees, and on relatively inaccessible hills. They are often rich in woodland hawthorn and lime (*Tilia cordata*) trees.

A wood that has been regularly coppiced for a long time will also have a variety of plants used to ancient cycles of shade and sunlight: particularly oxlips, anemones and primroses. Woodland has long memories: in the woods of Grovely Ridge, Salisbury, phosphate-loving plants are still living off the bones and burnt wood of long-vanished, 1,600-year-old Romano-British villages.[7]

Older woods may have a zig-zagging edge, where sharp corners have been carved into the wood's border by later fields. If an ancient wood's corners survive these invasions, they are often marked with mounds; and its sides are lined with substantial banks. Later woods – planned during the eighteenth and nineteenth centuries, when the landscape was chopped up in straight lines under the Enclosure Acts – have straighter edges, marked with flimsy banks topped with thin hawthorn hedges.

In recent years, England has become increasingly wooded. Over the last two decades, the country's woodland acreage has grown by more than three times the size of Greater London. So much new forest is being planted that some areas could even reach the level recorded by the Domesday Book in 1086, when 15 per cent of the country was covered in trees.

England's deforestation began a long time before then. Stonehenge's original astronomical use depended not just on having no trees around it, but also on a horizon uninterrupted by long grass, so that the precise alignment of stones could be ensured.[8]

Even at the time Stonehenge was being built, in around 2400–2200 BC, much of England had been deforested. It's thought that, by the second millennium BC, half of England was no longer wooded; by the end of the Roman period, the English wildwood had long gone.[9]

No trees, short grass – Stonehenge in the middle of the nineteenth century.

When the Saxons arrived in the fifth century AD, only about 30 per cent of England was wooded; late-Saxon farming reduced that to around 15 per cent. Tiny traces of pre-Saxon forest survive in a few places, like the Hertfordshire villages of Hadham, Widford and Sawbridgeworth. The Black Death in 1348 marked the first significant halt to the stripping of England – woods that survived until then often lasted for another half a millennium.[10]

Deforestation came late to some parts of England. Lancashire was densely forested in the Middle Ages – most of Manchester consisted largely of half-timbered houses until the Georgian period. Sussex was once so impenetrably dense with trees that it was the last southern county to accept Christianity. By 1700, that tree cover had largely gone: 300-year-old farmhouses in Sussex often shelter in the lee of windbreaks – useful stands of trees that were allowed to remain while all around was stripped bare.

The extent of British woodland was last thought to be at today's levels in 1750 – when forests were replenished after the agricultural revolution, before they were stripped again to build ships ahead of the Seven Years War (1756–63) and the Napoleonic Wars.

Over the next century and a half, forest cover dropped to below 5 per cent, before new growth turned things around from the 1940s onwards. The recent boom was largely helped by private buyers, encouraged by tax breaks. Private landowners now provide almost half of British tree cover.

All these things mean there are now 5,500 woods in the UK, covering 8,500 square miles. That's 9 per cent of the total land area, admittedly still one of the lowest percentages in Europe, where the average woodland cover is 44 per cent – forest covers 32 per cent of Germany and 29 per cent of France.

England's hospitable climate, its lack of mountains and really impenetrable wildernesses, and its limited size had their drawbacks as far as the survival of woodland was concerned – from early on in the Middle Ages, you could go practically anywhere in the country, with an axe under your arm, and get chopping.

We can, though, lay claim to one green record: Sheffield has the highest number of trees per head of any city in Europe. Our countryside may be more denuded than the Continent; but English cities remain exceptionally green, London among them.

In the rebuilding of Shanghai over the past twenty years, no new substantial parks have been built, and the few surviving city trees are in a terrible state. London is 40 per cent parkland; Shanghai 4 per cent. Even as the English have become more and more urban creatures, less than 8 per cent of British land is covered by urban development.

Because England has been so heavily cultivated for so long – because even its supposedly wild bits are in fact fairly tame – most of the country still has some agricultural use. Sheep and cattle graze the wild parts of Britain: the Welsh hills, the Cumbrian fells, the Scottish Highlands.

The total acreage of the UK is roughly 60 million acres.[11] Around three quarters of that is agricultural land. And, of that agricultural land, just under a quarter is arable. Arable farming likes it dry – from 15 to 35 inches of rain a year. So it tends to be concentrated on the drier, eastern side of the country; some parts of eastern England are technically classified as semi-arid. The relative flatness of the east is also better suited to the combine harvesters used on arable crops.

Yields climbed through the twentieth century, with greater use of fertilizer and pesticides, the introduction of those combine harvesters in the 1930s and the passing of the 1947 Agricultural Act. Under the Act, arable farmers were protected against the uncertainties of the market by subsidies in the form of guaranteed minimum payments, giving them the confidence to plan ahead. In the 1960s, wheat yields in particular grew, when the Government's Plant Breeding Institute developed a dwarf variety that could withstand bad weather better, and had more fertile ears.

The wide-open prairies of East Anglia – opened up even more over the last half-century for the combines, with hundreds of miles of hedges grubbed up – are still given over to traditional crops, like wheat, barley, mustard and peas. Colman's Mustard is grown in Carrow, Norfolk; malting barley in north Norfolk.

In among the wheat and the grass, there are more stretches of bright colour appearing across the country. The Scilly Isles, warmed by the Gulf Stream, turn daffodil-yellow in the spring; much of Hampshire goes flax-blue; purple lavender and borage are grown in Norfolk and Kent, home to the bulk of the twenty-six English commercial lavender farmers; while delphiniums are grown in Worcestershire to provide wedding confetti. The 120-acre field of tulips in Narborough, Norfolk, is the biggest tulip field in England.

Different vegetables thrive in different counties: more than 80 per cent of British tomatoes come from Sussex; Lincolnshire and East Anglia specialize in carrots; Lincolnshire and Bedfordshire are rich in Brussels sprouts, celery and potatoes; rhubarb is popular in the old mining areas north of Sheffield.

Even if farming still dominates the English landscape, as it has for the last 2,000 years, the type of farming has changed enormously in recent decades.

In 1997, Britain provided three quarters of its own food; in 2010, that dropped to 60 per cent, and the figure is falling by 1 per cent a year. EU set-aside laws – from 1988 to 2008, up to 15 per cent of farming land was left uncultivated – made their contribution to that decline.

Among the biggest changes is the near-disappearance of British orchards, down by three quarters since 1950. In Cambridgeshire alone, the number of orchard acres has shrunk from 10,000 to 2,100 over the past half-century. The Vale of Evesham in Worcestershire remains apple, pear, plum and asparagus country, but big patches of fruit-bearing trees have been grubbed up in recent decades.

The national collection of apple varieties – growing ever since Julius Caesar brought the apple tree with him to Britain in 55 BC – is still more than 2,000 strong. But the British apple has been living on borrowed time since the sixties invasion of cheaper South African, New Zealand and Australian apples – fruit grown from tree varieties that we exported across the Commonwealth in the first place.

Heavy grain subsidies from the EU in the seventies meant labour-intensive orchards were grubbed up and replaced by wheatfields, with their lower overheads. Imports of exotic fruit have also increased vastly over the last half-century, as the English diet diversifies: the apple has fallen way behind the banana in popularity.

Our orchards are just consolidating after half a century of decline, with efforts made to preserve older apple varieties like Howgate Wonder, a red, stripy cooker, propagated on the Isle of Wight in 1915, and the Blenheim Orange, propagated near Blenheim Palace in Woodstock, Oxfordshire, in 1770. In the seven counties of Bedfordshire, Norfolk, Hertfordshire, Essex, Lincolnshire, Suffolk and Cambridgeshire alone, there are still 250 varieties of apple, pear, plum and cherry tree.

Other declines are even steeper: just before the First World War, there were 7,000 acres of cobnuts under cultivation in England, mostly in Kent; by 1990, Kent was down to just 250 acres. The county had 46,600 acres of hop fields in the 1870s; it now has 1,000. The Garden of England now looks a little less varied than it used to.

Farm animals still determine the look of Britain, but they, too, are in decline. The pig population has fallen by nearly half over the last twenty years. Sheep numbers have fallen from 18.2 million to 15.4 million; even if Britain is still the largest producer of sheep meat in Europe, and very nearly self-sufficient in it.

Arable land still gives way in the west, and in the hills, to grass: the dairy heartlands of England run from Lancashire down through Cheshire to Shropshire; and, from the Vale of Gloucester, south to Cornwall.

But our historic landscape connection with dairy farming is winding down: over the last twenty years, the number of British cows has dropped by nearly a quarter. In 2008, Britain was self-sufficient in milk; by 2010, it was importing 1.5 million litres a day.

Much of England used to be milk country – the wet, temperate climate and fertile soils are ideal for grass-growing – but less and less so. The Chinese still say us Westerners smell of milk; but for how much longer?

4. A River Runs through It: Why You Live Where You Live

Not much space for swelling into hugeness; no great
wastes overwhelming in their dreariness, no great solitudes of
forests, no terrible untrodden mountain walls; all is measured,
mingled, varied, gliding easily one thing into another, little rivers,
little plains, little hills, little mountains . . . neither prison, nor
palace, but a decent home.

William Morris on England, *The Lesser Arts.*
Collected Works, vol. XXII

If I were deposited on the site of my flat in Kentish Town, north London, in prehistoric times, would I recognize it?

Would I find the top of the hill on which my late-Victorian villa sits, concealed by all that jungle and those woolly mammoths? Would I find my way down to the Thames, by tracking the route of its tributary, the Fleet? – it still runs down the bottom of my street, albeit cut and covered with roads and housing in the nineteenth century.

What about the hills at Woolwich, where the chalk downs approach the Thames? Could I identify the flat tributary valleys of the Thames, the Ravensbourne emerging at Deptford Creek, or the Wandle, running through Wandsworth?

The chances are, I'd be lost, even with the help of the most prominent features in the landscape. Still – whether I recognize

them or not – the reason why my flat is where it is, is precisely
because of those ancient landscape features, many of which survive today.

Most English cities are where they are for an ancient geological, or sociological, reason. You may be a Buddhist living in
Canterbury, but it's because St Augustine picked this spot for his
church that the city – and you – are there.

Ipswich – one of the biggest cities in Suffolk – is significant
today because it was significant yesterday. It was the only major
urban settlement in East Anglia until the Viking invasions ended
in the late ninth century.

In the sixteenth and seventeenth centuries, Norwich was the
second-biggest and richest city in the country after London. In
the fourteenth century, its walled centre was even bigger than
London's. Its modern prominence really depends on an even earlier incarnation as a Saxon town, around a spot called Westwic,
near the west end of modern Westwick Street.

Those ancient reasons for setting up a town are so deep-
rooted that they can survive long periods of obscurity.
Colchester – originally Camulodunum, after Camulos, the war
god of the Catuvellauni, a pre-Roman tribe – was the capital of
Roman Britain, but disappeared from view under the Saxons; it
isn't mentioned in a Saxon document until the tenth century.

Access to water dictated the site of most of these early English settlements. Monasteries were built close to water supplies
– for cooking, washing and drainage. The Norman cathedral of
Sarum, Wiltshire, was deserted in the fourteenth century
because it had no water supply; as a result, Salisbury Cathedral
was built in the valley below, and the town grew around it.
Neighbouring Wilton, once Wiltshire's most important town,
was eclipsed by Salisbury when the River Avon was forded by
Harnham Bridge, diverting the main road away from Wilton.

If rivers were medieval A-roads, estuaries were Roman,

Viking and Saxon motorways: the places where most riverborne traffic entered England; where the water was so deep that the biggest ships could dock easily. The ancient importance of river and sea traffic explains why so many English towns are still sprinkled around estuary mouths. Many of our eighty-one estuaries – a fifth of all the North Sea and Atlantic tidal inlets in Europe – are still given over to industry and ports.

Even if you're a Londoner who never uses the Thames, it's because the Romans did rely on it so heavily that you're living there. And it is water that still dictates the boundaries of Londoners' lives. Like rats, the water table is never far away from you: when a London basement is dug out, you almost always have to build in pumping systems and flooding alarms to keep the ground water at bay.

The plan of the City of London remains broadly Roman, nestling next to the Thames, and roughly skirted by its Roman wall. Made out of Kentish Ragstone, probably quarried in Maidstone, the wall was built in around AD 200; Kentish Rag was also used on St Paul's Cathedral, Canterbury Cathedral and the Tower of London.

Londinium was settled at the most easterly fordable point of the river before it grew too wide; a point where the tide can bring ships forty miles inland. Anyone downriver of that lowest fordable point – that is, anyone without a boat – necessarily had to use the London crossing first. Upriver, as the water narrowed, you could build any number of bridges.

Improved technology over the centuries has allowed rivers across England to be forded further and further downstream: like the Queen Elizabeth II Bridge, the M25 crossing over the Thames between Thurrock and Dartford, opened in 1991. When the Severn Bridge was opened in 1966, it was the longest bridge in the world; now it's flanked by the 1996 Severn Bridge, further downstream and more than three times the length.

"Now let's see what happens . . .'

From Ronald Searle's *Merry England, etc.*, 1956.

That lowest fordable spot on the Thames was where the Romans built the first London Bridge out of wood, 169 feet downstream from today's London Bridge. It was rebuilt by the Normans in stone in 1176. That bridge – the only fixed crossing east of Kingston upon Thames until 1730, when Putney Bridge was built – was replaced in 1831 by the bridge that ended up in Arizona in 1971.

The southern end of London Bridge became a natural settling point, too. It's where Southwark Cathedral, the oldest cathedral in London, was begun in AD 606. Roman London's road network revolved around the bridge, and the river – Roman settlements at Fulham and Putney were also river crossing points.

When the Romans invaded in AD 43, the London area contained a few ancient British settlements. Otherwise, it was little more than a sprawling series of marshes flanking the banks of the Thames; marshes formed by tributaries leading down to the flat river basin.

Above these marshes were two gravel-capped hills, now in the City of London – survivors of a 50ft-high gravel terrace that once ran parallel to the river.

These hills produced reliably dry positions from which to launch a boat. The need to cross from south to north – connecting Kent and Sussex, the counties where the Romans landed, with the rest of the country – was of paramount importance.

It's telling that the Romans chose the further bank – i.e. the north – as the basis for Londinium, embattled with walls and a fortress; the area that still roughly marks the square mile of the City of London. Both those crucial gravel-capped hills were on the less marshy north side of the river. The marshiness of the river's southern side also meant fewer train and Tube lines were dug through the subsoil – thought to be quicksand – as late as the nineteenth century. As a result, many more trains are run on viaducts through south London than they are north of the river.

The marshiness of the south bank explains why the north was settled first; and why the major administrative and commercial areas of the city were founded there. It also explains why south London has been unfashionable for centuries. This polarized approach just doesn't happen in other cities like, say, Paris, where the Rives Gauche and Droite share the commercial, administrative and architectural honours.

That derogatory attitude to south London has been around for a while. Even in 1901, the novelist Walter Besant called south London 'a city without a municipality, without a centre, without civic history ... with no intellectual artistic, scientific, musical, literary centre, with no local patriotism or enthusiasm. One cannot imagine a man proud of New Cross.'

The north–south divide also explains why, Lambeth Palace apart, the majority of the city's grandest buildings with the oldest origins – Westminster Abbey, the Houses of Parliament, St Paul's Cathedral among them – are on the north bank of the Thames.

Those two gravel hills north of the river were the hub of what became Londinium, founded in around AD 50, seven years after Claudius's armies invaded England. On one hill was the Temple of Venus – still London's principal religious hill, it now supports the dome of St Paul's, the fifth cathedral to stand on the site since AD 604.

The other hill was occupied by the heart of Roman government – the Forum. The spot continued to be strategically significant: the old Royal Exchange, now a series of upmarket shops, is on the site today, but, from 1565 to 1939, it was the City's commercial centre, right next door to the Bank of England.

Between the two hills ran a stream called the Wall Brook; the street running along its course is still called Walbrook. Other small streams, like the Fleet at the bottom of my street, were buried later – as was the Holbourne river, whose deep valley now passes beneath Holborn Viaduct. The Westbourne was dammed to form the Serpentine; the Tyburn stream produced the lake in St James's Park.

Beyond the confines of the City, other islands, poking above the marshes, were the first villages to be settled. Medieval London parish churches were scattered along the Thames. Their names – Battersea, Chelsea and Putney – reflect the Saxon for island, 'ea' or 'ey'. Westminster Abbey, the site of a Saxon church, was also built on one of these 'ey' islands – Thorney Island. Eyots, small, mid-river islands, have the same etymological root.

Risk from flooding obviously increased the closer you got to the river. In the suburbs, villages like Wimbledon and Clapham

Common were settled on higher ground, often ranged around flat grazing commons.

Ancient villages downstream from London – Erith, Purfleet, Gravesend, Woolwich, Greenwich – were built on chalk hills. In between these high points, the soft alluvial land was easily dug out to produce the London Docks. The Thames was the site of the first great enclosed docks in the country: the West India (1799–1806), the London (1800–1805) and the East India (1803–6).

Right up until the creation of the canals in the eighteenth century, roads were so unreliable that the Thames was one of the principal arteries of England, carrying stone, grain and timber in vast quantities. The Thames pumped life into towns all the way along the riverside – Oxford, Reading and Henley among them.

London's significant political, religious and commercial buildings are still on the river bank or near it, including Parliament, Westminster Abbey and St Paul's. And most royal palaces are on or close to the river: Hampton Court, Windsor, Whitehall, Buckingham Palace, Greenwich and Richmond.

Today, though, the Thames has never been so empty since before the Romans arrived. London may be built around the Thames, but it turns its back on the water. Londoners can go years without crossing the river or walking along it. Once a week, I bicycle across the river to teach in south London. As I thread my way through the traffic jams on Waterloo Bridge, I'm struck by how little traffic there is down below me, on what was once the busiest river in the world.

Still, for all its modern emptiness, the river remains at the heart of London's foundation, as it does with other English cities. Manchester began life as the Roman fort Mancunium – thus Mancunians – in the first century AD, settled on a spur of land by the River Medlock. The medieval city was built on a sandstone hill where the River Irwell met the River Irk.

Leicester – the best spot to cross the River Soar – was a town for half a century before the Romans arrived in AD 43.

Cambridge, the highest navigable point of the Cam, began life as a river-crossing town, called Durolipons by the Romans, on a gravel ridge north of the River Cam. Four Roman roads crossed the river here: Akeman Street, running north-east to south-west; a connecting road to Ermine Street; the road to Braughing and Great Chesterford; and the road from Colchester to Leicester. Any traffic from further north was squeezed down towards Cambridge by the near-impenetrable Fens.

Southampton is where it is because the Channel narrows between Cap de la Hague, near Cherbourg, and Portland Bill. The city's unique position – affected by tidal oscillations along the Channel, as well as across it – gives Southampton a double high tide. With three hours of high water, that still gives enough time to dock and turn round the biggest of ships.

There are usually further geological reasons why a particular riverside spot is chosen for an ancient settlement. Liverpool was settled on a peninsula between the Pool of Liverpool, a tidal creek, and the River Mersey; it was also built around a hill, a low one made of the same sandstone used to build much of the city.

Winchester was sited on a gravel spur projecting into the Itchen Valley; the cathedral crypt is still often flooded because it was built on the valley floor. Worcester was first settled in the fourth or fifth century BC, on a ridge of gravel and sand next to an ancient ford across the Severn.

York is on a terminal moraine – a ridge of accumulated glacial debris across the marshy plain – producing a dry east–west walkway above the ancient swamps, across what is now the Vale of York, itself formed by a lake dammed with ice. Where the Ouse crossed these heights, the Romans, in AD 71, built Eboracum, which became York.

Access to the River Avon, and from there into the Bristol

Channel, is the main reason for Bristol's site. The city nestles in the Avon valley, between, to the north, the Cotswolds, and the Mendip Hills to the south. Bristol was England's main port for trade with Wales, the West Country, Ireland, Western Europe and America. The port specialized in West Country goods – leather, wheat, food and wool. The geology surrounding the port was helpful, too – with good building stone, alluvial clays, gravels, sands and coalfields nearby.

Bristol and Bath were the only Roman towns of any size in Somerset; in large part because of their site on the River Avon.

Bath had another reason for its prominence – it had the only naturally occurring hot springs in England. That's why the Romans built a spa there in AD 43; why it became England's first big modern spa town in the late seventeenth century, and why it later became the pre-eminent Georgian city in the country.

It's also why Bath got both its modern name and its ancient one, Aquae Sulis – the Waters of Sulis, the Celtic goddess worshipped at the spring before the Romans came.

What's in a Name?

Earlier this year, I caught the last sunshine of a spring Bank Holiday weekend, and took a thirty-mile bike ride between Shotover Hill, Oxfordshire, and Ivinghoe, Buckinghamshire.

After climbing Shotover Hill, the road flattened out along a ridge, on the old route from Oxford to London. Ivinghoe Beacon was quite a climb, too, but the profile of the hill was slightly different: with a slightly concave slope leading up to the peak, dipping down to a flat ridge beyond.

I only know these things because I bicycled past them. If I had been Margaret Gelling, the leading historian of British place names and president of the English Place-Name Society for twelve years, who died in 2009, aged eighty-four, I wouldn't have had to look at a map, or read a book, to work out what these places looked like.

Just from their names, Dr Gelling would have known not only what these places looked like, but also a pretty good chunk of their history, too. She would have known that the 'over' in Shotover derives from the Anglo-Saxon term *ofer*, meaning a flat-topped ridge with a convex shoulder. The 'shot' comes from *sceot*, meaning a steep place.

The 'hoe' in Ivinghoe is also a precise term. Literally meaning a heel, a hoe looks like an upside-down foot, with the heel sticking up in the air, and the concave indentation of the instep sloping down to ground level.

For thousands of years, this island has been intensively settled and cultivated by man – from Bronze Age man through Iron Age, Roman, Anglo-Saxon, Viking and Norman man. They left behind them a dense web of place names, describing the physical and sociological features of the place where they lived.

Even as much of England gets covered in concrete, tarmac and out-of-town shopping centres, those ancient place names survive beneath it all, giving clues as to how those places originally looked – and often still look.

The vast majority of English place names are derived from the Old English spoken by Germanic immigrants who came here in the fifth and sixth centuries, after the Romans left in AD 410.

There aren't many Anglo-Saxon buildings remaining – there are thought to be only around 250 surviving churches with some Anglo-Saxon element in them. But the Anglo-Saxon names live on.

Our language was only given the Anglo-Saxon name 'English' – or *englisc*, in fact – in the ninth century. And it was under the Anglo-Saxons, too, that England started to develop a distinctive English look.

Not only did the Anglo-Saxons name most of modern England, but they also decided where most modern settlements are. Practically every modern village and town appears in the Domesday Book, a survey that largely consists of settlements founded before the Norman invasion.

Some Celtic terms for ancient landscape features, such as *penn* (head) and *cruc* (hill, mound or tumulus), were borrowed by the Anglo-Saxons from the Britons who were there before the Romans. The Thames comes from the Celtic *Tamesa*; the Avon from *afon*, meaning water, as does *isca*, the root of the Rivers Usk and Esk.

Celtic names survive in greater numbers in Wales and Cornwall, where the British fled the Anglo-Saxon advance. The popular Cornish prefix 'Tre-', as in Tremaine and Tregarn, comes from the Celtic *trev* or *tre*, meaning a village or homestead.[1]

But, otherwise, today's place names were mostly first used 1,500 or so years ago by those Germanic immigrants, to describe landscape contours. The names practically always survive; as do the contours, unless they've been completely concealed by new settlements or motorways.

That connection between geography and name doesn't exist in more modern countries that use borrowed names; like in, say, America, where Exeter, New Hampshire – unlike Exeter, Devon – doesn't mean the *castra*, or Roman camp, on the River Exe.

In the mid-nineteenth century, the American writer Ralph Waldo Emerson said his home country was 'whitewashed all over by unmeaning names, the cast-off clothes of the country from which its emigrants came; or named at a pinch from a psalm-tune'.[2]

To be fair, the American settlers weren't always quite as random as that. Many of those American place names, particularly in New England, are directly borrowed from the East Anglian towns the settlers came from – such as Yarmouth, Ipswich,

Haverhill, Cambridge and Boston. An estimated 71 per cent of
the first Puritan pioneers to land in America in the early seventeenth century came from East Anglia.[3]

The scientific study of place names has been going on for
about a century – and Dr Gelling was the most prolific and original of all place name historians. They are a meticulous group,
keen on examining a small part of the country in detail, and
looking into the origins of every village, farm and field. Most of
them content themselves with studying one county over a lifetime. Dr Gelling mastered three.

For the English Place-Name Society, she wrote the official
surveys for Oxfordshire in 1954 and Berkshire in 1976. At her
death, she had done practically all the work for Shropshire.

Dr Gelling knew all the clues inside out, and the tiny differences between them. She knew that *dun* in a place name means
not just a hill, but also a hill that was the site of a large village;
that a settlement name incorporating versions of the word *beorg*
tended to have a single farm or contain a church.

Leah – meaning clearing, wood, glade or forest – is by far the
most common topographical term. Bexley, Bromley, Radley,
Chorley, Headingley, Madingley, Washingley . . . all of them
incorporate the term. Water also defines English place names to
a great extent; another very common suffix is 'ford', as in
Oxford and Hereford; 'bridge', as in Tunbridge Wells, Stock-
bridge and Trowbridge, isn't far behind.

Once you know a few verbal tricks like this, place names begin
to split naturally into their constituent parts. The Midlands are
indeed Mid-Land. At Meriden, Warwickshire, there is a tapering cross which is supposed to mark the centre of England.
Lambourne, Berkshire, splits easily into 'lambs' stream'. *Burna* is
Old English for stream or brook (itself derived from the Old
English *broc*). *Burna* is often used – in chalk country, in particular
– to describe rivers that dry up intermittently.

Names can be extremely precise in their topographical descriptions: like the Gordano Valley, near Bristol, visible from the M5, meaning 'an open valley with a triangular shape'; *gelad*, as in Crecca gelad, which morphed into Cricklade, Wiltshire, means a 'difficult river crossing'. Sometimes, admittedly, place names can be a little more ambiguous. Endings derived from *-ieg* can refer to a place with drainage canals (like Wantage), or land liable to flooding.

You also get a feel for who founded a particular town or village. Norse words were incorporated into place names in the late ninth and tenth centuries, after the arrival of the Vikings. The Vikings landed on the east coast between the Thames and the Tyne and filled their place names with words like 'beck' (river), 'fell' (hill) and 'thwaite' (forest clearing). You'll find them particularly in the Danelaw – the Viking-dominated land north-east of the line that runs roughly from Liverpool to the Thames Estuary.

Because of the powerful topographical effect on place names, villages with the same landscape end up with the same name, but with different pronunciations – they were named long before a standard pronunciation was settled on.

Gillingham – 'a homestead of Gyllas family', from Old English *ham* (village, homestead) and *ingas* (family, followers) – is pronounced with a soft 'g' in Kent, and a hard 'g' in Dorset. Mildenhall ('a nook of land of a woman called Milde or a man called Milda') is pronounced as it's spelt in Suffolk. In Wiltshire, it's pronounced 'Minal'.

If only Dr Gelling had lived to see the row in the Kent village of Kenardington in July 2009. Victoria Cocking, a parish councillor in Church Road, Kenardington, was receiving misdirected post, meant for Church Road in neighbouring Kennington. And so she began a campaign to change the name of her street to Church Lane, although opponents of the move thought there were ulterior purposes.

'It has always been Church Road – not a posh-sounding lane,' said Geoff Cornes, another parish councillor, 'The persons behind this change want to increase their social standing and up the value of their homes. Evidently Church Lane must have a nicer ring to it and be softer on delicate middle-class ears.'

Geoff Cornes was certainly right that there is a distinction between the terms, if not a class one. 'Lane' comes from the Old English, meaning narrow or hedged in. 'Road' is also derived from the Old English *rad*, meaning 'a journey made by a horse', i.e. a thoroughfare strong enough to withstand pounding hooves. 'Road' only became established in its current sense in the sixteenth century, used by, among others, Shakespeare (who spelt it 'rode').

Incidentally, Church Road, Kenardington, remained Church Road.

Dr Gelling wasn't content, though, with merely compiling a list of suffixes and prefixes used in place names. She used these clues to compose an original history of how Britain developed over the last 1,500 years.

Before Dr Gelling came along, place name historians tended to think that place names were imposed by elites in a top-down way: thus names like Kington, Herefordshire – a king's tun, or manor – or Knighton, Powys, meaning a knight's tun.

Dr Gelling showed how many Anglo-Saxon place names must have been coined by ordinary locals, who named their villages after landscape features.

Where other historians concentrated on places that got their names from people's houses and farms, she directed her attention to how the natural world inspired those names. Our Anglo-Saxon ancestors were skilled observers, adept at dreaming up accurate place names to fit the exact shape of the surrounding countryside.

Just as the Eskimos reputedly have dozens of different words for snow (in fact the Sami civilization in Arctic Scandinavia and Russia have many more), the Anglo-Saxons had forty different words for hill. And Dr Gelling worked out that they all meant distinct varieties of hill.

You can see why the Anglo-Saxons had to be so precise. In the days before maps or widespread literacy, the best way to direct someone to an unknown destination was to describe its exact physical features – 'the tall, hump-backed hill by the stream' or whatever it might be.

So, a place ending in -*dun* (the North and South Downs were originally Duns) meant a flat-topped hill that was easy to build on. Those ending in -*hoh*, like Ivinghoe, the destination of my bicycling trip, were sharply projecting, heel-shaped hills. Endings in -*hop* meant a valley or, more precisely, a remote place enclosed by hills.

Dr Gelling had one further triumph. She had always been convinced that the ancient Celtic Britons weren't exiled to the fringes of the country by later invasions. Too many Celtic place names survive, predating the arrival of the Anglo-Saxons in the fifth century AD. Place names incorporating words like *avon* (river) or *hamps* ('a dry stream in summer') pointed to a continued Celtic presence.

Can you imagine, she said, Anglo-Saxons going up to the ancient Britons, and saying, 'Look here, before I cut off your head, just tell me the name of this place.'[4]

It was more likely that the ancient Britons were allowed to stay on in their old haunts and stick to their old names. In 2001, Dr Gelling was proved right. DNA tests showed that most of us living in south England share DNA with pure-blooded Celts.

What's in a name, Dr Gelling asked. And she got her answer – a staggering amount.

5. Why English Towns Look English

Nor will the singular beauty of the chimneys escape
the eye of the attentive traveller.

William Wordsworth on the Lake District

The Englishness of English buildings is a slippery idea to catch
hold of. There just aren't that many indigenous architectural
features around.

Those sash windows on the rectory have seventeenth-century
French origins. That tracery in the cathedral windows was inspired
by Gothic churches in medieval France. The Ionic pilasters on the
manor house facade came from Palladio's sixteenth-century palazzi
in the Veneto. The rounded curves of its gables are Flemish, as is
that crow-stepped arch on the church porch.

Where buildings become archetypally English is in the adap-
tation of those foreign architectural features – an example of
our make-do-and-mend, hodgepodge approach to the visual
arts, our taste for the compromise over the *grand projet*, and our
preference for customizing other people's ideas rather than
creating our own.

That classical manor house has a steeply pitched slate roof to
deal with all our northern rain; while Palladio's villas outside
Vicenza have flat, or nearly flat, roofs.

The English cathedral will usually be bigger than the French
cathedral that inspired it – a reminder of our pre-Reformation
days, when we were referred to as 'the pious English'.

In time, we also developed our own customized English

version of northern Continental Gothic architecture: Perpendicular Gothic, which emerged at Gloucester Cathedral in the 1330s, and lasted until around 1530.

Perpendicular Gothic is all extremely tall, wide, straight-mullioned church windows, together with fan-vaulted ceilings. The style bled, too, into the ultra-English, secular, domestic style of the sixteenth century: as seen in tall, blockish Elizabethan houses, such as Longleat and Hardwick, articulated with large, rectangular windows – useful for illumination in our gloomy English winters.

As a contemporary wit put it, Hardwick Hall was 'more glass than wall'; and the light, airy, Perpendicular churches were called 'lantern churches'. If southern European medieval churches had been built with as much glass, you'd have roasted to death during summer masses.

The flat-topped towers of Perpendicular Gothic churches are an English anomaly, too; as is the tendency to have a flat end to Perpendicular chancels, unlike rounded Continental ones. The flat, square blockiness of English churches can be traced back to Anglo-Saxon churches; a square blockiness that doesn't appear so much in churches in Kent – these were influenced more by the round-ended Gothic churches of northern France.

An English tendency for repetition of square and rectangular architectural units is picked up later on, across the country, in the long, unremitting lines of Georgian and Victorian terraced houses.[1]

In domestic Tudor housing, too, the English could hardly be accused of being internationally unique: they followed a natural combination of timber frames and in-filling that existed across Europe.

But, again, they customized the style in a peculiarly English style suited to the weather, with overhanging, jettied storeys on the first floor – a useful way of sheltering the ground floor and the front door, while producing a dripping edge to drain the upper floors into the middle of the street below.

Climate is also the defining factor behind the crowning achievement of English architecture – the ornamental chimney.

The first surviving English fireplace appeared in the Tower of London in 1081, the first chimneys in the early twelfth century. The earliest decorated chimney anywhere in the world is at Old Sarum Castle, just outside Salisbury. The castle chimneys, built between 1120 and 1140, are extremely ornate.[2]

Throughout the Middle Ages, chimneys got more sophisticated, reaching the height of complexity on the skylines of Tudor palaces, with red-brick chimneypots twisting into tightly spun corkscrews. In the sixteenth century, chimney styles turned classical, clustering together into groups of Doric columns, as they do on the roof of Burghley House, Lincolnshire, finished in 1587.

Meanwhile on the Continent – even if they indulged in the heights of the baroque and the rococo elsewhere on their buildings – their chimneys remained austere and unadorned.

Much of our architecture is shaped by Continental influences, Italian ones in particular. But the ornamental chimney, at least, is ours; as is the mass-produced, simpler domestic chimney – a late-sixteenth-century agricultural boom led to a chimney boom across the country.

Early industrialization and the mass construction of terraced houses continued the boom into the nineteenth and twentieth centuries, giving us the widest variety of chimneys in the world. The National Clayware Federation's 1964 catalogue lists 500 different types of chimneypot, from the fluted beehive to the beaded cannon-head.

Chimneys vary distinctly according to county, too: in the Cotswolds and north-east Norfolk, chimney stacks are at the gable ends; in Suffolk and the south-east, they're planted squarely in the middle of the timber-framed buildings.

How fitting that we should lead the world in chimneypots – it chimes with our taste for the homespun, the unflashy, the slightly jokey, along with the need to keep the chill off, in our damp northern climes.

It is in the idiosyncratic combination and arrangement of buildings, too, that a particular architectural setting looks typically English. The beguiling village combination of church and rectory, for example, doesn't exist anywhere else in Europe.[3]

Difficult as it is to characterize all 13,000 English villages in any uniform way, they also tend to be laid out in a limited number of peculiarly English ways.

First, they tend to be extremely old – most date back to the Anglo-Saxons, some as far back as the fifth century. Their sites were chosen for economic reasons – near rivers or springs, and close to fertile soil. They were about the same size and roughly equidistant from each other, with that distance varying from county to county, according to local prosperity and soil fertility. In more remote Devon and Cornwall, villages are around six miles apart; in prosperous East Anglia and the East Midlands, the gap is more like three miles.[4]

The wealth and fertility of lowland England, in the southeast, also meant that surviving villages are most thickly concentrated there. Deserted villages are mostly found in the Midlands and the east; there are thought to be over 2,000 of them in England – largely the result of the Black Death and the Norman enclosure of the royal forests. From the twelfth century onwards, there was also considerable monastic demolition of certain villages, like Old Byland, North Yorkshire, removed by the Cistercians to build Rievaulx.

This coincidence of age, geography and Anglo-Saxon origins means that ancient villages tend to share a rough ground plan, built along one of three patterns: villages strung along one street, or along two streets at right angles to each other; those arranged around a square or green, often to protect animals from predators; and those with houses thrown together in an apparently random ragbag.[5]

While cities have expanded out of all ancient recognition, most villages today aren't that much bigger than they were a century after the Norman Conquest; they still cluster around those ancient ground plans. The average village size in 1086, according to the Domesday Book, was around 150 inhabitants; not that much smaller than today, and about the same size as prehistoric hunter-gatherer clans.

According to the Oxford evolutionary anthropologist Robin Dunbar, 150 is also the maximum amount of friends you can conceivably juggle, because the number has been hard-wired into the human mind over the millennia.

Dunbar's two criteria for his broad definition of friendship are: you must be willing to lend one of these friends £5 and you must contact them at least once a year.[6] With more than 150 inhabitants, communities – or groups of friends – grow too large and fall apart. At 150 or below, everyone knows everyone else and is prepared, in theory, to fight for them.

The Dunbar number chimes with the standard size of military units: companies have 100–150 men; platoons are around thirty-strong. At that smaller level, of thirty or fewer – a platoon, say, or among members of an extended family – people are even prepared to sacrifice themselves in defence of the group; a uniquely human trait.

As with higgledy-piggledy villages, so with towns. Symmetrical town planning isn't a naturally English thing. That's one of the reasons town planners have brought such destruction to provincial towns in the last half-century, by trying to impose unnatural order and symmetry on pleasingly chaotic street patterns built up over centuries.

There are several factors behind the English opposition to

planning: the country's long history, which leads to a semi-random accumulation of layers of historical development, relatively unaffected by disasters, manmade or natural; the English taste for picturesque shabbiness; and a liking for old things, closely allied to a dislike of change and an opposition to being dragooned into *grands projets*.

Defence was behind the foundation of the first English towns, the grid-like camps, or *castra*, set up by the Romans: Manchester, Chester, Colchester and all those other towns and cities with 'chester' endings. They were often sited, too, at river crossings, like Cambridge and Canterbury, or at road intersections, like Alcester and Dunstable.

The earliest towns then developed organically and asymmetrically, often around a castle or cathedral standing on one side of a square, rectangular or triangular market place.

This commercial aspect was crucial in the origins and development of most towns. As early as the tenth century, King Edward the Elder passed a law decreeing that buying and selling must be done in a market town, and watched over by a town reeve; thus the number of towns with names like Burnham Market, Market Drayton and Market Harborough. 'Chipping' – as in Chipping Norton and Chipping Ongar – and 'cheap' as in Eastcheap and Cheapside, come from the Anglo-Saxon *cheapen*, 'to buy'.

Markets often dominated an unusually wide main street – as in Marlborough, Wiltshire, originally home to a big sheep market, or Thame, Oxfordshire, site of an important cattle market.

Triangular market places, like the one in St Albans, Hertfordshire, stretched away from one broad end – up against the abbey, or another major building – and then narrowed to a point as the market petered out.

Over time, English towns were moulded into a series of rough-edged palimpsests, building on the foundations of an earlier civilization, with each new layer sprawling wider and wider, part obscuring the older layers. It made sense to construct your biggest buildings on top of, or next to, those of the earlier civilization, absorbing their history and kudos, often incorporating their stones, walls and ditches.

London's Guildhall is built on the site of the only amphitheatre in the Roman city. The Anglo-Saxon church of St Nicholas, Leicester, was constructed over the palaestra, or wrestling school, of the old Roman baths. The chancel window of St Nicholas practically touches the Jewry Wall, a large fragment of Roman masonry. Dover's Saxon church, St Mary in Castro, incorporates tiles from the neighbouring second-century AD Roman lighthouse.

Early monasteries were often constructed within Saxon forts; the church at Breedon-on-the-Hill, Leicestershire, is built on an Iron Age enclosure. The street pattern of Devizes, Wiltshire, shadows the walls of the Victorianized Norman castle; The Brittox gets its name from the bretesque, the old stockade on either side of the approach to the castle.

Saxon Bristol is visible in its modern street plan, around Leonard Lane, Bell Lane, St Nicholas Street and Tower Lane – an almost circular boundary that stretches east of the High Street around the site of the ancient castle. Bristol's thirteenth-century city walls were wrapped around the old Saxon defences.

Oxford (with its walls built in 1224–40), York (with walls from 1250) and Newcastle (with walls from 1265) were encircled at about the same time; not just for defence, but also to regulate booming regional trade.

You could walk across most medieval walled cities in less than an hour; as you could ancient ones – fifth-century BC Athens only extended a few miles beyond the Parthenon. London's Roman wall, marking the boundaries of the city, was only three miles long, enclosing 330 acres. These cities have of course long outgrown their Roman or medieval city walls, even if the principal Roman cities in Britain were as big as any across the empire; only four cities in Roman Gaul were bigger than Londinium.

You can chart the medieval expansion of British towns beyond their city walls through the pattern of church-building. Ancient churches, built in the days before there were many tombstones, often don't have a churchyard. Rome only gave permission for graveyards to be built around churches in AD 752; and it wasn't until the eighteenth and nineteenth centuries that headstones and tombs were erected in great quantities. Georgian graveyards were often planted with English yews; Irish yews were popular under the Victorians.

Once sanctioned, those graveyards filled up quickly. The mass of bodies built up over the centuries – there are around 10,000 in an average country churchyard, with generation laid on top of generation[7] – can raise the level of the graveyard above the surrounding country by several feet.

It was often the church – or abbey or monastery – that led to a town being settled in the first place. Evesham, Worcestershire, grew up around the Cistercian abbey built on a site chosen for the soil's fertility. The town of Ely expanded around a Saxon monastery and the later cathedral, on a site picked for its remoteness in the fenland marshes. Ely's medieval isolation was so great that it was effectively ruled by the Bishop of Ely, not the monarch; it was only absorbed into Cambridgeshire in 1836.

These palimpsests of towns and cities developed fresh layers through the medieval period, into the modern age. Still, in many English settlements, the Georgian and Victorian layers are the most visible, particularly in London, and particularly in the form of the terraced house.

After the Fire of London, the rows of new terraced houses migrated west from the City of London – the natural direction for prosperity to spread, with the prevailing wind sending the city's noxious air off to the east (see Chapter 1). London still remains more built up to the west; and the eighteenth- and nineteenth-century terraces in the west tend to be bigger and more expensive than those in the east.

Throw in a declining royal court in the seventeenth century, and an increasingly powerful Parliament, and it was natural that new developments should go up in and around Westminster. The first symmetrical piazza in England was built by Inigo Jones at Covent Garden in the 1630s. The first garden square was St James's Square, close to Westminster, built in 1661. It was paid for by Henry Jermyn (as in neighbouring Jermyn Street), the Earl of St Albans, held up as the founder of the West End – in the days when the West End was still at the real western end of London.

Garden squares soon spread to the provinces. St James's Square was followed by Queen Square, Bristol, laid out in 1699, mirroring London's Bloomsbury Square, with two streets entering at all four corners of the square, each at right angles to the other.

The organic, higgledy-piggledy accumulation of garden squares of differing sizes – across London and other English cities through the seventeenth, eighteenth and nineteenth centuries – is a peculiarly English phenomenon. They also made English cities unusually green. When, in 1828, Earl Grosvenor was building the Grosvenor estate in Mayfair, he asked the developer, Thomas Cubitt, 'Will you ensure you bring a little country into the town by having garden squares?'

Nikolaus Pevsner thought London garden squares, informally connected to each other in a loose rhythm, were the city's principal contribution to the history of European town planning; so unlike Baron Haussmann's boulevards, carved through Paris in the 1860s, the Emperor Trajan's symmetrical Forum in Rome, or indeed Mussolini's thumping great triumphal straight roads, sliced through ancient and medieval layers of the city in the 1930s.

1. Northern Gothic: this 1647 view, by Wenceslaus Hollar, from Southwark to the Tower of London, reveals an unplanned jumble of half-timbered houses wrapped round the Gothic church of St Olave's.

2. Southern classical: Christopher Wren's post-fire plan for the City of London, 1666, looking east, St Paul's in the foreground. Wren's even grid, boulevards and symmetrical hubs were killed off by the English dislike of the grand project.

3. Barns, the treasuries of medieval England. Manor Farm Barn, Harmondsworth – called 'The Cathedral of Middlesex' by John Betjeman – was built in 1426 to store the grain for Winchester College. The barn was constructed on cathedral lines, with aisles either side of a nave, supported by a dense web of pointed Gothic arches.

4. Liverpool Street Station, built in 1875 to resemble a Gothic cathedral. The station was designed on the medieval Latin Cross church plan.

5. Grandness disguising small-scale, domesticated usefulness. In 1824 John Nash built the first semi-detached houses in England, in Park Village East, Regent's Park. Two houses lie behind the unified skin of a single, grander, classical villa. The pub, *right*, was built on a traditional corner site.

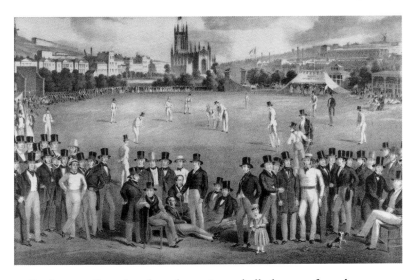

6. Cricket was first played on the springy chalk downs of southern England. Here, Sussex take on Kent at Brighton in the 1840s. Among the Sussex players is John Wisden, founder of the eponymous cricketers' almanac. In the background, a familiar combination: a chaotic collection of classical terraces jostle around the Gothic church.

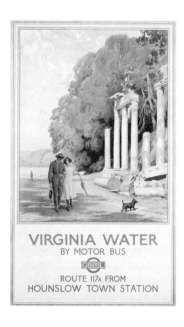

VIRGINIA WATER
BY MOTOR BUS

GENERAL

ROUTE 117A FROM
HOUNSLOW TOWN STATION

7. Follies: affection for the past mingled with a romantic attachment to decay. Virginia Water, Windsor Great Park, and the second-century AD columns from Leptis Magna, Libya.

8. When the Savoy opened in 1889, it was the first British hotel to have hot and cold running water, electric light throughout and 'ascending rooms', or lifts. Only some rooms were en suite – there were sixty-seven bathrooms for 250 bedrooms.

Telephone No. 2830.   Telegraphic Address: 'SAVOY HOTEL,' LONDON.

THE SAVOY HOTEL AND RESTAURANT,
Victoria Embankment, LONDON.
"THE HOTEL DE LUXE OF THE WORLD."

Containing 250 Apartments, 60 Private Sitting Rooms, and 67 Bath Rooms. Shaded Electric Lights everywhere, and no Gas used. The finest River and garden view in London, giving a Panorama of the Thames from Westminster to London Bridge.

Luxurious Suites on every floor, with Private Bath Rooms, &c. No charge for Baths, Lights, or Attendance. Large "Ascending Rooms" running all night. Top Floor Rooms equal in every respect to the Lowest. Large Central Courtyard with Fountain, Plants, Flowers, &c.

THE SAVOY HOTEL AND RESTAURANT.

THE SAVOY HOTEL AND RESTAURANT

THE SAVOY RESTAURANT.
The Finest and Only Open-air Restaurant in London.

In the GRAND RESTAURANT Breakfasts, Déjeuners Fourchette (Lunch), and Dinners are served à la carte either in the Rooms or on the wide Terrace Balcony (overlooking the Thames), which is enclosed with glass and warmed in cold weather, but open in warm weather.

SAVOY LUNCHEON SERVED ON THE TERRACE, 4s.

There are several Private Dining and Reception Rooms with wide Terrace Balconies, specially adapted for Private Parties, Wedding Breakfasts, Receptions, and "At Homes." Guests may engage tables in advance by wire or letter. The Cuisine and Cellars rival the most famous Continental and American Restaurants.

In the SALLE A MANGER, Breakfasts, Luncheons, and Dinners are served at separate Tables at the following fixed prices, viz.:—

	s.	d.
Breakfast, Plain	2	0
Ditto with Meat or Fish, etc.	3	6
Savoy Dinner, at separate Tables	7	6

Dinners served in Private Dining Rooms, from 10s. 6d. per head for not less that Four Persons. Table may be engaged beforehand at the Reception Office.

THE BALL ROOM.
Beautifully Decorated and admirably adapted for Wedding Breakfasts, Public, Regimental & Masonic Banquets.
Chef de Cuisine, M. ESCOFFIER, from the Grand Hotel, Monte Carlo.
Acting Manager, L. ECHENARD, from the Midland Grand Hotel, London.
General Manager, C. RITZ, Proprietor, Hotel Minerva, Baden-Baden, and Provence, Cannes.

9. The Shambles, York, voted Britain's most picturesque street. The fourteenth-century street of old butchers' shops – with timber-framed, jettied upper storeys leaning at drunken angles – evokes a natural, organic, literally shambolic beauty.

10. Cornwall, England's granite county. Here, in 1936, stonemasons at Carnsew Quarry, Penryn, cut Cornish granite into blocks for the piers and buttresses of the new Chelsea Bridge.

11. Pleasure in walking, in unspecialized clothes. Man, sheepdog, sheep and drystone walls, Yorkshire, 1965. More than half the 70,000 miles of drystone walls in England are in Yorkshire, Cornwall, Derbyshire and Cumbria.

12. Dressed for unpredictable weather – second layer needed on Scarborough's South Bay Beach, 9 August 1952. Above looms the Grand Hotel, a High Victorian colossus built in 1867 by Cuthbert Brodrick in Mixed Renaissance style. When opened, the Grand, the greatest hotel in Europe, was the first hotel of that name in the world.

13. Motorways get off the ground – just. In September 1959, Jayne Mansfield opened the Chiswick flyover in west London. 'It's a sweet little flyover,' she said. Little was the operative word – it was a quarter of a mile long.

14. The stones beneath Caversham Road (the author's street), north London, resurfaced in 2011. The Dartmoor granite kerbstones have been 'chitted', or roughened, to prevent slipping. The newly exposed Victorian street is made of sarsen silcrete setts – small cubes of sandstone from Cranborne Chase, Dorset.

15. The garden square, a triumph of English urban planning: Queen's Square, Bath, built by John Wood the Elder in 1736. To the right, the north side consists of seven houses grouped together to form a single Palladian facade.

16. Why England doesn't look like England: the Bull Ring, Birmingham, bombed in 1940 and twice rebuilt, in 1967 and 2003. Solid, barely adorned chunks of glass and steel swamp the tapering, prickly, Gothic outline of medieval St Martin in the Bull Ring.

On an early trip to England in 1930, Pevsner was particularly taken with the garden squares of Bloomsbury. He liked the way they had been arranged, in haphazard relation to each other, with no focal point – the result of centuries of an independent bourgeoisie developing the city in an organic way, with no overarching plan forced on them from above. The only thing that Pevsner took against was the anti-social taste for fencing and locking up the gardens – a reflection of the English cult of property ownership.

Rows of terraced houses started snaking north of St James's Palace in the early eighteenth century. By the end of the Seven Years War in 1763, they had spread north and west of Cavendish Square. Development was particularly intense in the square bordered by Portland Place to the east, Oxford Street to the south, Edgware Road to the west and the New Road, later Euston Road, to the north.

Euston Road was built in the eighteenth century by the Duke of Grafton, also the Earl of Euston, then owner of much of the land around the modern Euston Station. He designed it expressly so that, every working day, 1,500 cattle could get to Smithfield Market from the west, without blocking Holborn and Oxford Street. (Cattle transport had a lasting effect on the English landscape, and townscape – many of the lanes that lead into agricultural towns were originally drovers' roads. You can spot a drovers' road by its name – there are Bullock Roads, Drove Roads and Cow Lanes across the country, particularly in the Midlands.)

Much of London's development was at the hands of aristocratic urban landowners like the Duke of Grafton. The Howard de Walden family, the Duke of Westminster, Earl Cadogan and Viscount Portman own vast swathes of the city centre today. The Russell family – in their later incarnation, the Dukes of Bedford – owned most of Bloomsbury between 1175 and 1850, and still control a big chunk of the area.

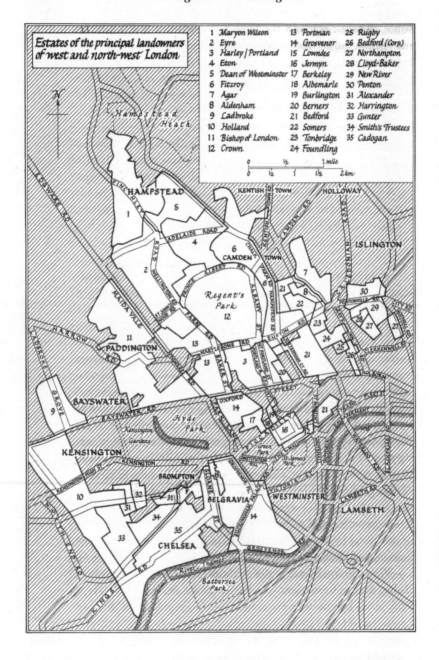

Estates of the principal landowners
of west and north-west London

1	Maryon Wilson	13	Portman	25	Rugby
2	Eyre	14	Grosvenor	26	Bedford (Corp.)
3	Harley / Portland	15	Lowndes	27	Northampton
4	Eton	16	Jermyn	28	Lloyd-Baker
5	Dean of Westminster	17	Berkeley	29	New River
6	Fitzroy	18	Albemarle	30	Penton
7	Agar	19	Burlington	31	Alexander
8	Aldenham	20	Berners	32	Harrington
9	Ladbroke	21	Bedford	33	Gunter
10	Holland	22	Somers	34	Smith's Trustees
11	Bishop of London	23	Tonbridge	35	Cadogan
12	Crown	24	Foundling		

That continuity of urban land ownership by single families is uniquely British – a reflection not just of the power and wealth of the aristocracy, but also of sustained democracy, respect for property rights, and a lack of revolutions and apocalyptic economic crises. You can add in a near-continuous monarchy for over a millennium, whose landholdings have been astonishingly robust: the Duchy of Cornwall, owned by the Prince of Wales, was set up by Edward III in 1337 and still owns 160 miles of coastline, most Cornish rivers, the Isles of Scilly and more than 54,000 hectares of land.

The lack of English revolutions has astonished those who are more used to them in other countries. Otto Hintze, the early-twentieth-century German historian, said England was made up of living fossils, dependent on a feudal system that had been toppled practically everywhere else in Europe.[8]

In the eighteenth and nineteenth centuries, English cities were largely built by a combination of these landowners, working in conjunction with developers. Because the landowners controlled large stretches of virgin land in the expanding cities, the organized building of long terraces was possible.

Landowners worked hand-in-glove with developers, through the peculiarly English intricacies of the leasehold system. The landowner let plots to the developer, who then paid for the construction of the terraces and sold them to leaseholders. Once the initial lease expired, those terraces became the property of the landowner. On the security of this deal, the developer borrowed the funds to pay the construction costs.

To provide further finance, the developer often built a pub first – that's why a pub is often on a corner site, because it was the first building in a row of terraced houses. The pub not only brought in money from patrons; it provided a place for builders to eat, drink and sleep in. In extremis, the pub and its licence could be sold off to pay for finishing off the terrace.

When John Nash built the Quadrant, at the bottom end of Regent Street, in the early nineteenth century, he developed several houses for himself. He lent the money for building other properties in the Quadrant to his plumbers, glaziers and brick-layers. They then did work for free on each other's houses, and on those owned by Nash – now not just the architect, but also the developer, speculator and all-round wheeler-dealer.

The state may have intervened on a massive scale in private life over the last century, and wrecked big patches of our city centres. But, still, our cities – and our sewers, railways and canals – remain essentially Georgian, Victorian and Edwardian; and built by private hands, not public ones, with an unusual degree of freedom.

Because there has been no over-arching planning authority – no Trajan, no Haussmann, no Mussolini – London, and most English cities, haven't ended up with the straight, wide boule-vards of Paris or Fascist Rome.

English cities have few dominating axes or ordered plans. As a result, they present less of a grand spectacle, and look less bewitching from the air than rooftop cities like Paris or New York – no grand avenues, no pleasing grand-scale geometry. But on the ground, at eye-level, they present more surprises – more half-glimpsed side streets, more curves, more variety of scale between alley, dead end and main street.

The unit on which the English city largely depends is the ter-raced house, multiplied into varied matrices of squares, crescents, circuses and terraces, forming long, looping lines across the cityscape.

On the Continent, fragmented urban land ownership meant mass urban housing couldn't be built in the same way. Parisian aristocrats owned grander, detached private houses, or *hôtels*, with walled courtyards separating them from the street. Even the English rich were squeezed right next door to each other in

Mayfair terraces, in inflated versions of the terraced houses lived in by the vast majority of the working and middle classes.

Squeezed-together, low-rise, small-scale terraced houses are unusually English. They are often what first strike foreign visitors travelling into London through the suburbs; Spaniards in particular, according to a Hispanophile friend of mine. (They are also surprised by carpets in pubs; paying when ordering drinks; raised railway platforms; people not looking you in the eye; and town centres deserted after 5.30 p.m., except on binge-drinking weekend evenings.)[9]

Those visitors are struck, too, by the back gardens seen from railway trains; in particular, the contrast between the rough-and-tumble views you get of the back of terraced houses, compared to their neat fronts. The unadorned, symmetrical, Georgian and Victorian fronts of the terraced houses disguise higgledy-piggledy back garden extensions, side-returns and garden sheds, framed by a mesh of washing lines and football nets.

Just as the land-owning structure of England – with large tracts of land owned by individuals – meant terraced houses could be planned in those long lines, their gardens, too, could be neatly aligned with the continuous lines of railway track.

Because Britain was the first country to build railways, those railways were often built before the Victorian, Edwardian and inter-war suburbs that grew up around them. With newer railway lines, like the Channel Tunnel Rail Link, you don't see so many neat ends of gardens from the train, because the line slices through pre-existing streets.

Foreign visitors are also often surprised by how small the houses are at the end of those gardens. They are indeed small; largely because they're houses, not flats. Half the new homes in Germany, Italy and France in the 1990s were flats. In England, in 1996, only 12 per cent of new homes were one- or two-bedroom flats; 30 per cent were houses with four or more bedrooms.

On top of that, 65 per cent of British houses are home-owned (2010 figures); in Continental Europe, the figure is half that. This overwhelming English desire to own a house, rather than rent a flat, despite shortage of funds, leads to an inevitable conclusion – smaller houses.

The average new British home is now 76 square metres, compared with 109 square metres in Germany. That pattern has been around for a while: in 1791, a German historian, Johann Wilhelm von Archenholz, said the English 'prefer the most miserable cottage hired in their own name, to more convenient apartments in another house'.

It's no coincidence that British estate agents refer to houses by the number of bedrooms; if they defined them by floor area, as they do in America and much of Europe, we would rumble how short-changed we are. British journalists buttress the convention: our newspapers are unique in recording someone's wealth by detailing the number of bedrooms in their house.

In our densely packed towns and cities, with old housing stock and limited room for new developments, the logical result is that, instead of building bigger houses, the English add on to existing ones. The average kitchen has almost doubled in size since the 1920s. That's why you get all those side-returns, loft and basement conversions, and higgledy-piggledy extensions, the ones seen from railway lines that so astonish Spaniards.

You can also diagnose our obsession with home ownership in our complex property law. Gazumping, stamp duty and the 999-year lease are all unusually English institutions.

Particularly that last one – long leases satisfy the British desire for home ownership: both freeholder and leaseholder get to share different types of possession of the same property. A 999-

year lease also shows an unusually strong national faith in the enduring strength of a secure, property-owning democracy.

That faith is wrapped up with the long survival of the rule of law in England. A lack of invasions since 1066 – and of civil wars, for over 350 years – has led to a confidence that property rights will last for ever, and so to the high percentage of home ownership in England. The related idea of 'An Englishman's home is his castle' was first invoked in English law in 1623 by Sir Edward Coke, a jurist and MP. The English language has long been rich in references to an affection for property ownership, like 'There's no place like home' or 'As safe as houses'.

The Germans and the French may have ways of translating the word 'freehold': *Freibrief* and *nue propriété*. But the concept is unrecognizable on the Continent, where landowners don't have the same rights as freeholders; that's why Napoleonic roads could be so straight, and breezily bulldoze through private land.[10] English common law enshrined the protection of private property. And the appearance of Trust Law, from around 1600, provided further protection.

It was the power of the private English landowner that prevented the realization of Sir Christopher Wren's grid plan for London after the Great Fire of 1666.

Wren wanted a series of wide boulevards radiating from his new St Paul's Cathedral, interconnecting with a straight-lined grid; like Haussmann's Parisian boulevards, or New York's chessboard street plan that gradually spread north through Manhattan Island in the nineteenth century.

But private landowners and developers – who either owned or were responsible for rebuilding the charred ruins of the City – did not approve of Wren's axial plan. The design would have forced them to dance to someone else's tune: ordained from on high, it cut across the pre-Fire boundaries of their building plots.

In the end, a new generation of classically inspired, seventeenth-century terraced houses was built on the footprint of the pre-Fire, Gothic, medieval city; but the winding, asymmetrical, medieval street pattern remained almost unaltered. Wren's fifty-one post-Fire City churches were also mostly built on the site of pre-Fire churches.

The dogged English taste for the small-scale, for natural development, for the unplanned, for curves and slow-revealing views, had triumphed over the symmetrical, overarching *grand projet*. Today, the City of London, for all its metal, glazed, right-angled skyscrapers, retains its cramped, squiggly, ancient street pattern. You can still comfortably fit the medieval plan of the City on to the modern one.

After the second obliteration of the City during the Second World War, a new financial centre of concrete, steel and glass skyscrapers was erected over the next sixty years – but still on that medieval plan. Then came the ring of steel – the one-way systems, street closures and concrete barriers imposed on the City as a security and surveillance cordon, after the IRA bombed the Baltic Exchange in 1992, and Bishopsgate in 1993. The ring of steel wrapped a roughly circular, ghost barrier around the medieval plan, but those higgledy-piggledy, curving lines remain much as they were half a millennium ago.

Wherever you do see a sudden straight, wide avenue in a medieval English city, it's likely to be a Victorian 'improvement'. The ones in London include Aldwych, Charing Cross Road, Victoria Street, Kingsway and Queen Victoria Street (the name Victoria's a useful giveaway).

These avenues produce the kind of dull, un-English uniformity that Joshua Reynolds diagnosed in the regularity of Wren's City plan.

The forms and turnings of the streets of London and other old towns are produced by accident, without any original plan or design, but they are not always the less pleasant to the walker or spectator on that account.

On the contrary, if the city had been built on the regular plan of Sir Christopher Wren, the effect might have been, as we know it in some new parts of the town, rather unpleasing; the uniformity might have produced weariness.

Joshua Reynolds, Thirteenth Discourse (1786)

Wren's defeat by the power of individual property rights was not unusual. Extended prosperity over many centuries in most English cities means that any explicitly geometrical town plans are often obscured by the asymmetrical demands of commerce and private residential development.

You can spot fragments of the old, roughly rectangular Roman Wall of London, but modern streets are often carved through those fragments, as opposed to being aligned with them.

In York, you can still walk the 2.5-mile-long walls of the playing-card-shaped fortification built by the Romans in AD 71 on the north-east bank of the River Ouse. They are the longest, and best-maintained, Roman city walls in England. York's main streets, too, are laid on top of the Roman grid street pattern. Stonegate follows the line of the Via Praetoria; Petergate runs along the Via Principalis.

Much of York's Roman grid remains. But the ancient, right-angled tramlines are largely obscured by the much thicker encrustation of medieval Gothic development.

York flourished between 1068 – when William the Conqueror built two castles either side of the Ouse – and the seventeenth century. As the city prospered, overarching Roman order gave way to typically English, faintly shambolic development. Religious, secular and private buildings were constructed independently of each other, at different times, in different Gothic styles.

In 1130, York was the fourth-biggest town in Britain; by the 1660s, it was the third-biggest, behind London and Norwich. Over those 500 or so years, nearly fifty parish churches – in the Early English, Decorated and Perpendicular Gothic styles – shot up across the city.

Many of those parish churches have been deconsecrated and converted, or were damaged in the Second World War. But, still, as you ramble through the winding, medieval streets, you keep catching oblique views of Gothic church spires.

For all the stamina of York's classical city walls, the asymmetrical, medieval street plan – and the bristling, chaotic confection of Gothic, crocketed spires, pointed windows and ogee arches – ultimately conquered the right angles of Roman order and geometry.

Across England, irregularity triumphs over symmetry. Giuseppe Tomasi di Lampedusa, the Sicilian author of *The Leopard*, said of London in the late 1920s, 'This city is perhaps the only one that can evoke the same emotions as nature – indeed it isn't a city, but a wood in which, together with the most dismal trees, houses have grown, too.'[11]

Even in the stripped-down, modernist age, a love of shambolic, tumbledown shabbiness, allied to a taste for historicism, remains deep in the English soul.

We still prefer the warped, ancient look; the same look that Bram Stoker appreciated in Dracula's Whitby: 'The houses of the old town are all red-roofed and seem piled up one over the other anyhow.'

For all the modern tyranny of right angles in steel and glass, England remains rich in these piled-up houses, jumbled up together in pleasingly chaotic streets like medieval Abbey Street, Faversham, Castle Street, Warkworth, or Totnes High Street winding up from the river, looping itself round the castle. Winchester, Wells, Durham, Stamford and Beverley are all

entangled with curving, tortured street patterns that have merci-
fully avoided the town planner's ruler and protractor.

Irregularity remains the English norm, even when it's dressed
up in the ordered clothes of classicism.

Bath, though pretty much entirely classical, is also very English
in the asymmetrical plan of its classical terraces. In eighteenth-
century Bath, the two John Woods, a father-and-son pair of
architects, took the English terrace – developed a century earlier –
and bent and folded it into crescents and circuses for the first time.

While each individual house may be symmetrical and classically inspired, the combination of thousands of houses laid
across Bath's rolling hills in unpredictable loops, curves and
lines, set at oblique angles to each other, is thoroughly English.

That said, several Norman towns and cities were started on a
regular grid plan, or within rectangular borders: including
Bury St Edmunds, planned by its Norman abbot before 1086;
Stratford-upon-Avon, which had its original charter granted in
1196; Leeds, whose borough charter was granted in 1207; and
Liverpool, also given its borough charter in 1207.

But the clean, straight original lines of these town plans have
been largely blurred by later demolition and building. The grid
laid down in Cambridge by King Edward in AD 917 has been
almost completely obliterated by the university, with only a few
fragments surviving. The same goes for the Saxon grid plan
imposed on London, now concealed by more than a millennium's worth of new developments.

These early grids and planned towns were, in any case, the
exception in English town-building. It was hard to start a town
from scratch without unified ownership of a virgin site by a
single individual. However big the landholdings of the aristocrats of London, no single landowner dominated the whole
city.

Barrow-in-Furness, Cumbria, was in single ownership, and

so could be designed in an un-English way, with complete top-down control, leading to a unified, symmetrical plan.

A tiny fishing village of thirty houses in 1843, Barrow expanded with the discovery of hundreds of thousands of tons of iron in the neighbouring Furness orefield; by 1876, the town was home to the biggest steelworks in the world. In 1854, James Ramsden, the 23-year-old locomotive superintendent of the Furness Railway, bought the Hindpool estate in Barrow. In 1856, he laid out the surviving, even grid of terraced streets.

Whitehaven, also in Cumbria, followed the pattern – a large patch of undeveloped land wrapped around a small seaside village, owned outright by the Lowther family. From 1666, a grid plan was laid down to house workers in the town's shipyards and coal port.

Whitehaven, Cumbria, in 1839. A grid plan was laid out by the Lowther family in 1666. The roads leading into the town remain relatively unsophisticated.

A similar degree of control, again combined with undeveloped land, meant the Bishop of Sarum could impose his own new grid plan on Salisbury in the 1220s, when he moved operations from Old Sarum, up on the hill, down to the new cathedral site. That planned grid of streets still exists in Salisbury's centre.

As England filled up through the Middle Ages – and existing towns and cities sprawled and thickened – there was little opportunity for starting from scratch like this, until the revolutionary garden city experiment of the twentieth century. The same degree of unified planning control held by the Bishop of Sarum, James Ramsden and the Lowthers was exerted over the first garden city in the world: Letchworth, Hertfordshire.

Letchworth was founded with private money in 1903, on the initiative of the garden city pioneer, Sir Ebenezer Howard. It was built on six square miles of virgin land outside Hitchin, bought by First Garden City Ltd, the company founded by Howard. Welwyn Garden City followed, in 1920, using the same model of virgin land, purchased by Welwyn Garden City Ltd, another newly incorporated company.

Because of its healthy supply of virgin land, relatively late development and large private landholdings, Scotland has many more planned villages than England. In England, villages began to materialize on a substantial scale in around the tenth century, and were often founded much earlier; in Scotland, they are usually more recent.

Before the eighteenth century, rural Scottish settlements mostly consisted of clachans or fermtouns – where groups of families shared tenancy of the farmland, and lived and worked in a roughly assembled group of farm buildings and houses, often inhabited by their animals, too. In the eighteenth century, as agricultural yields increased, landlords got more interested in their estates, and began to build planned villages. Among them were Newcastleton, Roxburghshire, built by the

Duke of Buccleuch, and Monymusk, Aberdeenshire, built by Sir Archibald Grant.

New planned fishing villages were constructed along the Scottish coast, too, not long after the establishment of the British Fisheries Society in 1786. Rural estates were cleared – like the Duke of Sutherland's in north-east Scotland, in the Sutherland Clearances of 1807, when his tenants were exiled to newly built seaside villages, while their old land was let to sheep farmers, at higher rents.[12]

Because these planned towns are so rare in England, we feel instinctively wary of them. We have become so used to towns being a gradual, organic juxtaposition of new and old – of Georgian next to medieval, next to Edwardian – that any town thrown up in a single brief period feels oddly contrived.

The same taste for happenstance, instinctive patterns of settlement over long stretches of time, can be seen in the surviving ancient haunts of London's professional classes. Barristers are still cloistered in the four Inns of Court near Holborn, as they have been for 600 or so years. The upper echelons of the medical profession are still clustered in and around Harley Street, near Regent's Park in London, even if the classifications may have blurred a little.

Doctors used to be confined to Wimpole Street, and dentists to Harley Street. Now the Howard de Walden estate – which has owned the land for 300 years (the de Waldens are descended from the Harleys who built Harley Street) – is a little more easy-going, although so-called 'fringe medicine', or homeopathic practitioners, are still unlikely to get leases from the estate.

The reason why those doctors and dentists are still there goes back to the eighteenth century, when the Barber Surgeons were founded just down the road in Soho Square. When they expanded north, they sought refuge in the Howard de Walden estate; it was handy, too, for rich patrons moving into nearby Cavendish Square. Marylebone is still home to the British Veterinary Association, the Royal College of Nursing, the General Dental Council and the Royal College of Midwives.

Theatres also moved to the West End after the Restoration of Charles II in 1660. Before then, theatres like Shakespeare's Globe were confined to the South Bank, next door to the cockpits and brothels of Southwark, in the so-called Liberties – beyond the cities of Westminster and London, and so beyond the control of the aldermen. Even after the theatres moved to the West End, they were restricted by law. Until the Theatres Act of 1843, only the patent theatres, licensed in 1660 by Charles II to perform 'spoken drama', were allowed to put on plays. The two London patent theatres were the Theatre Royal, Drury Lane, and the Theatre Royal, Covent Garden, now the Royal Opera House. The Theatres Royal in Bath, Liverpool and Bristol were also given letters patent.

New professional classes are still making fresh, instinctive claims to particular areas of London. Hedge funders have settled in Mayfair, drawn there by its grandness, central location and architectural beauty. It helps that hedge fund offices are small – and can easily be accommodated in a single terraced house, with no need for the vast steel and glass office blocks of the traditional merchant banks of the City. Hedge funds began in the 1940s in America but took off in London in the 1990s to accommodate the new practice of shorting shares – betting they would go down rather than up. As hedge funds prospered over the last decade, bankers set up funds in Mayfair in their droves; although there was a culling of the herd after the 2008 crash.

The closest the English got to large-scale town planning was with the creation of seaside resorts – an idea invented by the English.

Scarborough, in Yorkshire, was the first seaside town, cultivated for the health-giving properties of the sea from the late
seventeenth century. Before then, the idea of prizing the sea for
its healthiness or beauty would have seemed distinctly odd – the
oldest buildings in Scarborough face each other, not the seafront.[13]

In the 1620s, a mineral-water spring, with supposedly thera-
peutic effects, was found on a cliff above Scarborough's south
beach. In the 1660s, a Dr Witte published *Scarborough Spa*, which
suggested that the sea water was a 'Most Sovereign remedy
against Hypochondriack Melancholy and Windness'. It could
apparently cure epilepsy, apoplexy, vertigo and catalepsy,
cleanse the stomach, and put an end to scurvy, asthma, and black
and yellow jaundice.

Dr Witte also advocated bathing every day – a fashion soon
adopted by men, who swam naked out at sea, having been taken
there by boat; and women, who stuck to the shallow water,
safely covered by their bathing dresses, and taken to the sea by
horse-drawn bathing machines to preserve their modesty.

The old fishing town soon developed assembly rooms, a bathing house and, in 1826, an iron footbridge across the valley to
the new promenade on the clifftop above. Towering over South
Bay was the Grand Hotel – the first hotel of that name in the
world, and then the greatest hotel in Europe.

Other seaside towns followed, boosted by George III's
patronage of Weymouth in the late eighteenth century:
Brighton took off in 1750, its appeal added to by the Prince
Regent's first visit in 1783; Margate in 1769; Melcombe Regis
in the 1780s; Bognor Regis in the 1820s. The seaside holiday
really became an institution with the railways – Cromer and
Great Yarmouth, in Norfolk, both mushroomed in the mid-
nineteenth century.

The arrival of the chartered railway trip helped. Thomas

Cook, the travel agent, planned the first chartered public rail excursion on 5 July 1841, when he arranged for 570 campaigners to travel from Leicester to Loughborough for a temperance rally.

In 1871, the Bank Holidays Act – dreamt up by Sir John Lubbock, MP for Maidstone, to give bank workers the chance to watch a day's cricket – completed the triumph of the British seaside holiday. Charing Cross and Fenchurch Street stations were overwhelmed with day-trippers on the first bank holiday in August that year. By the 1890s, around 360,000 Londoners headed to the coast for the August Bank Holiday.

Through the nineteenth century, seaside architecture was developed to entertain the new tourists. The first bandstand wasn't actually by the sea; it was built in 1887, at Dartmouth Park, West Bromwich, Staffordshire, near the iron foundries. But the idea quickly migrated to seaside towns.

The first municipal beach hut was built in Bournemouth in 1909 by Frederick Percy Dolamore, the town's chief assistant borough engineer and surveyor. It survives today; in February 2011, it was given a special plaque, commemorating Bournemouth as the home of the beach hut. Bournemouth now has 1,900 beach huts, and there are 20,000 altogether strung across the British coastline – descendants of the Victorian bathing machines.

Most seaside towns have preserved their eighteenth- and nineteenth-century characters, thanks in part to the rise of cheap air travel. Just as concrete tower blocks were spreading across England in the late 1960s, so foreign package tours were getting cheaper and cheaper. The poor seaside towns may have lost custom to Majorca and Tenerife, but they kept their pretty buildings – why rebuild a town that can't attract visitors?

Seaside towns apart, the English opposition to large-scale planning has continued to the present day, but with perversely disastrous effects. One reason why so many fine towns and villages have a patch of dreary, homogeneous developments on their outskirts is because it is so difficult to get attractive, new, one-off houses past government planning rules. Those rules took up some 1,300 pages of legislation until the Government introduced proposals in 2011 to cut them down to fifty-two pages.

Because it's hard for private individuals to wade through the petty bureaucracy, only big building companies can afford to fight the planning battle. That battle takes a long time, consumed with endless appeals. During that delay, demand and capacity build up; when the permissions are finally granted, a large-scale, unoriginal, edge-of-town development is often the result.

From the Restoration until very recently, cities expanded outwards, naturally, organically, in a series of low-rise, domestic-scale streets of terraced houses. The English love of the individual family home meant that Georgian, Victorian and Edwardian buildings were kept low-rise – connected to each other horizontally, not vertically. Their scale was reined in, too, by the structural limitations of early building materials.[14]

In the boomtime developments of London and other principal English cities over the last twenty years, the market has conspired to produce high-density, high-rise developments.

This is partly due to the arms race in show-off projects, trying to outdo each other in pushing the city skyline higher and higher. The London horizon in particular is now dominated by skyscrapers built over the last thirty years: from the NatWest Tower, now Tower 42, the first skyscraper in the City of London, built in 1979, through to the Gherkin, the Cheese-Grater and the latest, the Shard.

The increased vertical axis of English cities has also been a result of planning restrictions. Buildings are constructed on footprints that can't expand outwards, because of those planning restrictions and the confined, crowded nature of our old cities.

And so the only option is to build upwards. As developers try to realize vast profits, the architect becomes the developer's frontman, squeezing as much as he can on to the site, in a pile 'em high, sell 'em cheap way. The extreme vertical axis that results is the complete opposite of what has gone on in England for the preceding several thousand years.[15]

The days of instinctive, improvised development, free from planning control – which produced the haphazard collection of English garden squares that Pevsner admired so much – are gone.

Towns and cities are now developed by dirigiste, centralized diktat, declaring what can and can't be built. Gone is the instinctive, untrammelled spirit that produced the typical English look: a hodgepodge of periods and architectural features, sprouting up independently of each other, but working together in serendipitous harmony.

Ironically, it is modern nimbyist planning restrictions – a hallowed English ritual you can trace back to the seventeenth-century opposition to Christopher Wren's City of London grid plan – that have dumped those blockish, right-angled towers of steel and concrete on England's cities, and sprinkled faceless brick boxes around the edge of its villages.

6. Georgian Hedge Funds: How Greedy Landowners Enclosed Our Fields and Drove John Clare Mad

The mournful peasant leads his humble band,
And while he sinks, without one arm to save,
The country blooms – a garden and a grave.
Where then, ah! where, shall poverty reside,
To 'scape the pressure of contiguous pride?
If to some common's fenceless limits stray'd,
He drives his flock to pick the scanty blade,
Those fenceless fields the sons of wealth divide,
And ev'n the bare-worn common is denied.

Oliver Goldsmith (1730–74), 'The Deserted Village'

In May 1939, on the eve of war, H. E. Bates wrote, 'Most of the English countryside as we see it today is manmade . . . the part most completely shaped by man is this plain, fundamental chequerwork of flat field and hedgerow.'

Chequerwork is perhaps the wrong word; it implies too much order, too many right angles. Fly over the Midwestern states of America – as I did recently, over Iowa – and you will see one huge green chequerboard: flat, mile-square field after flat, mile-square field.

These geometrical field shapes grow out of a vast, featureless landscape, acquired in one go by a single landowner, or parcelled out in even chunks by government – like the forty acres and a mule granted by the American Union general, William Sherman, to freed slaves as he occupied Confederate territory in 1865. Forty acres, or one sixteenth of a square mile, is a commonly used land measure.

English fields rarely look as symmetrical as that, but some fields are more symmetrical than others.

The single most powerful factor in producing a measure of symmetry was enclosure. Under this system, common land – heathland, woodland and rough grazing – and open fields, once cultivated in unfenced strips, were fenced in, and divided by hedges into single fields. The system also brought an end to common rights – where commoners could graze their animals or collect hay, even though they didn't own the land. Instead, the uses of the land were granted entirely to its private owner.

The enclosure of much of England in the eighteenth and nineteenth centuries is the biggest ever single factor in changing the national landscape.

Most of England is now enclosed, but the date when enclosure took place makes all the difference to the way it looks today. Much of our ancient countryside – the West Country, the Welsh and Scottish borders, Essex and Kent – was divided in this way in the Middle Ages.

In these areas – often wilder and more remote – there had never been much of a fashion for open-field farming. Instead, when the fields were first claimed from heath and forest in the Middle Ages, or even earlier, they were immediately confined in small, sheltered fields.

Meanwhile, the broad plains of the Midlands lent themselves that much better to open-field farming; so they were divided much later, in the eighteenth and nineteenth centuries, as private landowners cottoned on to the greater profits that came with enclosure.

Over the centuries, those ancient landscapes, enclosed at an earlier stage, built up a thick web of woods, ponds and pollarded trees; their roads, footpaths and ancient, mixed hedges are alluringly crooked, their fields more likely to be irregular. The people in this ancient countryside tend to live in isolated farms, small towns and hamlets.

That said, some ancient civilizations were keener on symmetry than others. In southern Dartmoor, the moors are still divided into neat parallel lines by low stone banks, or Bronze Age 'reaves' – barriers used on arable and pasture land. They wander out of true every now and then, but their overwhelming force is towards order – their lines often leap over a sunken river and continue their straight course on the other side of the valley.

A similar pattern of hedges, on roughly parallel axes, can be seen near Bungay, Suffolk. The Dengie peninsula, in south-east Essex, was divided up by the Romans – or possibly as early as the Iron Age – into a grid of differently sized rectangles. There's a similar Roman grid at Holme-next-the-Sea, Norfolk; and another Bronze or Iron Age grid in Tadlow, Cambridgeshire.[1]

But symmetrical ancient features are the exception. Most prehistoric fields – and most of the ones that predate the Middle Ages – are irregularly shaped. They often vary in size to meet the differing needs of their farms. On the Lizard Peninsula, in Cornwall, the smallest, most intensively cultivated fields are wrapped closely around the farmyard, with the larger fields further away, ranged around the smaller fields in a roughly circular pattern.

Great age is also apparent in the depth of country roads, particularly in Devon's ancient sunken lanes, flanked by banks topped with thick, brambly hedgerows. These are often formed by two-fold ditches – where the spoil from the excavated road was piled up on either side to create the semi-tunnel effect.

Age can be diagnosed, too, in the profile and density of those hedges. In Devon and Cornwall in particular, the ash, elm, oak and sycamore hedges can be extremely old. Some of those at

Land's End are Bronze Age, their thick, humped masses blasted into shape by salty Atlantic winds for more than 2,600 years.

England's earliest hedges were planted in the neolithic period, in around 4000–2500 BC. But extensive enclosure was first carried out in earnest by the Romans, who came up with the simplest way to grow a hedge: smear plant seed all over a piece of old rope, and bury it in a shallow trench.

The Anglo-Saxons accelerated the practice of enclosure; the word 'hedge' comes from Old English *haga*, meaning an enclosure, itself derived from the Saxon word for the hawthorn fruit. The first mention of a hedge being planted was at Kington Langley, Wiltshire, in AD 940: 'the hedgerow that Aelfric made'.[2]

If not planted by man, hedges have grown naturally along the line of fences, off which birds drop plant seeds; occasionally they are thought to be ghosts of ancient woodland, like a hallowed stretch of lime hedge in Shelley, Suffolk.

Hedge-laying continued through the Middle Ages. Richard I, a keen hunter, insisted that his tenants keep their hedges at four foot six or lower, the height a deer could comfortably clear. In the fourteenth century, increasing numbers of open fields were enclosed. More arable land became pasture, as cattle and sheep grazing was extended – animals need more fencing in than crops. Woodland, scrub and common land were increasingly cultivated, too.

After the Black Death, in 1348–50, farmworkers were in a more powerful position, because of the sheer shortage of labour. More of them were given their own plot to plough. Fields were often divided up into areas that were a furlong – an eighth of a mile – in length, the accepted distance that could be ploughed in a single day.

By 1700, about half of the arable land in Britain – around 4.5 million acres – had been enclosed. The rest was open field – hedgeless fields, divided into narrow, long strips in the same way they had been since the Anglo-Saxons.

Celtic fields that predated the Anglo-Saxons were smaller and squarer, partly because the Celtic plough was so simple that the fields had to be double-ploughed – horizontally and vertically, in a grid-like pattern. The more sophisticated Anglo-Saxon plough allowed a field to be ploughed in one long, straight line.

All that open field has been enclosed since, with the rare exception of a few acres here and there, notably at Laxton in Nottinghamshire, Braunton in north Devon and in the fields around Eton, Berkshire.

In a few places, you can still see signs of pre-enclosure ridge and furrow farming, and the old custom of ploughing in strips. A 1591 estate map for All Souls College, Oxford, shows ridge-and-furrow strips marked with the names of the tenant farmers; it tallies accurately with a 1950s aerial photograph of the land.

The ridges and furrows, running downhill, to help drainage, were made by a plough drawn by eight oxen, going up and down the traditional half-acre strip, or 'selion', from the French for a furrow. As the oxen reached the end of their run, they would prepare to turn around in a swerving line, lending a curving, reversed S-shape to the selion.

Not everywhere was enclosed. Today, there are still great tracts of uncultivated land in England – around 5 million acres of common, waste and wild land survive, of the 32.7 million acres that make up England. The 914,307 acres of common land in England are controlled by ancient common rights, usually owned by villagers, or a lord of the manor. That lord may be the local authority: Newcastle City Council owns the Town Moor in the city, where the June Fair, the Hoppings, takes place.

Common land includes the 'Strays' in York, road verges in Herefordshire and chunks of mountaintop in the Lake District. Surrey – with its once remote heaths – has more common land than any other county. There are fewer commons in the

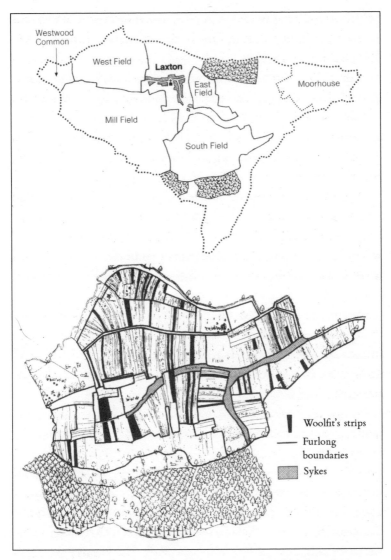

The English countryside before enclosure – Laxton, Nottinghamshire, in 1635. The first picture shows the irregularly shaped, open fields. The second shows the hedgeless strips cultivated by different farmers in South Field. The black strips are those worked by a single farmer, William Woolfit. A furlong is the name of a single block of land cleared for cultivation. The grey areas are sykes – grazing places for tethered cattle and horses.

Midlands, so comprehensively enclosed after 1750. Epping Forest and Hampstead Heath are both commons, owned by the Corporation of London.

Not that common status necessarily means preservation. Greenham Common, owned by the Borough of Newbury, was converted into an airfield in 1941, before being lent to the American air force. With their cruise missiles, they in turn lured the Greenham Common protesters to the site. In 2002, the Greenham and Crookham Commons Act returned the common from the hawk to the barn owl, as it became wild common land once more.

Ancient hedges, planted in the pre-modern age, tend to be rambling things that just about agree to make up a four-sided field, and only very rarely one with approximately right-angled corners. They follow the wandering natural boundaries of the country: old roads and hollow ways, woods, the crests and troughs of hills and valleys, with little sign of those dead straight lines that come of centrally planned subdivision.

In Ireland, the roads, and roadside hedges, are that much straighter: the Grand Jury, the local county government body, built the Jury Roads – straight as a die until they reach the demesne of the local manor house, where they swing round the estate wall.

Older English hedges often follow the line of ancient tracks, which in turn originally followed the route of cows and sheep across fields – and they don't walk in straight lines. Humans are different from cows: their footpaths cut straight across irregular ancient fields. Well, English footpaths do; in France, the footpaths carefully and politely go round the field's perimeter. On most of the Continent, public access stops as soon as you hit private land.[3]

Private property rights are robustly protected in England – witness the effect they had on stopping Christopher Wren's grand scheme for the City of London (see Chapter 5) – but so are easements and public rights of way.

There is a thick, bristling selection of species in an old hedge: among them blackberry, elder, dwarf oak, maple, honeysuckle, wild clematis, hazel, wild rose, sallow, blackthorn and hawthorn. Their make-up varies from county to county. Holly is popular in the Pennines; alder and willow are prominent in Sussex's wet river valleys; gorse is used in the New Forest, and Scots Pine in East Anglia; there are cider apple trees in Herefordshire hedges, cherry trees in Norfolk's.

Soil makes a difference: in the Vale of the White Horse, Oxfordshire, the hedges, planted on clay covered with sands and gravels, are unusually tall. Buckthorn grows on the chalk of Essex and Hertfordshire.

Age is the defining factor in producing a range of species in a single hedge. Six hundred plant species, 65 bird species, 40 butterfly species and 20 types of mammal have been found in British hedges. To work out the age of a hedge, use Hooper's Rule, named after its inventor, Dr Max Hooper.[4] Because hedges accumulate more species over time, and earlier hedges were planted with more species, the rule goes like this: count the number of different species in a thirty-yard stretch of hedge, not including common plants like blackberries and ivy, multiply the figure by 110 and you'll calculate its age. Ancient hedges show the work of generations of woodsmen, too, thick as they are with pollarded trees and coppice stools.

The hedge is particularly well designed for wildlife. A useful covered highway for birds, it's also a refuge from the pesticides and the plough of the neighbouring field. It creates sheltering planes at different angles, providing moisture and shade.

A hedge's raised banks also place some flowers directly in the sun. In County Durham one spring, bicycling west out of Chester-le-Street, I noticed the sunny side of the road was thick with primroses at the foot of a south-facing hedge; on the other side of the road, below the north-facing hedge, there was a single primrose in a quarter-mile stretch. In spring, bluebells, white anemones, violets, campion and lady smocks often join the primroses around the foot of the hedges. In summer come meadow-sweet, foxglove, wild roses and bay willow-herb.

Most hedge styles depend on cutting back stems three quarters of the way through, and laying them flat, overlapping with each other. Hedges are laid in different ways, to cater for different animals. In the Midlands plashing style, the hedge is cut back, and the branches wrapped around ash stakes, producing a hedge strong enough to support a leaning bullock; in the southwest, sheep are kept back by lower, denser hedges; the beef cattle of Leicestershire are restrained by thick, tall, bullfinch hedges.[5]

While many hedge styles are in decline, as they are grubbed up to make bigger fields, there is one increasingly popular roadside style – called 'Motorway' – where branches are laid in parallel with the flow of traffic, to limit damage from, and to, passing cars. In the early 1960s, gorse, which likes poor, acidic soil, was also planted alongside the first motorways; it is still prominent alongside the M3.

England's enclosure was largely completed by a series of parliamentary Acts from the eighteenth century onwards, as strip-farmed open fields were replaced by larger, more regular, if not completely symmetrical, ones.

You can divide England up between that ancient countryside (in the West Country, the Welsh and Scottish borders, Essex and Kent) and this newer, centrally planned countryside, divided up under the eighteenth- and nineteenth-century Enclosure Acts.[6]

That planned countryside runs down a central strip of England: through the landscapes of the Midlands, stretching up into Norfolk, Lincolnshire and Yorkshire, and down into Dorset. Almost 2,000 Enclosure Acts were passed between 1760 and 1815, largely in those areas, with each parish requiring its own Act.[7]

Under the acts, those old open fields, bordered by low earth banks, with grass paths and narrow cultivated strips, were gradually turned into what you see today in those landscapes that were enclosed later: a quilt of roughly square, small fields enclosed by hedgerows and ditches, divided by straightish roads. The resulting landscape, as designed by enclosure commissioners, was not only more regular but also barer, with few woods or footpaths, fewer, straighter roads and plainer hawthorn hedges, planted in straight rows.[8]

Where pre-enclosure farmhouses were usually found in the village, new ones were now needed in the middle of the freshly enclosed land. And so they were called things like New Ground Farm or Newlands Farm; or given names that chimed with eighteenth-century events contemporary with the Enclosure Acts, such as Hanover Farm, Bunkers Hill or Quebec Farm.[9]

When local landowners took over this land and enclosed it, the landlords' fortunes improved enormously. They could grow what they wanted, and graze their cattle away from possibly diseased neighbouring livestock.

But not everyone loved the hedge. The new hedges were loathed by smallholders who'd reaped a comfortable if basic living from pre-enclosure common land. And enclosure had a disastrous effect on the landless. The landlords only took on a relatively small number of employed farmhands. Thousands of other farmworkers were made destitute; poorhouses spread across the country in the eighteenth century.

John Clare (1793–1864), the poet and labourer from Helpston, Northamptonshire, wrote bitterly about enclosure: the uprooting of trees and hedges, the draining of the fens and the ploughing of the pastures. Driven to distraction by enclosure – and not helped by an extremely sensitive disposition – Clare descended into mania and spent the last twenty-three years of his life in Northampton General Lunatic Asylum. The English countryside we get so lyrical about these days had some agonizing birth pangs.

When Clare was fourteen, in 1807, his home village was enclosed by Act of Parliament. In order to increase yields, commons and waste ground, where labourers like Clare previously got their firewood and grazed their animals, were turned into large, privately owned fields. Where fields once stretched outwards from the village, like spokes from a hub, they were now divided into those rough rectangles, with no direct connection to the village.

Enclosure effectively privatized the country. Within the newly defined boundaries, it allowed the development of private aristocratic pursuits, chiefly the intensive rearing of the pheasant. The most common gamebird in the English countryside, the pheasant isn't in fact native; neither is the rabbit, introduced in the early Middle Ages. The pheasant, of south-west Asian origins, is thought to have been introduced by the Normans.[10]

The bird flourished in the copses, game crops and woods which, under enclosure, were either preserved or freshly planted to keep up fresh supplies of game. By the late eighteenth century, pheasant-rearing was a significant part of the English country life. Hunting, too, had its own effect on the landscape in good fox country. In 1770s Leicestershire, fox coverts – spinneys with thick undergrowth, each of around 1–8 hectares – were created in abundance.

But all this was at the expense of the old rural smallholder and labourer; like John Clare, who wrote 'Helpston Green' in response to the vagaries of enclosure.

> Ye injur'd fields ere while so gay,
> When nature's hand display'd
> Long waving rows of willows grey
> And clumps of hawthorn shade.
> But now, alas, your hawthorn bowers
> All desolate we see
> The tyrant's hand their shade devours
> And cuts down every tree.
> Not trees alone have felt their force,
> Whole woods beneath them bow'd;
> They stopt the winding runlet's course,
> And flowry pastures plough'd;
> To shrub nor tree throughout thy fields
> They no compassion show;
> The uplifted axe no mercy yields,
> But strikes a fatal blow.

In this brutal way, around 4.5 million acres of open field – a seventh of England – were enclosed along these lines, with around 200,000 miles of hedges planted between 1750 and 1850, as much as in the previous half a millennium. Most of the new, post-1700 hedges were straight – a bending stretch in the middle of a straight hedge is often a lonely section of ancient hedge that was absorbed into the new order.[11]

England is now left, then, with four main types of fields. The first are the ancient, smaller fields, often preserving the double-curve 'selion' shape. The second kind were created by medieval or Tudor enclosures: on a larger scale, with boundaries a furlong in length, marked out with winding, mixed hedges. Those fields enclosed under the later parliamentary Acts have near-straight, thin hawthorn hedges, obliterating the curving, small-scale lines of the old open-field strips. And modern fields

– the fourth sort, planned long after the Enclosure Acts – are, if anything, even more symmetrical.

The Enclosure Acts were also behind the large-scale creation of allotments. Allotments first appeared in the late sixteenth century: as common land was gradually gobbled up, commoners were allotted land next to their tenanted cottages as part of their wages. The 1806 Enclosure Act, enclosing Great Somerford, in Wiltshire, was the first legislation specifically setting aside land for the labouring poor. The 1845 General Enclosure Act further declared that 'field gardens' must be set aside whenever land was enclosed. Under the 1887 Allotment Act, local authorities had to set aside such land if it was in demand.

Railways increased demand for allotments. The first railway companies rented land to their workers on excess land either side of the tracks – that's why you still see so many of them from train windows. The demands of the Second World War meant allotments hit a new peak, with 1.5 million plots under cultivation, and 6,000 allotments in London's parks alone. There are now 297,000 allotments in England.

These different histories mean allotments vary in size, although the classic simple dimensions were thirty strides by ten and the average plot now measures 250 square metres. There are varieties in produce, too – with leeks popular in the damp northeast, chrysanthemums in Yorkshire and roses in Nottinghamshire.

The strong identities, and administrative structures, of different English counties led not only to different allotment shapes, enclosure practices and field shapes, but also to different types of gates. Sweet chestnut gates are popular in Kent; oak gates are common in Sussex, where oaks were once so thick on the ground that the tree was called the 'Sussex weed'. Most gates have five bars, but you can find six in Cornwall and Devon. Different counties use different combinations of vertical, horizontal and diagonal bars.[12]

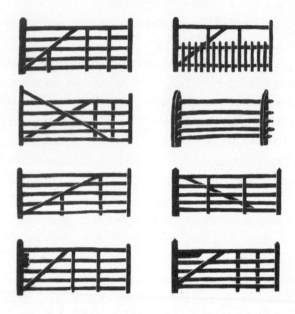

County varieties of field gates, *from top, left to right*: Warwickshire; Weald, Sussex; Devon; Cumbria; Essex; Northumberland; Gloucestershire; Buckinghamshire.

Barns, too, vary from county to county. Staffordshire barns have chequered patterns, produced by absent bricks, to ventilate the hay, straw or grain; square holes in the barns of the Yorkshire Dales let owls in to catch rats; Cotswold-stone barns favour triangular holes. There are, though, shared features across counties: double doors on barns are usually positioned to allow carts in on the windward side, to blow away the chaff and dust when the winnowing and threshing are done.[13]

The grandest medieval barns were extremely elaborate structures. It's not surprising, considering that farming was the backbone of the English economy before the Industrial Revolution; and the barn was essentially the farm's treasury building. John Betjeman called Manor Farm Barn in Harmondsworth

'the Cathedral of Middlesex', and the romantic old poet wasn't using poetic licence.

Harmondsworth Barn was built in 1426 to store the grain that paid for the upkeep of Winchester College. At almost 200 feet long, the barn could hold an awful lot of grain. With all that money at risk, it then had to be built to the highest standards – cathedral standards, in fact.

Betjeman was architecturally correct in his praise. The barn was constructed by cathedral joiners, using the same principles that lay behind Westminster Abbey and Canterbury Cathedral. Like our Gothic cathedrals, Harmondsworth has aisles running along either side of a nave-like, central passage, all supported by a dense web of pointed arches.

A northern twist on the barn was the bastle – popular along a twenty-mile stretch of the English border with Scotland. Thought to derive from *bastille*, these are defensible farmhouses, with doors on the ground and first floors. Animals and stores were kept on the lower floor; the farmer used an outside ladder to get to the first floor, which he could whip away if under attack. The style continued, with more first-floor windows and thinner walls, even after the threat from Scotland receded.[14]

As fields were gradually enclosed, the way cities developed depended largely on who owned the fields on the edge of town. The shape of those fields often dictated the shape of the resulting developments: you can still make out the borders of the five fields around Brighton, covered with Regency terraces in the early nineteenth century, at the height of the city's fashionability.

Nottingham, full of slums in the nineteenth century, has plenty of high-density, multiple-ownership housing with not much green space. That's because the 1,100 acres of open fields on its fringes were under rights of common pasture through the early nineteenth century, and so couldn't be developed. With no breathing space for the town to expand, its centre was intensively

developed. Every garden and orchard was taken over for hous-ing. By 1845, those neighbouring open fields were finally enclosed but it was too late – Nottingham's slums had appeared.[15]

In Leicester, by contrast, where the three big open fields out-side the town were first enclosed, and then given over to urban development, there was more breathing space. Today, the city still feels more prosperous than Nottingham. It has larger gar-dens and wider streets, lined with bigger houses, often with four large bedrooms. With more land available, each house took up a bigger footprint, and had fewer storeys.[16]

Stamford, Lincolnshire, is the picture postcard town where *Middlemarch* was filmed in 1994. The only reason it is so picturesque – and costume drama producers love it so much as a film set – is because of the pattern of development; or lack of it. In the nine-teenth century, the open fields surrounding the town were owned by the Marquess of Exeter, who lived in Burghley House, the sixteenth-century palace on the edge of Stamford. The marquess refused permission for those fields to be enclosed or developed. At the same time, he insisted that the new railway stopped at Peter-borough, fourteen miles away, and not at Stamford.

As a result, the marquess killed off any burgeoning commerce in the town. Grass was said to grow in Stamford's High Street in the late nineteenth century. But he also made Stamford the frozen idyll it remains; while Peterborough was cruelly over-developed, its fine medieval cathedral wrapped in a hideous ring road, lined with grim shopping centres.[17]

Enclosures didn't necessarily mean hedges. The fenlands are bordered by narrow, straight drainage ditches (an eighth of England is still drained through the Fens) rather than hedges.[18] And drystone walls take the place of hedges wherever there is good building stone beneath the turf – particularly along the ribbon of limestone running north-east to south-west across England, from Yorkshire down to Dorset.

More than half of the 70,000 miles of drystone walls in the
country are in Yorkshire, Cornwall, Derbyshire and Cumbria.
The drystone walls of the Pennines were largely built after enclosures from the sixteenth century until the turn of the nineteenth
century, by landowners keen to maximize income from their
sheep. A parliamentary Act of 1801 produced most of the drystone
walls in the Yorkshire Dales. The drystone walls of the Cotswolds
were principally built under enclosures between 1760 and 1825.

Drystone walls are really two walls joined together by regular 'through-slabs', with an infill of small stones. If properly
built, they can last a century or more. And they're still being
built, at a cost of around £25 per yard. Drystone walls on both
sides of the track between Blea Moor Tunnel and Ribblehead
Viaduct, north Yorkshire, have recently been rebuilt.

It's not just in the country that the hedge controls the lie of
the land. In towns and cities, older garden walls still run along
the hedge line of the old fields. That's why the biggest, oldest
trees in your garden tend to run along your back wall. If you
look at a pre-urban map of a city, the old hedge line will often
shadow the modern shared wall running between the back gardens of parallel terraces.

More recently, hedges have become the dividing lines of the
suburbs. When Dame Henrietta Barnett set up Hampstead Garden Suburb in north London in 1907, she stipulated that building
plots should be divided by hedges, trellis or wire fences, but
never by walls.

Suburbia fell deeply for the hedge, as an echo of rural England.
Privet is the classic suburban hedge, singled out by fashionable
critics for withering criticism. In an unusually snobbish attack on
suburbia, George Orwell took against 'the same long, long rows
of semi-detached houses, the stucco front, the creosoted gate, the
privet hedge, the green front door. The Laurels, the Myrtles, the
Hawthorns, Mon Abri, Mon Repos, Belle Vue.'[19]

Urban hedges in fact vary considerably: with holly in Osmaston, Derbyshire, rhododendron and laurel in Bournemouth and fuchsia hedges in Cornwall. Guinea Gardens in Birmingham has unusually high hedges; in parts of Nottingham, detached gardens, with front doors set into the hedges, are now Grade II listed.

A similar snobbish attitude has grown over time towards the Leylandii tree; a tree that appeared as the suburbs were developing. It was first propagated in 1881 by Sir John Naylor in Leighton, Powys; his son, Christopher, developed the tree further (and changed his surname to Leyland in order to bag an inheritance – thus the name).

Hedges still divide much of England then: in ancient, crooked countryside, in the more symmetrical fields enclosed in the eighteenth and nineteenth centuries, and in semi-manicured rural suburbia on the fringes of our towns and cities. Even the suburban hedge fits squarely into the peculiar English affection for the countryside; a natural – if neatened and straightened – device for connecting the country to the fringes of town.

The hedge, particularly the crooked hedge, remains idiosyncratically English. Elsewhere across the world, smaller estates and a peasant farming tradition meant farmland was sliced and re-sliced into rectangular strips.

In France, the Napoleonic Code absorbed Roman law and ended primogeniture. The Code declared that inherited property must be divided into thirds. One third went to the wife, another was split between the children equally, and the last third was disposed of as the deceased wished. This led to constant sub-division of estates between heirs, and the repeated imposition of new, straight boundaries. An increased hunger for land meant hedges often weren't used much, if at all. They took up too much valuable space; wire and timber fences were much less land-hungry.

The collectivization of many French farms after the war added another layer of dirigiste organization – and more right angles and straight lines. Still, pockets of France retained their hedges, notably Normandy, where Allied troops had to fight their way through the thick, tangled undergrowth of the *bocage*. American GIs even referred to the *bocage* as hedgerows. The Normandy landscape is not unlike Devon's, with mixed pasture and woodland, and deep-burrowed lanes.

That apparently unplanned look of ancient English country-side at its best shares much of the same organic, free spirit behind the asymmetrical, unplanned street pattern of English cities. And often for the same reasons: rich landowners and commercial farmers privately developing their land, free from overarching, central planning. Whenever control did became more centrally planned, as it did in those eighteenth- and nineteenth-century Enclosure Acts, then England looks less and less like England.

Where the countryside still looks quintessentially English, it's often because of the country's class structure.

When the Government performed its U-turn over the sell-off of Forestry Commission land in February 2011, it cast a revealing light on the changing relationship between class and land ownership. The Forestry Commission, founded in 1919, is the biggest landowner in the country, with 2,571,270 acres – and 1.4 billion trees. Progressive land sales to companies, charities and government agencies like the Commission, as opposed to private individuals, mark the biggest change in British land ownership over the last 150 years.

In 1872, twelve out of the top thirteen landowners in the country were aristocrats; the other one was the biggest land-owner of all, the Church of England, with 2,130,000 acres (the Church now owns 210,000 acres). Today, the top five landowners are: the Forestry Commission; the National Trust, with 630,000 acres; the Ministry of Defence (592,800 acres); company pension funds (550,000 acres); and utility companies (500,000 acres). Aristocrats have largely been replaced by public bodies at the top of the tree.

That's not to say that the aristocracy and the monarchy don't still own an awful lot of land. The Crown Estate controls 358,000 acres; that figure would be over 23 million acres if you added in the foreshore and the seabed, out to the twelve nautical miles limit – all officially owned by the Queen.

'Officially' because, although the Crown Estate is strictly owned by the Queen, it is not her private property to play around with. Income from the Crown Estate goes to the Treasury. In return, the Queen receives her Civil List payment, or she will until 2013, when the Coalition Government has arranged for her to be paid directly from Crown Estate coffers.

The 36,000 members of the CLA (Country Land and Business Association), 0.6 per cent of the population, own half the rural land in the country. A third of British land is still owned by aristocrats and rural gentry. The Duke of Buccleuch and Queensberry remains the eighth-biggest landowner in the country, with 240,000 acres in Dumfriesshire, Selkirkshire, Northamptonshire and the outskirts of Edinburgh. The top ten British landowners own a million acres between them, in a country of 60 million acres altogether.

Still, even that is an improvement on 1873, when a sort of second Domesday Book, *The Return of Owners of Land*, was published: then, 7,000 men owned 80 per cent of England. After the First World War, with the loss of so many heirs to great estates on the battlefield, and the increase in taxes, a quarter of British land changed hands in four years;[20] the biggest change in land ownership since the dissolution of the monasteries.

The First World War, income taxes and death duties were

supposed to have done for the aristocracy at the beginning of the twentieth century. Those death duties did in fact wipe out a lot of estates and great houses, particularly in the First World War and its immediate aftermath. But those estates that survived the crash, and further dips in land values after the Second World War, are now sitting pretty.

In a land-starved, people-packed country, landowners can sell off tiny twenty-acre portions of their estates to a supermarket, raise millions and keep their hands on those hundreds of thousands of acres they've clung on to. Sir Reggie Sheffield, Bt, David Cameron's father-in-law, who owns 3,000 acres of Lincolnshire and two stately homes, says he survives on a small private income 'garnished with a few planning permissions'.[21]

Continued domination of the landowning tables by the English upper classes is reflected in the landscape. Even the vast acreage of land sold by the aristocracy over the last century and a half is still shaped by their previous ownership of it.

And the biggest class influence on the English landscape derived from primogeniture. In 1856, Ralph Waldo Emerson, the American writer, said of English country houses, 'Primogeniture built these sumptuous piles ... Primogeniture is a cardinal rule of English property and institutions. Laws, customs, manners, the very persons and faces, affirm it.'[22]

Primogeniture also means English country houses have retained their contents, too. On the Continent, the great palaces and country houses have been ransacked, not just by revolution, but by partible inheritance: with every new generation, there's another division of the spoils.

Emerson was talking about country houses, but he might just as well have been talking about the land around those houses. Still today, big parts of the English countryside are undeveloped because they are owned in great blocks by individual landowners – who, if they can get planning permission, will tend to develop on the edge of their estates, leaving the core of their landholdings unchanged since they were enclosed and land-scaped three or four centuries ago.

Primogeniture, and the practice of titles usually passing through a single male heir, means the British aristocracy has remained relatively small. In the late eighteenth century, there were 365,000 nobles in France, 479,000 in Spain and 580,000 in Russia. There were fewer than 10,000 in England.[23]

That meant there was more land to go round for a tiny club of grand landowners. Estates have for the most part remained large in England, with little of the land-grabbing division and sub-division of other countries. This is true of some counties in particular. Of Norfolk's 1,324,160 acres, eight estates have over 10,000 acres; fifty-six have more than 1,000 acres.

These large landholdings mean villages are often small, as development has been limited, first by the landowner and now by planning restrictions. The churches, often built by that rich landowner, are disproportionately big. In Norfolk, some villages amount to little more than a large medieval church with a farmhouse next door.

There hasn't always been primogeniture in England. King Alfred (849–99) became king, despite the legitimate claim of his eldest brother's oldest son. By the time William the Conqueror invaded, primogeniture was still only an expectation, not a legal requirement. Even William the Conqueror passed over his own oldest son, Robert Curthose, in favour of a younger son, William Rufus. By the thirteenth century, primogeniture had become established English law, although the British throne has only followed strict primogeniture lines since George I's accession in 1714.

Not everything was subject to primogeniture in England; by tradition one of the few things that doesn't go to the oldest son is jewellery – usually passed down the female line in families, unlike in most Continental countries. And certain families have always been able to inherit titles and estates through the female line. When Lord Mountbatten was killed in 1979, his daughter, Lady Patricia, inherited the title by special remainder, because he had no sons.

Parts of England weren't subject to primogeniture, either, even into the modern age. The Anglo-Saxon gavelkind system, whereby property was distributed between all sons, including illegitimate ones, survived in Kent from the eleventh century until 1925, when it was legally abolished in Britain. The 1925 Administration of Estates Act also removed the primogeniture law that had lasted in much of the rest of England for more than half a millennium.

'Gavelkind' is a Kent dialect word, derived from Old English. It literally means a form of land tenure held by 'gavel' – that is, rent or fixed services other than military service. But it soon came to mean a type of inheritance split between sons. The word was adopted in Wales and Ireland, too, where gavelkind survived English occupation.

William the Conqueror supposedly let gavelkind survive as a concession to the men of Kent, while primogeniture became standard elsewhere throughout his kingdom. With its similarities to German Salic Law, gavelkind was probably introduced by German immigrants to Kent in the fifth century. Those Germans settled as freeholders, as was the German custom, not as feudal tenants.

The gavelkind legacy led to smaller fields and smaller estates in Kent. That's why Kent remains largely a place of farmhouses and hamlets rather than estate villages. There are still relatively few big estates, country houses, parks or grand landowning families in the county.[24] Land was enclosed earlier, too, in Kent, with little of the open-field farming which remained popular in the Midlands long after Kent had given up the practice.

Centuries of gavelkind left a legacy that survives today: in

Wales, the division of property between sons led to smaller fields and farmhouses than in England. It also led to bigger rows, as Welsh brothers engaged in bloody battles over their shared inheritance.[25] Only to the immediate west of the Welsh border, where primogeniture was introduced earlier, and some of the Marcher lordships built up significant landholdings, are there larger estates on the English model.

Scotland, too, tends to have smaller fields – based on the crofting system, introduced to the country in the eighteenth century. Each tenant farmed his own smallholding of around five acres, as well as sharing rights of common grazing with neighbouring crofters.

You can also see more close-knit field patterns in much of Ireland. Under the Penal Laws of the sixteenth to eighteenth centuries, when an Irish Catholic landowner died, his property was forcibly split between his children. Shared inheritance between large Catholic families led to fields being divided and sub-divided into smaller plots than in England.

Fields are smaller in Ulster as well. The Scottish settlers, who came over in the early seventeenth century, were given mammoth estates. One family, the Montgomerys, had 100,000 acres in County Down when they arrived at the beginning of the seventeenth century. But they also brought 8,000 tenant farmers with them – so each farm, and its attendant fields, ended up being pretty small.

Because of the big landed inheritances that come with primogeniture, English landowners can afford to be liberal with their hedges, allowing a generous amount of land either side of them – the traditional three- to four-yard strip between crop and hedge, used for turning machinery.

Or at least they used to be more generous. Since 1945, 250,000 miles of hedgerow – more than half of all English hedges – have been grubbed up, particularly in the prairies of East Anglia, where vast combine harvesters find three-point turns tricky. A lot of thickly hedged England was also opened up with the change from pasture to arable land during the First and Second World Wars. In the 1930s, only 1 per cent of Leicestershire farmland was arable; by 1982, that figure had climbed to 51.85 per cent.

After the last war, even more hedges were grubbed up, woods were cut down, farmhouses removed, marshes drained, grassland ploughed, and fertilizers and pesticide used intensively on bigger, more open fields.

Still, the stripping of the hedges is slowing: in recent years, many hedges have been replanted. Since the 1997 Hedgerow Regulations, you have to get planning permission to rip up a hedge. Even with all that grubbing up, hedges remain a defining feature – perhaps the defining feature – of the English landscape.

7. A Love of the Picturesque

Are Britons here? They go abroad, feel calls
To trace old battlefields and crumbling walls.

Mephistopheles in Goethe's Faust (1832)

In March 2010, a competition was held to find Britain's most picturesque street.[1]

The winner was the accurately named Shambles in York – a fourteenth-century street of old butchers' shops, with timber-framed, jettied upper storey, leaning at drunken angles, teetering over the street from either side and practically kissing each other in mid-air above your head.

It's serendipitous that the Shambles should win a picturesque competition. In its natural, organic, literally shambolic beauty, the street captures many of the ideals of the eighteenth-century Picturesque movement – which contributed, and still contributes, enormously to a peculiarly English type and sense of beauty.

As first defined in the 1703 *Oxford English Dictionary*, picturesque literally meant, 'in the manner of a picture; fit to be made into a picture'. The word is derived from the Italian, *pittoresco*, meaning 'in the manner of a painter'. 'Landscape' was originally an artistic term, too, derived from a Dutch painter's term, *landskip*, meaning a picture of a view, as opposed to the view itself.

But you don't have to know the eighteenth-century origins of the term to understand that there is something more to the meaning of picturesque than mere suitability to be painted. The word encompasses an apparently happenstance, wild, accidental beauty, even if the beauty is choreographed by a hidden human hand. An asymmetrical, tumbledown Cotswolds village is picturesque; the imposing, ordered splendour of, say, Versailles isn't.

The English aren't good at immaculate, idealized beauty – whether it's in their clothes, their art or their teeth. The beauty that springs up, unbidden, from apparent neglect is more their thing.

Their ideals remain those of the Picturesque movement; particularly when it comes to imitating Nature – better a splodge-shaped lake fringed with shaggy-profiled oaks than an arrow-straight canal flanked by a thousand-yard avenue of pleached limes. The English countryside as a whole – apparently wild, but in fact manicured for centuries – is innately Picturesque.

The specific aesthetic, upper-case term 'Picturesque' only took a proper foothold in 1782, when the Rev. William Gilpin published *Observations on the River Wye, and Several Parts of South Wales, etc. Relative Chiefly to Picturesque Beauty; made in the Summer of the Year 1770.*

But that Picturesque taste for the natural, wild, romantic look began earlier in the century. In 1711, Joseph Addison wrote in the *Spectator*, 'For my own part, I would rather look upon a tree in all its luxuriance and diffusion of boughs and branches than when it is . . . trimmed into a mathematical figure.'

At about the same time, Queen Anne did away with the symmetrical box hedges at Kensington Palace, because she didn't like the smell. Before the natural look took over, English gardens and landscapes had been controlled with martial precision – geometrical walls shadowing those lines of clipped box hedges, alongside rectangular grids of paths and flowerbeds.

Alexander Pope, writing in 1731, suggested that the English landscape should be rich in curved lines, obscurity and variety, an evocation of rough, wild nature.

> To build, to plant, whatever you intend,
> To rear the column, or the arch to bend,
> To swell the terrace, or to sink the grot;
> In all, let Nature never be forgot.[2]

On the Continent, nature and surprise were alien concepts in the manmade landscape; and symptomatic of the Englishness of English literature, too, according to Voltaire.

> Up to now the English have only produced irregular beauties ... Their poetical genius resembles a closely grown tree planted by nature, throwing out a thousand branches here and there, and growing lustily and without rules. It dies if you try to force its nature and trim it like the gardens of Marly [a small royal palace on the edges of Paris, with elaborate, geometric gardens].

Voltaire had spotted the emerging roots of a consciously wild tradition of English gardening. That tradition had many manifestations over the next three centuries: a revolt against anything too artificial – iceberg roses, say – created by horticulturalists; a taste for the nearly wild Tenby daffodil over louder, new, pink-centred species; the popularity of English cottage gardens at the Chelsea Flower Show.

The tradition culminated in today's ultra-English garden look: ragged-edged borders, teeming with apparently unruly plants, with rough-mown paths curving through overgrown grass dotted with wildflowers.

This natural look progressed through several degrees of cultivation. 'English landscape was invented by gardeners imitating foreign painters who were evoking classical authors,' Tom Stoppard wrote, in *Arcadia*, 'Capability Brown doing Claude, who was doing Virgil.'

We like to think of ourselves as a cool, level-headed, northern race, but a streak of the warm, wild south runs through our landscape. Take a look at some of Claude Lorrain's paintings of Greece and Italy, and you could be forgiven for thinking you were in deepest Wiltshire.

Claude was a Frenchman – born in around 1600 in the Duchy of Lorrain; thus the name – who lived in Rome for most of his life. And yet several paintings, like his *Landscape with the Judgement of Paris*, look distinctly English.

Rambling, deciduous trees tumble down to a gently bubbling, rock-fringed lake, flanked by a ruined folly. If it weren't for Paris's toga and the goddesses' topless gowns, you'd hardly believe it was ancient Greece. Greece, ancient or modern, never looked as dark green as this. This similarity – between rural England and rural Greece painted by a Frenchman to look like seventeenth-century Italy – is no coincidence.

Fifty years after his death (in 1682), Claude was central to the English appetite for contrived wilderness. Other artists also inspired the new generation of English gardens: Poussin, Gaspard Dughet and Salvator Rosa among them. Roman poetry, by Ovid, Virgil and Horace, encouraged the movement, too, as Tom Stoppard pointed out.

But it was Claude's paintings that dominated the scene from the 1730s onwards. Twenty-seven of his paintings were sold in London auction houses between 1731 and 1759. Frederick, Prince of Wales, hoovered up as many Claudes as he could. In the early 1740s, engravings of forty-four Claude landscapes were snapped up by the public from an enterprising Covent Garden printmaker. Another successful set of Claude engravings appeared in London in 1772. As late as 1794, a drawing room in Butcher Row, east London, was painted with a mural copy of Claude's *Pastoral Landscape with the Arch of Titus*.

His Arcadian vision was copied across England in the parks of country houses, from Blenheim Palace to Stowe. At Stourhead, Wiltshire, Henry Hoare, of the banking family, was so keen on

Claude that some historians have suggested the whole garden is a copy of Claude's painting *Aeneas on Delos*. These new landscapes were designed to look natural: clumps of trees wrapped round lakes, clearing to reveal views to the far horizon; and, just like in Claude's *Judgement of Paris*, dotted with temples.

Claude's pictures had a particular influence on Capability Brown's managed landscapes. Lancelot 'Capability' Brown cultivated a natural look, even if it was a carefully contrived natural look; the nickname came from his confident assertion to potential clients that their acres showed tremendous capability for improvement.

By the 1740s, Capability Brown was hard at work, following Pope's advice and emulating Claude's brushwork, removing walls, canals, tree-lined avenues and centralized fountains, ripping up flowerbeds and topiary, and making straight lines wavy.

A Brown-style park attached to a country house became an essential feature, with thousands of them landscaped through the eighteenth and nineteenth centuries, right up until the agricultural depression of the 1880s. Brown's 280 commissions ended up covering more than 123,000 acres of Britain.

His ideas inspired gardeners across the world for a century and a half: in Les Jardins Anglais of France and the Englischer Garten of Munich; even in Central Park, New York, whose designer, Frederick Olmsted, emulated Brown's pastoral Arcadia. Sheep were only removed from Central Park in the 1930s; Sheep Meadow, a big, open space used for concerts, demonstrations and sunbathing, survives today.

To foreign sensibilities, the English landscape, whatever it gets called in different countries, is asymmetrical, untethered and faintly shambolic, with serpentine lakes, winding drives and paths, and trees grouped in apparently random clumps around an off-centre lawn.

Brown's intention was that you shouldn't notice quite how

contrived the 'natural' look was. The resulting look – still surviving at dozens of stately homes – was a smooth, rounded one,
with vistas of intertwining hills, and ornamental lakes.

The newly cleared landscape was articulated with those
clumps – or plumps – of exotic trees. These clumps were originally planted in deer parks in the early eighteenth century as fox
coverts and game cover. Gradually, they were shifted, for scenic
effect, to hilltops – where many of them survive. They're often
made up of beech trees, like the Seven Sisters on Cothelstone
Hill, in the Quantocks, or Wittenham Clumps, near Abingdon,
painted by Paul Nash in 1943–4.

Nature was artfully manipulated: those hills were often
sculpted out of gentle slopes; the lakes formed by damming thin
streams – at Petworth, West Sussex, Brown moved more than
60,000 tons of earth and laid a mile of underground brick
plumbing to feed the lake.

Brown's serpentine lakes (he designed 150 of them) and rivers
were a reflection of the taste for curved lines over straight ones
and, in particular, for the 'line of beauty', the term coined by
William Hogarth in 1753 for the shallow, elegant, undulating
double curve threaded through English landscapes, and English
buildings.[3]

That same swerving line runs right back to the swirling,
intertwining line of window tracery and stonework in Decorated Gothic work of the early fourteenth century, and feeds
into the curving lines of Georgian lakes, paths and lawns.

'There's none of your straight lines here,' wrote David
Garrick and George Colman, in *The Clandestine Marriage*, in 1766,
'but all taste – zigzag – crinkum crankum – in and out – right
and left – to and again – twisting and turning like a worm, my
lord.'

In Coleridge's *Kubla Khan*, written in 1797, Xanadu's gardens
were 'bright with sinuous rills'.

The dislike of the straight line continued into the early nineteenth century. In the 1830s, Sir George Tapps Gervis, a local landowner, started developing Bournemouth; his aim was planned asymmetry along Picturesque lines. He laid out a series of Italianate and Tudor villas, well spaced around broad, tree-lined streets that had to wind along irregular lines. There is still no formal promenade in Bournemouth for this reason; and the older bits of town are criss-crossed with curving roads and footpaths today.

By the 1750s, Capability Brown took to bringing the park, thinly disguised as countryside, right up to the walls of the house. The trick was perpetuated by the ha-ha – a hidden ditch that kept animals from the house, but allowed views to run, apparently uninterrupted, all the way from your front door to the horizon.

The ha-ha was a French device, first used in England at Stowe in 1730. Stowe was typical of a new desire for a selection of different sculptures, buildings and viewpoints scattered across the landscape. There were so many at Stowe that Horace Walpole referred to 'the Albano glut of buildings' there.

Stowe was where the architect and designer William Kent first 'leapt the fence and saw that all nature was a garden', as Walpole put it in 1735. All the same, it was a natural garden that demanded some pretty heavy-handed planning: in 1710, thirty-two houses and 180 people were removed, mostly to the nearby village of Dadford; the bishop refused to remove the church and so it remained at Stowe. Across England, villages were razed to make way for new parks and country houses, such as Castle Howard and Harewood House in Yorkshire, Milton Abbey in Dorset, Compton Wynyates in Warwickshire and Nuneham, Oxfordshire.

'The omnipotent magician Brown appears,' said the poet William Cowper of this kind of vast landscape surgery, all done with wheelbarrow and spade, 'He speaks, the lake becomes a lawn, woods vanish, hills subside and valleys rise and streams as if created for his use.'

Others were less admiring. Even when Brown was alive, his over-designing was criticized. Another poet, Richard Owen, said he hoped he would die before Brown, because he would like to 'see Heaven before it was "improved"'. In *Arcadia*, Tom Stoppard says of a Brown landscape that it's manicured down 'to the right amount of sheep tastefully arranged'.

Uvedale Price, one of the guiding lights of the Picturesque movement, said of Brown, 'Whoever views objects with a painter's eye, looks with indifference, if not with disgust, at the clump, the belts, the made water, and the eternal smoothness.'

Inspired, too, by the landscape architect Humphry Repton (1752–1818), the Picturesque movement promoted a new, rougher, wilder approach.

Landscapes should be irregular, with asymmetrical patches of trees. Repton took against right angles – his favourite approach to a house was at a 45-degree angle. Landscapes should be designed like paintings, with a foreground, middle ground and background. The garden in the foreground was allowed some ornamental planting and geometrical shaping, or dressed ground, as Repton called it. Beyond the flower beds and lawns, often marked off with a ha-ha, the middle and background should be infused with wildness and nature, full of irregularity, contrast and surprise, as opposed to predictability and symmetry. These characteristics transfer easily into human ones, peculiarly English ones – oddness, quirkiness, freedom, humour and a relaxed shabbiness.

The Picturesque movement also began the tradition of the touring holidaymaker, the igniting spark behind the modern caravan and the holiday cottage. In 1770, William Gilpin and Thomas Gray, the poet, made a trip down the Wye in search of 'nameless beauties', settling on the view of Goodrich Castle, Herefordshire, from the river as 'correctly picturesque'.

Twelve years later, Gilpin published the travel book *Observations on the River Wye*, which formally enshrined the Picturesque movement. The Wye Valley soon became a popular holiday destination. The heritagization of the country for the benefit of the city dweller had begun; and so had the myth that rural life was a thing of bucolic pleasures, not back-breaking poverty.

Foreign holidays, too, were taking their first tentative steps, building on the established tradition of the Grand Tour. Tourism is a relatively modern creation: Thomas Coryate (b.1577) is said to be the first Englishman to have travelled purely for the sake of travelling. By the late eighteenth century, English gentlemen were travelling in droves to the Continent, clutching their Claude glasses – small, tinted mirrors which instantly converted any scene in the Roman *campagna* into a mini-Claude painting.

That apparently rough and ready Picturesque look wasn't confined to the country; it crept into English towns, too. Compare the Tuileries in Paris – vegetation-free paths, dead-straight lines of geometrical parterres, and lime trees manicured to look like topiary, running at right angles to the long, straight Rue de Rivoli – with, say, St James's Park; where willows dip clumsily into the water, and snaking, pitted paths follow the undulating line of the lake; where the oaks are left to their messy, shifting outlines, part obscuring, part shaping the ever-changing views of Buckingham Palace and the Foreign Office.

The contrast between Continental neatness and English roughness is still enshrined in the Continental mind. A friend tells me that, near her house in Zutphen, Holland, the untidy local Dutch farmer – with his ripped bin bags and defunct agricultural machinery crowding his farmyard – is known as the *Engelse boer*, the English farmer.

And it's not just Dutch farmers who are neat, my friend tells me; even the builders wear neat, clean jeans and ironed shirts – unlike their English counterparts. That idea of Dutch cleanliness goes right back to seventeenth-century Delft – to domestic scenes painted by Pieter de Hooch of the town in the 1660s, with mob-hatted women dusting wood-panelled drawing rooms and scrubbing down dairies, lined with easi-clean Delft tiles.

Wrapped up with the Picturesque movement and its affection for unmanicured nature was the new cult of the ruin; and the emerging English conviction that old things are better than new ones, particularly if they're a little battered.

There's nothing we like more than the crumbling remains of a village deserted after the Black Death, or a field's ridges and furrows that have survived since the Middle Ages; nothing, perhaps, except a great old building that's been left to rack and ruin.

The English cult of the ruin goes back at least as far as 1613, when John Webster wrote in *The Duchess of Malfi*, 'I do love these ancient ruines: We do never tread upon them, but we sette Our foot upon some reverend history.'

Sir John Vanbrugh, architect of Blenheim Palace and Castle Howard, was the first Englishman to campaign for the protection of threatened ruins. Preservation of old buildings is now a sacrosanct pursuit in England; but Vanbrugh was considered distinctly odd in 1709 when he tried to save Woodstock Manor, the decaying medieval pile opposite the site of Blenheim.

Old buildings, Vanbrugh said, 'move more lively and pleasing reflections than history without their aid can do'. Invoking the same principles as the Picturesque movement that followed, he added, of the manor, 'It would make one of the most agreeable objects that the best of landskip painters can invent.'

The Duchess of Marlborough, Blenheim's patron, did not agree, ordering the demolition of Woodstock Manor. But the taste for ruins had begun. At nearby Rousham, Oxfordshire, in 1740, William Kent continued the trend, using two Gothic ruins as 'objects in a landscape'.

'The British Character. Passion for Ruins', by Pont in *Punch,* 8 September 1937.

This taste for ruins bled into an eighteenth-century taste for follies, too. Somewhere, buried deep in the English artistic mind, is the overpowering English desire to crack a joke. Follies are a punchline in stone – the little building on the horizon that takes the edge off the grandness of the great Palladian pile in the valley below.

There are follies all over the world, but Britain remains the

international folly capital. Stowe, begun by the Temple–
Grenville Whig dynasty in the eighteenth century, has more
follies than anywhere else on the planet. Among the highlights
are pavilions by Gibbs, Doric and Corinthian arches, a men-
agerie, Dido's Cave, Vanbrugh's Rotondo, Queen Caroline's
Monument, and temples to Venus, to Ancient and Modern
Virtue, to Friendship and to British Worthies.

The taste for classical ruins was borrowed, too, from earlier
landscape painters – particularly, again, from Claude Lorrain,
who took a cheeringly free approach to classical archaeology.

In one picture, *Pastoral Landscape with the Arch of Titus*, Claude
transplants the ruined arch from the Forum at Rome, and slaps
it next to some of the greatest hits of imperial architecture – the
Colosseum, Claudius's aqueduct and the Ponte Nomentano. He
then lumped all of this together into an elegiac, rural capriccio,
very much the same effect the landscape architect Charles
Bridgeman was striving for at Stowe.

Follies were originally just that – foolish buildings that
showed folly in the builder. The first folly was reputedly a castle
in the Welsh borders, built in 1228 by Hubert de Burgh. No
sooner had he put it up than it was ordered to be demolished
because a new peace treaty had been signed with the Welsh. The
mix-up meant the building was given the Latin name, Stulti-
tiam Huberti – Hubert's Stupidity, or Hubert's Folly.

By the time the folly craze got going in the early eighteenth
century, the word had lost its critical undertone. It came to
mean what it usually means now – an entertaining building,
rather than a stupid one.

Fawley Court, Buckinghamshire, until recently the Divine
Mercy College for the Marian Fathers, a Polish Catholic institution, is the spiritual home of the folly. And its spiritual father is
John Freeman, Fawley Court's owner, who, in 1731, was responsible for the earliest building to combine all the classic folly

elements. Fawley's sham Gothick ruin has a genuine Perpendicular Gothic window punched into a tumbledown wall. At its heart, a charming domed room is decorated in faux-primitive style with knucklebones and pebbles, its floor tiled in a swastika pattern in the days before the Hindu symbol was hijacked by the Nazis. Statues on plinths once lined a processional route leading to a chunk of altar from the ancient Greek city of Pergamon on Turkey's Aegean coast.

The ingredients of the ideal British folly were fully realized at Fawley – a mixture of the antique, the Gothic and the jokey. Freeman's greatest joke of all survived even his death. In 1731, he built a sham long barrow, near Fawley, at Henley. Perhaps the folly lost its comic value for the archaeologists who excavated the barrow two centuries later, when they came across an urn with an inscription carved by Freeman, admitting responsibility for the prank.

For all the pleasure of follies, they needn't be entirely fanciful. Their beauty can outweigh their humour; as at Virginia Water, in Windsor Great Park, home to the best ancient ruins in the country – the second-century AD columns from Leptis Magna, Libya, artfully rearranged in a ruinous tableau in 1826 by Sir Jeffry Wyatville for George IV. Some columns lie broken on the ground; others stand alone, bereft of their capitals, as if this damp, forgotten corner of the Roman Empire on the Berkshire–Surrey border had been sacked by Vandals just yesterday.

The Virginia Water ruins are definitive English folly material: combining an affection for the past with a romantic attachment to decay. This peculiar love of old things overlaps with an English architectural conservatism and revivalism, entrenched more recently in our strict planning laws.

Our obsession with history is unusual, even when it comes to its academic study. Political science is a much more popular subject across the Continent. In Germany, in around 1900, political science was deliberately substituted for history – then considered to be an ungainly mixture of anecdotes and pointless articles. In many other Continental countries, history is a subject that stops at the end of primary school.

Even our electricity pylons hark back to a pre-electric age. The first generation of pylons was introduced in Britain in July 1928, in Bonnyside, Edinburgh; the last of the 26,000 pylons was installed in the New Forest in September 1933.

Planners insisted the new 150ft-tall pylons should be prettier than existing Russian and American designs. So Sir Reginald Blomfield, the conservative, classical architect who built Lambeth Bridge and the Menin Gate at Ypres, was brought in to design gradually narrowing, steel-lattice pylons – evoking the shape of the original ancient *pulon*, the Egyptian-style doorway that's narrower at the top than at the bottom.

The poet Stephen Spender described the Blomfield pylons as giant, nude girls. In October 2011, it was announced that the next generation of pylons would be rather slighter girls – a third shorter than the old ones, built to a simpler, T-shaped design, designed by Bystrup, a Danish firm.

Throughout recent design history, the English have been unusually given to repeated imitations of a previous age. Three of the great national clichés – the double-decker bus, the black cab and the red phone box – all satisfy the English desire for old-fashioned things.

The double-decker, unchanged from its 1954 original design, lasted on London streets until 2005. Boris Johnson's replacement, unveiled in February 2012, is directly inspired by it.

Even the curved top of the phone box – the red K6 designed by Sir Giles Gilbert Scott in 1935 – was in conscious imitation of the early-nineteenth-century 'trampoline ceiling' in Sir John

Soane's house, now the Sir John Soane Museum, in Lincoln's Inn Fields.

And the current black cab, the TX4 (2007 to date), and its predecessors (the TXII, 2002–6, and the TX1, 1997–2002) are in direct imitation of the Austin FX4, the definitive cab, produced from 1958 to 1997. That in turn was an imitation of the even more old-fashioned Austin FX3 (1948–58).

This taste for historical revivalism has been strong in England for centuries. It's remarkable, even if we don't remark on it much, that the train stations of the great new railway age in the mid- to late nineteenth century were built to look like medieval Gothic cathedrals. John Betjeman pointed out that Liverpool Street Station was built on the Latin Cross plan of a Gothic cathedral, complete with triplets of Early English Gothic lancet windows; the original station canteen was exactly where the altar would be. St Pancras's train shed has a pointed Gothic arch, while its attached hotel, the Midland Grand, was a confection of Venetian and Lombardic Gothic, combined with details borrowed from Westminster Abbey, and from Winchester Cathedral and Salisbury Cathedral.

Historical revivalism was at work through the eighteenth and nineteenth centuries. England's Palladian country houses were inspired by Andrea Palladio's late-sixteenth-century palazzi in the Veneto; Victorian Gothic Revival churches happily imitated fourteenth-century designs – and the Gothic Revival appeared in England half a century before it materialized on the Continent.

It doesn't matter much if those historical styles are mixed up in the same building, either. Perhaps the most famous building in the country, the Houses of Parliament, is a mixture of Perpendicular Gothic, in its detail, and classical symmetry, in its plan, reflecting the tastes of its two architects: the arch-Gothic revivalist, A. W. Pugin, and the classically minded Sir Charles Barry.

St Paul's Cathedral, for all its vogueish, early-eighteenth-century classical skin, is built on the archaic Latin Cross ground plan of the Gothic cathedral; and it's supported by another Gothic device, the flying buttress.[4]

Jokey historical buildings, follies included, go down particularly well with the English – like the McDonald's on the London Road, leading out of Oxford, done up in gleeful OTT Mock Tudor style.

England was the first country, in fact, to mix architectural function and form so dramatically. Nineteenth-century cotton warehouses in Manchester and Pall Mall gentlemen's clubs, like the Reform and the Travellers, were dressed in the clothes of Genoese merchant palazzi. Victorian Holloway jail, in north London, was disguised as a medieval castle. The 1762 summerhouse at Kew Gardens was designed by Sir William Chambers as a ten-storey Chinese pagoda. Those ten storeys also expose the knockabout, carefree English approach to architecture; genuine pagodas are supposed to have an odd number of storeys, the implication being that only God can provide the perfection associated with an even number.

The English love to pump up the fantasy in these playful buildings. In places like Strawberry Hill, Twickenham, the Gothic Revival got much more fantastical than its original medieval inspiration ever did, reaching Disneyland extremes of inflated machicolations, gingerbread crenellations and the sort of candle-snuffer towers designed for wimple-wearing maidens to let their hair down from. But, still, this is essentially high-camp larkiness; the innate artistic conservatism of the English means they are reluctant to create, or fully embrace, serious, revolutionary artistic and architectural styles.

So, our foray into baroque architecture at the turn of the eighteenth century produced some fine, original architecture by

Vanbrugh, Hawksmoor, Wren and Thomas Archer. But it barely matched the frothy excesses of German and Italian baroque. Evelyn Waugh said of the baroque that it 'has never had a place in England; its brief fashion was of short duration; it has been related to the holidays – a memory of the happy days in sunglasses, washing away the dust of the Southern roads with heady southern wines'.[5]

Hogarth thought the baroque never took off properly in England because 'Religion, the great promoter of this stile in other countries, in this rejected it.' For much the same reason, austere, iconophobic English Protestant churches are short on the paintings and frescoes that fill Italian Catholic churches.

That innate conservatism explains, too, why we never hit the heights of German, wedding-cake rococo. Our monarchy and aristocracy, reined in by the Civil War and an increasingly democratic Parliament, didn't have the Continental degree of untrammelled power; power not only over the people, but also over interior decoration. In those countries where baroque and rococo decor ran riot – Austria, France, Italy, Spain and the constituent parts of Germany – their blue-blooded patrons ended up paying for their excesses with their heads, or at least with their political power.

Our architectural ardour is also cooled by our geographical position. Before the early-seventeenth-century arrival of Inigo Jones, the first British architect to understand classicism, England was essentially a northern Gothic country.

Until Inigo Jones, our towns and cities were more Germanic- and Dutch-looking than Italian; more curly gables and higgledy-piggledy half-timbering than symmetrical columns and neat pediments. Compare that look with ultra-classical Rome, which still today has only one Gothic church, Santa Maria sopra Minerva, also Rome's first Gothic church when it was finished in 1370.

There had been earlier bursts of classicism before Inigo Jones. There's a strong classical feeling to the tomb of Henry VII in the Henry VII Chapel, in Westminster Abbey, sculpted by an Italian, Pietro Torrigiano, in 1512. The pilasters on the Christ Church Gateway at Canterbury, dated 1517, are among the first substantial classical architectural details in the country.

Still, Jones was the first English architect to build English classical buildings which completely, and correctly, absorbed the rules of classical architecture as they had been developed in ancient Greece and Rome, and Renaissance Italy.

For some time after Jones's first buildings went up – the Queen's House, Greenwich (1619), the Banqueting House, Whitehall (1622), and the Queen's Chapel at St James's Palace (1627) – England remained a Gothic country.

Claude de Jongh's 1630 painting of London Bridge shows a Gothic city of medieval, half-timbered houses with pointed gables. In the whole cityscape, there is just one classical building, on the river bank; the building, on the site of Cannon Street train station, no longer survives.

Within 200 years of this picture being painted, England had become a classical country, principally through the enormous success of the classically proportioned terraced house. These days, very few of those pre-1600, Gothic buildings, churches apart, survive in our big cities – they are now largely eighteenth- and nineteenth-century classical metropolises, notwithstanding the survival of Gothic cathedral cities, like Norwich and York. We had been obsessed with classical literature since the Middle Ages; after Inigo Jones, we became obsessed with classical architecture, too.

Despite all this, we retained elements of that northern, Gothic coolness in our architecture. Our medieval churches and cathedrals of course remained Gothic – and the Victorian imitations of those churches, during the Gothic Revival of the mid-nineteenth century, are necessarily Gothic, too. The rural skyline is still punctured by Gothic church spires; much of the urban skyline, too.

In his fifty-one City churches, built after the Great Fire of London, Christopher Wren may have used classical features, principally Doric and Ionic pilasters, but those pilasters were wrapped around the essentially Gothic skeleton of a spiky spire, an outline never seen in ancient Greece or Rome.

English villages, which mostly avoided bombing or modernization through the centuries, are more likely to be filled with pre-1600 cottages. That's why a Brueghel, painted in Gothic northern Europe, can be easily imagined in a rural Suffolk village or the Yorkshire Dales; less so in Birmingham or Leeds.

But even those Gothic, pre-Inigo Jones houses were part-classicized a long time later. The biggest alteration was the replacement of the diamond-paned, casement window – pointy and Gothic in feeling – with the even, symmetrical, classical sash window, introduced from France in the late seventeenth century.

When Charles I was beheaded at the Banqueting House, Whitehall, in 1649, he stepped to his execution out of a first-floor casement window on to a raised stage, in order to raise viewing figures and ensure that word got round that the king was really dead. Half a century later, those windows were replaced by sashes, which remain there today.

This bodged combination of classicism and northern Gothic, of the fiery south and the cold, puritanical, conservative north, makes for an unusually English look. That English conservatism, along with what you might call English preservationism, also means that building styles tend to last for unusually long periods.

Charles I stepped through a casement window to be executed at the Banqueting House in 1649. Inigo Jones designed the steeply pitched roof to cater for the English rain.

In 1362, Henry Yevele, Master Mason of the King's Works, designed the nave of Westminster Abbey in almost exact imitation of the earlier Gothic part of the building that had been started a century before. English Gothic architecture barely changed between Gloucester Cathedral's chancel in 1350 and its Lady Chapel in 1450. The principles of Palladian architecture, too, remained much the same from 1715 for a century or so.

For all their foreign origins, both Gothic architecture and Palladianism morphed into idiosyncratically English styles. They worked, and can even be considered archetypally English, because they were playful, instinctive impersonations of foreign influences, which were then adapted to accommodate the

English weather, English taste and the logistics of everyday English life.

That peculiarly English, alluring accommodation of influences doesn't come through in more carefully planned, consciously old-fashioned, modern pastiches, executed in a short time. That's the problem with somewhere like Poundbury, Prince Charles's model village in Dorset, begun in 1994 to a plan by Leon Krier, and still expanding.

Poundbury may be built in imitation of the classic organic hodgepodge of the traditional English town, with curving, asymmetrical streets, alongside a mock-eighteenth-century, Palladian fire station and a faux-medieval town hall. But what jars at Poundbury is the impractical, slavish imitation; like the installation of modern windows, blocked up in emulation of original windows elsewhere that had been blocked up from 1696 to 1851 for a genuine reason – to dodge window tax.

You get the same awkward shiver down the spine in the new generation of American suburbs, designed to look like a series of Victorian villages, and blended together to produce seamless, sprawling developments. Something that feels harmonious when it has been built up naturally and organically over several centuries feels artificial when it's all built in one go. The English like oldness – and modern tributes to oldness – but they don't go for elaborate, over-designed tweeness.

This desire to copy or adapt the old, rather than plunge headlong into the avant garde, is for a simple reason: England is an old country, still full of old buildings, despite the modern horrors inflicted on many towns.

It also helps that England can still, just about, afford to be proud about its past. For at least the last century, it's been on the right side in its conflicts, certainly in the First and Second World Wars, anyway. There's little need for an English equivalent of the German compound noun *Vergangenheitsbewältigung*

– 'coming to terms with the past'. Germans have had to use the word rather a lot since 1945.

A preponderance of old stones in this country makes it harder to insert new stones among them and still achieve any sort of harmony. The childish steel and glass tower blocks recently built by the Candy Brothers at One Hyde Park in central London – or the bright-orange one built by Renzo Piano at Central St Giles near Tottenham Court Road – look particularly hideous and infantile, when surrounded by older, more sophisticated, low-rise buildings.

New York and Chicago – for all their beauty – can absorb modern ugliness better because they are modern cities that have been high-rise for almost a century; the edges of their uglier skyscrapers are literally eclipsed by their taller neighbours, as opposed to standing embarrassingly proud of a predominantly low-slung cityscape like London's.

Most English cities have been scarred with some modern ugliness – more scarred than, say, French or Italian ancient cities. But the long continuity of monarchy, government and property rights in England means that few other countries have as ancient and continuous an administrative skeleton buried beneath the surface, ugly or not.

Much of that skeleton is dictated by geology or medieval law. Many parish boundaries, including hedges, earthworks and roads, were built by the Anglo-Saxons and Romans, and some date back to the Iron Age. A long stretch of the border between Lincolnshire and Leicestershire still runs along the Bronze Age track connecting the River Trent with the River Welland. The Roman road of Watling Street marks out the boundaries of twenty-five parishes.

As early as 1180, the parish boundaries of England were largely settled. A zig-zagging parish boundary suggests the land was divided into fields before the boundary was laid down, with the boundary tracking the ancient field edge. Earth banks in the middle of ancient woodland often mark parish boundaries, too.

Parish boundaries were also dictated by agricultural needs. On the Berkshire Downs, a single, long, narrow parish might stretch from the damp clay on the valley floor right up to a patch of field, high on the chalky uplands.[6] In the Yorkshire Dales, the long, thin parishes are defined by the natural lines of the river's edge and the watershed at the top of the hill; an area that neatly encompasses summer and winter grazing, as well as access to water.

Other boundaries, like the banks and ditches built by the Anglo-Saxons to mark the edge of their property, also survive; not least Offa's Dyke, which runs in an impressively straight line through the swerving, chaotic boundary of the modern Welsh border. Armourwood Lane, near Thorverton, in east Devon, follows the seventh-century boundary of Exeter Abbey's estate. The border between medieval monastery estates in Yorkshire, once owned by Fountains Abbey and Bolton Abbey, are still marked with ancient stone walls.

Other countries may have older buildings and landscape features, but they are less likely to be used for their original purpose, because of a greater incidence of war, revolution and invasion. England has been much battered by development since the Second World War; still, before then, it was remarkably unchanged. Queen Elizabeth I would have recognized much of England in 1945; even Queen Boadicea could have found her way round large areas of the country.

A surprising number of ancient English buildings retain their original use. Windsor Castle is the largest and oldest occupied castle in the world – there are older castles, but none that has survived for so long, largely intact, with their gilded occupants still in situ. There are more ancient parks than Richmond Park, south-west London; very few that have been so protected for so many centuries that, like Richmond, they have never been ploughed.

This liking for the past – for keeping things as they used to be – is reflected in our house-buying patterns. Only in England can oldness be sold as a term of approval by estate agents. 'Georgian', our favourite building style, is, after all, just another word for a building that's more than 180 years old.

The British pay a 27 per cent premium, an average of nearly £50,000, to live in spa towns, with their older, prettier buildings: properties in Boston Spa cost 85 per cent more than homes in the rest of West Yorkshire. Across the country, houses built before 1919 have risen in value by more than 450 per cent over the last twenty-five years, more than any other type of property: partly because there are fewer of them, they're bigger and they're in better locations, but also because we so much prefer older styles.[7]

We even prefer our new buildings to look old. The first twentieth-century building to be acquired by the National Trust, in 1974, was a mock-medieval castle – Castle Drogo, Devon, finished by Edwin Lutyens in 1930 – rather than an archetypal modern building, like, say, a Bauhaus block of flats or a nuclear power plant. The rebuilding of Shakespeare's Globe on the south bank of the Thames in 1996, the first thatched building to be built in London for 330 years, was another archetypal blast from the past.

Our love of old things leads to another English anomaly: living in a conservation area actually adds value to your house, even though it imposes restrictions on what you can and cannot do to your home.

Introduced by the 1967 Civil Amenities Act, conservation areas are designated by local authorities and English Heritage. Those authorities then control all demolition or developments, including the protection of trees. Any residents must get permission before they can make even small changes to the area's appearance: like cladding, new windows or satellite dishes visible from the street; all considered a bit déclassé, precisely because they're just too new.

Only in England is there something a little naff about having too sophisticated a hi-fi or too many television channels. Only in England are you more likely to find satellite dishes on a poor home than a rich one. In America, it's the other way round: richer houses have cable; poorer homes can only afford terrestrial.

Still, everything new grows old some day. Things that were hated when new become cherished once they've developed the patina of age. When gasometers were introduced to England in 1812, with the founding of the London Gas Light and Coke Company, they were thought to be horrible eyesores. By the time they were dismantling them at King's Cross to build the new Regent Quarter in 2011, there was a massive, and success-ful, conservation campaign for them to be reinstated.

The last 1,600 gas lamps in London are much prized, too: the ones outside Buckingham Palace, with royal crowns on top, are now listed. A similar turnaround in attitude applied to early electric street lamps, first introduced in London in 1878, and, indeed, for the power stations that produced their electricity.

It seems extraordinary now, but Bankside Power Station, now Tate Modern, was built in 1947 by Sir Giles Gilbert Scott to burn oil right on the banks of the Thames, opposite St Paul's, in the heart of the City. The era when central London was rich in industry seems remarkably recent; not least since Gilbert Scott's other great power station, Battersea, built in 1929, was less than a mile upstream. In the 1970s, more than 1.1 million people in London, almost a third of the workforce, worked in manufac-turing; in January 2011, 117,000 did, 2.5 per cent of the total.

There were objections when both power stations went up. But now, given the passage of time – not very much time; just over sixty years in Bankside's case – both power stations have been admitted to the pantheon of much-loved English buildings.

This conscious preference for old over new has been around in England since at least the seventeenth century. In 1625, Charles I fitted out Dover Castle in suitable style for his new queen, Henrietta Maria, the daughter of Henry IV, King of France. The queen was clearly disappointed. 'The castle is an old building made à l'antique,' wrote Leveneur de Tillières, the queen's chamberlain, 'where the queen was badly lodged with worse furnishing and her train treated with much less magnificence than was appropriate, considering the importance of the occasion.'[8]

That antiquarian taste is also allied to a reluctance to embrace creature comforts. When it comes to plumbing, we have lagged behind America for over a century. When the Savoy opened in 1889, it was the first British hotel to have electric light throughout instead of gas, hot and cold running water, and en suite bathrooms. Still, only some rooms were en suite – there were sixty-seven bathrooms for 250 apartments. All these creature comforts were introduced long after they had become standard in much humbler hotels in America.

One reason why the Midland Grand Hotel at St Pancras, reopened in 2011, had to close in 1935, after only sixty years in business, was because it didn't have any en suite bathrooms. It originally only had eight shared bathrooms for 300 rooms. The newly renovated building has just thirty-eight rooms, but they all have en-suite bathrooms, swimming with unguents.

The English still love old buildings, like the Midland Grand, that look charmingly asymmetric and picturesque on the outside; it's just that they've lost the taste for shambolic plumbing on the inside.

8. A Nation of Gardeners

Give the English a foot or two of earth, and they will grow
flowers in it; they do not willingly let go of the country – as the
foreign people do – once they have settled in a town; they are all
gardeners, perhaps country gentlemen, at heart. Abroad, the town,
even though it is really only a small village, nearly always starts
abruptly, brutally, at once cutting itself off from the country and
putting on the dusty and flowerless look of a city. Here we take leave
of the country reluctantly, and with infinite gradations, from the
glory of rosebeds and the full parade of hollyhocks to the last
outposts, among them grimy privet and grass where perhaps a sooty
aster still lingers.

J. B. Priestley, *English Journey* (1934)

'How many kinds of sweet flowers grow in an English country
garden?', goes the old English folk song.

If you're Jennifer Owen, who has spent thirty years studying
her back garden in suburban Leicester, the answer is fairly precise. In that time, she has counted 474 different plant species, 80
types of spider, 183 bug species, 375 kinds of moth and more
than 442 sorts of beetle.

Altogether, the retired ecology lecturer and zoology museum
curator has found 2,673 different species of flora and fauna. And
that's only a fraction of what's there – the total number of insect
species alone, in the average British garden, is thought to be
around 10,000.

Dr Owen's 1920s house on a busy street corner is unremarkable, as are her typical front and back gardens, laid out in 1927 – with 741 square metres of lawn, rockery, compost heap, herbaceous and mixed borders, hemmed in by a greenhouse, garage and garage forecourt.

From 1972 to 2001, helped by her husband, Denis, also a zoologist, Dr Owen netted butterflies and flying insects, trapped beetles and centipedes in a pitfall trap in the ground, and lured moths with a mercury vapour light trap. She noted down every flower she planted, every self-seeded plant and every weed.

Dr Owen's garden is more ecologically diverse than the lushest West African, Malaysian or Brazilian rainforest. When she returned from teaching in Uganda and Sierra Leone in the 1960s, she noticed that her back garden in Leicester had more butterfly species than her old tropical home; twenty-three, to be precise, with the small white butterfly the most common visitor.

The ecological variety of Dr Owen's garden is replicated across the country. The 8,000 square miles of British gardens – more garden per person than any other country – cover more land than all our national nature reserves put together. In Greater London alone, there are around 3.8 million front and back gardens, covering 37,900 hectares of domestic land, with about 2.5 million trees between them.

It's true that many of those gardens are being paved over – the amount of decking, terraces and paving in Britain increased by a quarter from 1999 to 2011. Trellises, too, have proliferated on top of garden walls over the last half-century, and more day-to-day things, like dahlias, vegetable patches and lime trees, have given way to exotics like gingko, eucalyptus, and fig and catalpa trees.[1]

Whatever the changes in flora, whatever the threat from decking, gardens remain some of the most diverse habitats in the country; particularly as British wildflower meadows have shrunk by 7 million acres since the war. When we look at the countryside, we think how unmanicured, how blissfully free of the hand of man it is. In fact, it is as far from its primeval, forested state as the city – perhaps more so.

City gardens, treated with many fewer pesticides, are more open to natural development than most farmland. Dr Owen's back garden is more fertile territory for plants and animals than the fields that circle the fringes of Leicester.

Across the country, the urban garden has evolved into a rare wildlife sanctuary; as agricultural land is increasingly farmed on an industrial scale, with weedkillers liberally applied and hedgerows grubbed up, particularly in the eastern counties. Where farmland is considered less valuable, as in, say, Cornwall, the hedges and the hedgerow trees tend to be left alone.

The older the city, the more varied the habitats, the better for the plants and animals. Railway lines act as green corridors through cities, not only for the seeds of plants like Oxford ragwort and buddleia, but also for foxes. A native English species, the fox arrived in central London only eighty years ago, after first migrating into the suburbs, or having its rural earths absorbed into sprawling suburbia.

A similar effect has produced the suburban deer. They are thriving, particularly around the M25, and in hotspots in East Anglia, East Sussex, Cannock Chase and the West Midlands. The deer population has doubled to 2 million in the last decade, with many of them marching into town along disused railway lines, now turned into footpaths and bike paths. Thanks to the Newlands forest project outside Manchester, muntjac and roe deer are encroaching on the city. And there are a number of recent reports of deer getting all the way into north-east London and the town centres of Stockport and Wolverhampton.

Many of the garden plants we think inherently English have even more exotic origins than the suburban deer. It's only because we've got so used to them growing in our back gardens that we forget how far they came to get there.

Runner beans come from South America, sweet peas from Sicily, and spinach from south-west Asia. Dr Owen's marigolds come from Mexico, her snapdragons from the Mediterranean, her poppies from the European Alps. Ground-elder, the scourge of gardeners, was introduced by the Romans.

Britain's temperate climate, on the crossing point between Continental and northern floral zones, makes it astonishingly accommodating to foreign arrivals. There are only thirty-three native species of trees in Britain – but its climate can accommodate hundreds more incomers.

There is no part of the earth's surface as small as Britain where such a diversity of plants can be grown. A garden in, say, Sleightholmedale, Kirkbymoorside, North Yorkshire, lies in the intersecting zone between the northern edge of the Continental flora zone and the southern edge of the northern flora zone. So you get a rare combination of the musk thistle and the heat-loving bee orchid growing next to northern plants like bird's-eye primrose and globeflower.

The fertile soils of England are unusually well-designed for a vast range of plants. The dry soils of Wiltshire and Herefordshire, meticulously sifted by ants into anthills, support a very precise flora: wall-leaved and thyme-leaved sandwort, the common mouse-ear, common rock rose and wild thyme. In Derbyshire, Lancashire and Cheshire, the sandwort there, known as leadwort, thrives on the lead in the soil.

Even pollution can stimulate the flora. After the heavy salting of the roads in the sub-zero winters of 2009–10 and 2010–11, salt-loving sea spurrey flowers were found as far as 100 miles inland, on motorway verges.

The great variety of our native soils suits not just a great variety of species, but also unusually large populations of individual species. Britain is home to half the world's bluebells, which can grow in a wide spectrum of our soils – clay and chalk, as well as slightly acidic, sandy loams.

Thanks to our northern climate, the Gulf Stream and our island nature, we are blessed, too, with the right amount of rain to produce England's distinctive greenness.

Hackneyed as it sounds, England is an exceptionally green country. James Ravilious, photographer, author and son of the artist Eric Ravilious, used black-and-white when he took pictures of Devon because, he said, it got rid of the green which so dominates the English landscape and is such a tricky colour to capture well.[2]

Nikolaus Pevsner was equally staggered by the effect of the colour on Durham. The green grass and trees, he thought, distinguished Durham from other European cities, like Prague and Avignon, that are also wrapped around dominant castles and cathedrals.[3]

Because we are so far north, and yet warmed by the Gulf Stream, we also get long, extended springs and autumns, unlike most other countries, which switch between the extremes of summer and winter with barely a season in between. Our subtly shifting seasons give a greater range of growing temperatures over a longer period of time.

In Mary McCarthy's 1971 book, *Birds of America*, the narrator, Peter Levi, prefers the extremes of weather in his mother's New England – its weather an exaggerated version of Old England's – to his stepfather's California, with its year-round warm temperatures.

'He had never liked California; he missed the winter. He hated his stepfather's garden in Berkeley, with roses and daffodils and tulips and irises all blooming at the same time, so that there was never anything to look forward to.'

In England – with four distinctive seasons, and some now

claiming a fifth, in the transition from summer to autumn – there is always something for gardeners to look forward to.

The British character is unusually well-disposed to producing gardeners, too. In a 2010 poll, over 60 per cent of the population said they had done some gardening in the previous four weeks.

That love of gardening doesn't just come from a conducive soil and climate. It's drawn, too, from the same source as the love of home-ownership – the desire to own land, a desire more easily satisfied in a country with secure land tenure over many centuries. Why buy land, or a house, if you think there's going to be a revolution tomorrow?

Still, it's sometimes easy to get a little too romantic about how deep-rooted our attachment to gardening is. Pliny said the ancient land of Albion got its name from the Latin *albus* – meaning 'white', in turn derived from 'the white roses with which England abounds'. Some garden historians have suggested that prehistoric plots of land, planted with henbane and opium, were the first British gardens – all a little too far back in the mists of time to be sure.

The oldest-known continuously cultivated garden is thought to be at Arundel Castle, Sussex, where the rose garden below the castle's south front is on the site of a herb garden mentioned in the twelfth century. Certainly by the medieval period, cottages had back gardens; and the chief characteristics of those gardens – long and thin, with private spaces fenced off from the neighbours – were in place. Early gardens were also relatively large, given the small dimensions of English houses. The typical gardens of classic, early-nineteenth-century cottages were 225 feet long by 45 feet wide, separated by brick walls.

From early on in the development of English gardens, sturdy walls, high hedges and robust fences were popular. The need for privacy is locked into the English soul, wrapped up with our island status, our damp climate, our long, dark winters – all of them conspire against sociability.

It's not that we're not interested in other people. We're obsessed with them, particularly when it comes to gossip. The number of newspapers and newspaper readers is proportionally greater here than anywhere else in the world. England is one of the first countries to have had a national portrait gallery.

'I had rather see the portrait of a dog I know, than all the allegories you can show me,' said Dr Johnson.

But we prefer to keep other people at arm's length – on canvas, in print, or glimpsed through a chink in the curtains. In Holland, you keep your downstairs curtains open the whole time, or have no curtains at all, to show you've got nothing to hide; in Amsterdam, they even install car window mirrors on the outside of their buildings, to watch the goings-on in the streets below.

We have a terrible fear of intimacy or socializing – thus our endless jokes, catchphrases, sarcasm, irony, understatement and banter, all conversational devices that keep intimacy and the serious exchange of private information at bay. Thus, too, our complex codes of manners. As Evelyn Waugh said, the English use manners to keep people away from them; the Americans to draw them closer.

Several years ago, the Foreign Office reported on a disastrous trade mission to Saudi Arabia. The more relaxed Arabs tried to get up close to the stiff English delegates, who then backed away. The Arabs were offended at the supposed rejection; the English were put off by the forced intimacy.

The English love of gardens is closely wrapped up with that desire for privacy, for a stretch of land where you know no one else will appear, where you can keep others at a distance. That desire increases with greater proximity to your neighbours. In the 1801 census, the English lived an average of 153 yards from each other; by the 1851 census, this had shrunk to 108 yards. In London, it fell from twenty-one yards to fourteen.

As we moved closer together, so we built more hedges, fences and garden walls. In 1857, Ralph Waldo Emerson noted that 'High stone fences, and padlocked garden gates, announce the absolute will of the owner to be alone.'

In Silverdale, Lancashire, and Shepton Mallet, Somerset, there survive several Victorian 'spite walls' – solid brick walls, the height of a house, built two feet from the front of a neighbour's home, to cut off any possible view of them.

It isn't just gardens that the English designed for privacy. Box pews in Georgian churches, wooden partitions in early-nineteenth-century coffee houses, snob screens in Victorian pubs; all of them were built to provide closed-off spaces. Only recently has all this changed, with the fashion for knock-throughs – sitting rooms leading into kitchens, kitchens opening out into the garden.

This yearning for privacy struck foreign observers early on. 'Intellectually, they were dead; lived only for their petty, private interest, for their looms and gardens,' wrote Friedrich Engels of the early-eighteenth-century English working class before the Industrial Revolution.[4] In the early nineteenth century, a French aristocrat said, 'the English detest being seen and will gladly forgo any prospect beyond their own limited boundaries.'

Our obsession with cultivating our own little private spaces explains why our public spaces are so often neglected. In France, there are elaborate public floral displays in summer; in Germany and Austria, perennials are planted on roundabouts and traffic islands.[5]

But there's a trade-off between private and public: private gardens in those countries are not nearly as sophisticated as ours, and there are fewer of them, too, with more flats and fewer owner-occupied houses. Increased home ownership over here

A yearning for privacy – 'During the hot weather, the Smythe-Robinsons of Tiddlington take their meals in a cool and shady spot of the garden', cartoon by H. M. Bateman, 1913.

means greater care of the gardens attached to those homes; but it also means worse care for public spaces.

This obsession with privacy, combined with the English taste for an unmanicured, picturesque look, lent an early individualism to English gardens. While Continental gardens grew ordered and symmetrical in the sixteenth century, mirroring the Renaissance ideals of the great classical buildings they bordered, England's gardens sought out an ambling, unpredictable line. Those English Renaissance gardens that there were usually had a wilderness in them. As early as 1624, Sir Henry Wotton, the first

proper architectural author in English, was writing, 'As Fab-
riques should be regular, so Gardens should be irregular.'

'Old roses should be allowed to ramp away into big bushes,'
Vita Sackville-West wrote of her garden at Sissinghurst, Kent,
'and allowed also to travel about underground if they are on
their own roots and come up in fine carelessness some yards
from the parent plant.'

'Fine carelessness' implies less lazy neglect than the studied,
artful creation of neglect. And it doesn't come cheap: when Vita
Sackville-West died in 1962, she left hardly anything in her will
– she had spent all her money on carefully producing the fine,
careless look. You can relate that fine carelessness to a national
gift for creation without prescription; to a common law built on
a million instances of judge-made law rather than Parliament
legislation; to an unwritten constitution and an undefined yet
established church.[6]

It's only because we've become so used to English back gardens
that we notice, and exaggerate, small differences between them;
rather than appreciate their considerable similarities. The exact
arrangement of a garden's features may vary, but it usually
approximates to a version of the classic English back garden.
The ground plan is usually a loose collection of rectangles: a
fairly neat lawn surrounded by borders on all sides, with a shed
and a stretch of terrace incorporated into the plan.

The lawn is at the heart of the English garden. And, if there is
a single most influential lawn in the country, it is the one at
Chiswick House, in west London. After Lord Burlington finished the house in 1729, in collaboration with William Kent, he
turned his eye to the garden. Clearing the stiff, formal lines of
the old baroque garden, Burlington and Kent transformed the
straight canal into a lake with serpentine banks, an early taste of
the Picturesque. By the lake, in front of the villa, they planted a

new, celebrated lawn (restored in 2010), with immense conse-quences for other country houses across England.

Those effects spread to back gardens across the country, spurred on by the invention in 1827 of the cylinder lawnmower, by Edwin Budding, a foundryman from Stroud, Gloucester-shire.[7] The new lawnmowers were often pulled by ponies that wore leather boots on their hooves to protect the lawn.

Before then, scythes had been used to clear grass, roughly, slowly and expensively – meaning lawns were largely confined to the rich. The new machine cleared large areas of land cheaply and quickly, leaving behind neat, even lines.

Vegetable patches in rural cottage gardens were now opened up, with a lawn at their heart. By 1841, the American landscape architect Andrew Jackson Downing was saying, 'The unri-valled beauty of the "velvet lawns" of England has passed into a proverb.'

The lawnmower didn't just popularize the lawn – it also helped to produce the modern urban park, and lay the ground for the Victorian boom in the national sports: rugby, football, cricket and tennis.

A border-fringed lawn also made a snug fit for the rectangu-lar plots laid out behind millions of English terraced houses from the seventeenth to the twenty-first century. The fashion for borders deepened with the introduction of carpet bedding – elaborately patterned, highly colourful floral displays, beloved of seaside esplanades – dreamt up by Cliveden's head gardener, John Fleming, in the 1840s.

This battle between the neat, ordered world of the carpet bor-der and Vita Sackville-West's fine carelessness still rages in the modern English garden. A recent survey declared that the ten most attractive features in an estate agent's photo of a property were a mixture of the ordered and the wild: tree-lined drive (ordered); perfect lawn (ordered); terrace (ordered); cottage planting (wild); wild meadow (wild); walled garden (ordered); romantic walk (wild); orchard (wild); kitchen garden (ordered); courts and pools (ordered).[8]

That conflict between ordered and wild often has unspoken class aspects, too, buried just below the topsoil. Over-neatened gardens, built on strict geometrical lines, are the antithesis of fine carelessness, as becomes clear in *South Riding*, Winifred Holtby's novel about Yorkshire municipal life in the 1930s. Greenlawnes, the Harrogate home of William Carne, a bloodless, soulless chiseller of an architect, is the archetypal neat garden.

> The house stood back from the road in a smart, prosperous, geometrical garden. The lawns had been mown, the hedges clipped, the begonias planted in unhesitating rows. There was a cubist bird-path, a crazy-paved sunk garden, a rubble tennis-court, a grass court, a rose-garden. The house was all white and chromium, and rectangular, with windows cut out of the corners.[9]

Holtby's intention is clear – the garden isn't just ugly; it's also not *comme il faut*.

When the BBC did a programme on Sissinghurst in 2009, the unsaid battlelines were laid between Vita Sackville-West's grandson, Adam Nicolson, and his landlord, the National Trust. Nicolson's bohemian taste for 'filth', as a term of affection, and 'admired disorder' – another euphemism for fine carelessness – clashed with the National Trust's desire for neat, ordered perfection.[10]

The battle flared into life when Nicolson woke up one day to find, to his horror, that a crumbling, antique stone statue had been replaced by an immaculate modern copy. Fine carelessness had lost out to untainted newness, thanks to the National Trust's obligation to preserve its houses and gardens in perpetuity; an obligation that militates against a gradual, pleasing crumbling into dust.

In 1979, the writer Philip Toynbee, a friend of Vita Sackville-West's son, Ben Nicolson, dreamt up the ideal practical joke to explode the aesthetic values beneath Sissinghurst's shambolic artfulness.

'The plan [was] to load up a lorry with hundreds of garden gnomes, drive down to Sissinghurst one night and plant them all over the famous and much-viewed garden of Ben's formidable mother.'[11]

A similar class battle over the shabbiness of the English garden takes place at Blandings Castle between Lord Emsworth and his Glaswegian head gardener, Angus McAllister. McAllister wants to build a gravel path through the yew alley at Blandings.

> 'Gravel path!' Lord Emsworth stiffened through the whole length of his stringy body. Nature, he had always maintained, intended a yew alley to be carpeted with a mossy growth. And, whatever Nature felt about it, he personally was dashed if he was going to have men with Clydeside accents and faces like dissipated potatoes coming along and mutilating that lovely expanse of green velvet . . .
>
> 'Most decidedly not. Try to remember, McAllister, as you work in the gardens of Blandings Castle, that you are not back in Glasgow, laying out recreation gardens.'[12]

We do allow a few carefully contrived spots of scrubbed-up gentility in our gardens – however unfashionable neatness is considered to be.

Nothing is more genteel than the conservatory – close to English hearts because it is so well adapted to deal with that peculiar English obsession, the weather. We are a nation of people who live in glass houses.

Of course conservatories crop up abroad, too, but it's striking that the word conservatory, or conservatoire, is normally used in Italy, France and America to mean a musical academy.

The desire to bring the outdoors indoors, to make the most of the daylight hours and to maximize the time spent gardening and looking at the garden is not stitched into their DNA the way it is in ours. England led the world when it came to developing the first conservatories, and taking the chill off the outside air while letting in as much of that precious northern sunlight as possible.

The first mention of conservatories is in the late seventeenth century. Glass was getting cheaper, thinner and finer, and people were beginning to understand the implications of the greenhouse effect, i.e. that glass allows heat to pass quickly through it and warm the room it encloses.

Conservatories were originally places for tender flowers or plants during the winter – literally a place to conserve them. They weren't quite the same as greenhouses, though: in those early days, conservatories tended to have beds of plants; greenhouses were for movable pots.

The race to build bigger conservatories heated up during the nineteenth century; a race led by Sir Joseph Paxton (1803–65), who in 1837 built the Great Conservatory for his patron, the Duke of Devonshire, at Chatsworth, Derbyshire – then the biggest glass building in the world, with specially customized panes, the largest ever made, at four feet long. He based his groundbreaking glass-and-metal-rib design on the strong engineering of the water lily leaf, after he saw that one of the duke's lilies could comfortably support his one-year-old daughter, Annie.

Paxton's success at Chatsworth won him the commission for the largest conservatory ever built – the Crystal Palace, built in 1851 for the Great Exhibition in Hyde Park, later transferred to Sydenham in south London. With 900,000 square feet of sheet glass, it required a third of Britain's annual glass output. The most famous building of the Victorian age, the palace had a huge influence on domestic fashion. Conservatories, mini-crystal palaces of iron and glass, cropped up across the country in the late nineteenth century.

As they became more popular, conservatories grew more integral to the house. Ornamental plants, once hothoused in greenhouses, were now brought to the conservatory to be shown off. Sir Walter Scott was astounded when he visited a house where 'the present proprietor had rendered the parlour more cheerful by opening one end into a small conservatory. I have never before seen this.'

Conservatories remain in Sir Joseph Paxton's image today. Some of them are topped off with spiky, decorative finials that recall the Paxton age of ornate, high-Victorian, Gothic architecture. They appeal to the English love of small, quirky buildings – reflected, as well, in our taste for follies.

The idea of sticking a little Gothic glass building on to the back of our classically inspired, brick, terraced houses would strike an Italian or French purist as being ludicrously chintzy.

But oh, how ludicrous and chintzy things appeal to the playful – especially the historically playful – parts of the English heart; particularly when you can stuff them full of flowers.

The conservatory is purpose-built for the English obsessions with gardening and being outdoors – or semi-outdoors, at least. As Jennifer Owen showed in the academic study of her Leicester garden, nowhere else on the earth's surface is there an area as small as Britain where such a diversity of plants can be grown. The extra few degrees of heat that come with glazing expand that diversity even more.

9. The Rolling English Road

We are a motorway race rather than an island race.

Will Self

Towards the end of *Withnail and I* (1987), a drunk Withnail is filmed careering down the M6 from Cumbria on his way back to London.

The only problem is, it's not the M6 from Cumbria, like it's supposed to be. A rogue sign in the background reveals that filming was done on the M25, just before London's orbital motorway was opened by Margaret Thatcher on 29 October 1986.

'M25' is emblazoned in huge white letters on the blue background of the motorway sign. But, still, it blends into the back of the shot, despite the mistake, because the style of that sign was the same as it would have been in 1969, when the film was set.

Motorways across the country are now practically uniform. You can forgive another motorist on the M25, Dennis Leighton, eighty-two, who, in December 2011, used the road to drive from Windsor to his daughter's house, fifty-five miles away, in Swanley, Kent. Thirty hours later, he still hadn't made it, having gone round and round the orbital system. Unless you happen to take in a local landmark or a change in the landscape, Berkshire, Kent and all stops in between end up looking fairly identical.[1]

The font of British motorway signs hasn't changed since 1958, when a designer called Jock Kinneir road-tested the style on the first bit of motorway to be opened in the UK, the 8.5-mile Preston bypass section of the M6, officially unveiled by Harold Macmillan.

That sans serif font on road signs, created in a series of designs by Kinneir and Margaret Calvert from 1957 till 1967, has been extraordinarily successful and long-lasting. It also looms larger in the national consciousness because of the British ban on motorway advertising, unlike in America and much of the Continent. (There's a similar contrast at Piccadilly Circus: only one side of the circus, owned by Land Securities Group, is plastered with advertising; the other sides, owned by the Crown Estate, ban advertising.)[2]

Kinneir thought the simple sans serif font on motorway signs was easier to read at high speed. He also mixed upper and lower case; signs in capitals only, Kinneir thought, smacked of authoritarian government.

In official terms, Kinneir's font is a refinement of Akzidenz Grotesk; later given its own name, Transport. The idea was to be modern, but softer and friendlier than European road signs – perhaps the reason why opponents called Kinneir's font common and fought for two years to change it.

As I write, there's another font row going on. In August 2009, IKEA changed its font from IKEA – in the IKEA Sans font, their customized version of the 1927 Futura font, a German Constructivist style – to IKEA, in the Verdana font, a 1994 Microsoft innovation designed to look good on a computer screen.

Kinneir's new font was combined with European signage conventions: triangular signs to warn motorists; circles for commands; and rectangles to give information. Different colour schemes were used for different roads: white lettering on a blue background for motorways; yellow road numbers and white lettering, on a green background, for primary roads; black letters on white for secondary routes.

Using pictograms on signs was another Continental idea adapted by Kinneir and Calvert. Calvert drew the signs, making them curvier and gentler than Continental equivalents.

For the farm animal warning sign, she based the cow on Patience, a cow on a relation's farm in Warwickshire. The girl in the 'School children crossing' sign was based on a photograph of Calvert as a child. She also dreamt up the idea of having an older girl leading a younger boy by the hand, to build an emotional connection in drivers' minds, and make them slow down.

The previous sign, of a boy in a school cap, was, according to Calvert 'quite archaic, almost like an illustration from Enid Blyton . . . I wanted to make it more inclusive because comprehensives were starting up.'

Kinneir and Calvert went on to devise the Rail Alphabet typeface for British Rail trains and stations in 1964. The metalware designer David Mellor designed the cutlery for the restaurant cars, and Gerald Barney, of the Design Research Unit, came up with the familiar BR symbol.

Like motorway signs, fingerposts, too, were standardized, under the Worboys Committee in 1964. Before then, different counties had different signposts – octagonal oak white posts with black pen-top-shaped finials were used in Sussex; Northumberland's were topped with handsome pointed acorns.[3]

England's motorway revolution began in earnest with the M1. Built by Sir Owen Williams and Partners, the M1 was first discussed in 1951, and given the go-ahead in 1955. It was officially unveiled in 1958, as the 'London–Yorkshire motorway', by the Transport Minister, Harold Watkinson, at a spot on the tarmac near Luton. The first fifty-five miles cut through Hertfordshire, Bedfordshire and Buckinghamshire in 1959, between what are now junctions 5 and 18.

England's first service station, Watford Gap, between junctions

16 and 17 of the M1, was also built in 1959, although there had been wayside eating places for centuries: the Clacket Lane service station on the M25 in Surrey is on the site of a stopover for pilgrims travelling to the Canterbury shrine of Thomas Becket.

The first AA petrol station, incidentally, was opened on the Bath Road, Aldermaston, Berkshire, forty years earlier, on 2 March 1919; petrol stations are now in decline, as small village outlets close down – of the 18,000 in the UK in 1992, fewer than half survive today.

Founded in 1905, the AA built much of the early road infrastructure: it installed thousands of direction posts and village signs, until responsibility was gradually handed to local authorities in the 1930s. Into the 1960s, the AA's uniformed motorbike patrolmen saluted oncoming members bearing visible AA badges; they would dispense with the convention, in order to alert motorists to imminent speedtraps.

More than 130 bridges were built on the first stretch of the M1, in six standard types. Many survive today: distinctly chunky in silhouette, reminiscent of prewar German autobahns, built of concrete, supported by elementary columns in the central reservation. The columns had no base or capital, but did have an abacus, a plain slab on top of each column. The retaining walls for the first motorways were also concrete; as they mostly remain today.

The lane system remains much the same, too, usually with three lanes in either direction. The standard width of our original motorways, widened when the first four-lane motorways arrived, is 105 feet, with 13 feet for the central reservation.

When we built those first motorways, we were a long way behind Italy, where the first motorway in the world was built in 1924; when Mussolini came to power in 1925, he encouraged further expansion of the network. Hitler, too, it must be admitted, was also a motorway progressive, enthusiastically backing autobahn construction projects after he became Chancellor in 1933.

Slow progress, due to parochialism and lack of money and space, meant our motorways never matched the scale and ambition of those Continental motorways. Still, in our characteristic, make-do-and-mend, postwar attitude, we were pathetically proud of what small projects we did complete – some comedown from the Victorian glory days of British engineering.

Jayne Mansfield opened the Chiswick flyover in September 1959, in an era when there was still some glamour left in road travel.

'It's a sweet little flyover,' Mansfield said, as she declared it open. Little was the operative word – it was a quarter of a mile long.

The new motorways were considered such thrilling wonders that there was a great fanfare when the M1 was opened; a workman was photographed sweeping the opening section of road to keep the new treasure spotless.

Barely half a century later, in July 2010, we had grown so tired of motorways that a list of the worst of them was published.[4] The M25 was voted Britain's most depressing road, with the 117-mile motorway singled out for particularly terrible traffic jams and extreme tedium.

Britain's top ten most depressing roads were, in order: the M25; the stretch of the M6 by Birmingham; the A1 Holloway Road, London; the M5 near Bristol; the M8 between Glasgow and Edinburgh; the A12; the M5 northbound between junctions 12 and 10; the A361 near Glastonbury in Somerset; the A30 near Bodmin in Cornwall; the A338 between Great Shefford; and junction 14 of the M4.

Over the last half-century, the biggest change to our roads – the one that has made that tedium worse – is the sheer amount of traffic. During rush hour, the car-borne population in Britain and Ireland is greater than the population of London. There are now 31 million cars in Britain, and rising. The inevitable result is the Great British Traffic Jam.

We have grown used to the standardization of our newer roads, particularly motorways slicing their unremitting, straight, flat lines through the landscape. But, before motorways were introduced under the Special Roads Act of 1949, English roads were more flexible, idiosyncratic things. Those old prewar roads, plenty of which survive, chimed with the familiar English taste for a touch of wildness. As G. K. Chesterton put it, in *The Rolling English Road*:

> Before the Roman came to Rye or out to Severn strode,
> The rolling English drunkard made the rolling English road.
> A reeling road, a rolling road, that rambles round the shire,
> And after him the parson ran, the sexton and the squire;
> A merry road, a mazy road, and such as we did tread
> The night we went to Birmingham by way of Beachy Head.

Wandering English hedges often track and shelter English roads, as Chesterton writes later in the poem: 'Why do flowers run behind [the rolling English drunkard, busy making the rolling English road]; and the hedges all strengthening in the sun?' In turn, the hedges and those early roads hugged the wavy contours of hilltops, valley floors and field edges.

Chesterton was right about the straightness of Roman roads. The Fosse Way – from the Latin *fossa*, meaning a ditch – runs between the Roman military camps of Exeter and Lincoln. It originally marked the border of early imperial territory before the Romans broke out of the south and headed north towards the Scottish border. And it is extremely straight – on the 182-mile stretch from Lincoln to Ilchester, Somerset, the road never veers more than six miles from a straight line.

Main roads today often still run along the course of old Roman roads. Where the A2 crosses the River Medway at Rochester, it runs alongside the old Roman road to Dover. Later called Waecelinga Straet by the Anglo-Saxons, it morphed into Watling Street, which runs all the way to the Roman fortress at Caerleon in Newport, south Wales.

Modern Rochester High Street was once part of Watling Street, running north of the cathedral and parallel with the nave; an ancient road-planning convention followed at Hereford Cathedral, too. Another convention was that minor Roman and Anglo-Saxon settlements tended not to be built too close to the road; that would have made them vulnerable to attacking armies.

This tendency for new transport routes to shadow earlier ones continued into the modern age. The M1 runs roughly parallel with the Grand Junction Canal, begun in 1790 by William Jessop, and the old Midland Railway – all following the flattest, straightest route north from London, passing through Watford Gap.

Leicester lies not only on the line of the 1768 Manchester–London stagecoach route, but also on the nineteenth-century Midland Railway, as well as the M1. Because it was on the Loughborough Canal by 1794, and the Leicester and Swannington Railway by 1832, the city's population increased from 6,000 at the beginning of the eighteenth century to 17,000 by 1800.

Celts laid the foundations for several Roman roads. Watling Street was originally an ancient Celtic trackway, later paved by the Romans. In 2011, archaeologists uncovered a Bronze Age livestock driveway near the A5 at Shrewsbury. In the first century BC, before the Romans turned up, the Celts built a cambered, forty-mile-long highway, surfaced with cobbles laid on top of a foundation of elder wood and silt. When the Romans arrived, they quickly adopted the highly sophisticated road for their own use.

For all their sophistication, Roman roads are responsible for the narrowness of our train seats today. The first Victorian trains were built to the same width as horse-drawn wagons; they, in turn, were designed to fit the ruts left in the roads by Roman chariots. The standard British railway gauge – 4 feet 8.5 inches – mirrors the specification for a Roman war chariot: that width, the Romans thought, accommodated a large horse's bottom, while also allowing for a little wriggle room on either side. As our own bottoms have grown bigger, those seats have grown more uncomfortable.

Similar ancient constrictions clog main roads leading out of town centres. These are often laid on top of old coaching roads, squeezed in on both sides by immovable Victorian terraces. Because they were built later, American cities, to a certain extent – and newer American suburbs to a greater extent – were designed for the car. Empty eight-lane highways lead out of small, out-of-the-way towns. Those wide, open suburbs tend to sprawl for miles beyond the city limits because of the vast, cheap American land bank.

Roman road junctions also dictated the sites of modern towns. Winchester, the Roman town of Venta Belgarum, is at the hub of six Roman roads; roads to Mildenhall, Wiltshire, and Silchester still run along two of those ancient routes. This efficient, extensive network of Roman roads also created the first English commuters: most Roman villas in Hampshire were within fifteen miles – or a day's ride – of Winchester town centre.

Heavy commuting traffic isn't a new thing. The traffic-relieving bypass goes back several thousand years. The Icknield Way – the Roman, possibly Celtic, road running through Berkshire and

Oxfordshire – often splits in two, where a side road is diverted through a village, before joining up again.

Even medieval bypasses didn't stop medieval traffic congestion. In 1285, Edward I wrote to the Prior of Dunstable about the crossroads of the Icknield Way with Watling Street, at Dunstable, complaining that the highways were 'broken up and deep by the frequent passage of carts'.

Ancient holloways – the deep-sunken lanes of England – are usually the result of similar erosion by wheels, rain and footfall, although occasionally they were laid along sunken ravines. They are most commonly found in the ancient landscapes of Sudbury in Suffolk, south-west Wiltshire and the Lizard Peninsula in Cornwall.[5]

Medieval roads swerved around all sorts of things – boulders, holes, tree trunks, dead horses – and those swerves became incorporated into the line of the road. If you drive along a minor, ancient road today, with a swerving hedge on the left, and a straight one on the right, the chances are that a farmer has nabbed the land to the right and fashioned a new straight border to it.[6]

Those medieval roads that are straight tend to be narrower than those laid down by the Enclosure Acts of the eighteenth and nineteenth centuries. Drove roads traditionally had wider verges to allow cattle and sheep to crop the grass as they were herded along. The post-enclosure roads were even straighter, too, running from village to village in as efficient a way as possible, unencumbered by the forest or wilderness cleared by enclosure. Older, bending roads fell into disuse, or became bridlepaths or rights of way.

Later, centrally planned roads usually had even, wide grass verges, thick with cow parsley and dog roses in the summer. Their dimensions were often laid down by diktat. New Somerset roads, laid in 1795, were 40 foot wide, with 12 feet of stone thoroughfare in the middle, flanked by 14 feet of verge on either side. The stone was a foot deep in the middle of the road; at the cambered edges, it narrowed down to 9 inches thick.

There were different widths for roads of mounting importance, a version of the later distinctions between A and B roads. In Norton Juxta Twycross parish, on the Leicestershire–Warwickshire borders, the 1748 enclosure document declares that the main road to London must be no less than 33 yards wide. The neighbouring minor road from Twycross to the market town of Ashby de la Zouch had to be no less than 22 yards, while other nearby roads are given the indiscriminate definition 'of a proper width'.[7]

Road dimensions were dictated by local conditions, the weather in particular. In winter, the main London–Exeter road could expand to a quarter of a mile wide where it ran through flooded parts of Salisbury Plain, as horses edged further and further from the waterlogged middle of the road.

Differing dates of enclosure heavily influenced the road map of England. In counties that were enclosed later on, like Leicestershire, enclosed in the Georgian period, the relatively few main roads were usually laid along the lines of heavily used farm tracks. This led to fewer roads than in, say, Devon, enclosed in the medieval period, where many more minor tracks were turned into roads earlier on, and have remained as roads ever since.

Enclosure practices also explain why you suddenly come across small country roads turning at a right angle at lone farmhouses in the middle of, say, Norfolk. Neighbouring parishes were enclosed at different times. A road heading out to a house on the border of one parish might be planned long before a later road to the house was built in a neighbouring parish. The later road, then, was connected with the earlier one at an extreme angle.

A similar effect occurs in parts of the Fens. In the seventeenth century, the roads were laid independently of each other, in allotted areas of two or three square miles. In the third great draining of the Fens, in 1650–55, each plot was individually planned by careless surveyors, who failed to consider the future disposition of roads in neighbouring allotments.

This led not just to roads connecting at strange angles, but also to roads that don't meet those in the neighbouring allotment at all – they just come to an abrupt halt, connecting with nothing. The effect is particularly noticeable around Littleport, Cambridgeshire.[8]

These independent arrangements for small chunks of England gradually disappeared through the seventeenth-century improvement of the roads, particularly with the increasing popularity, and efficiency, of stagecoaches.

The system of short stage traffic began under James I. Horses were changed at every ten-mile 'stage' of the journey; so it made sense to establish stabling at each staging point. The hamlets and towns at these staging points mushroomed, as the stables gathered around them an elaborate collection of lodgings, dining rooms and booking offices. Coaching inns had arrived; wayside hotels that grew increasingly elaborate until horse-drawn transport was eclipsed by the arrival of the train in the 1830s. They had a lasting effect on the look of English towns and cities – and on the standards of English hospitality.

Complaints about Fawlty Towers standards of roadside catering are nothing new. In *Henry IV, Part I*, Shakespeare sets a scene at the inn yard in Rochester, Kent.

'Peas and beans are as dank here as a dog,' says a guest, 'This house is turned upside down since Robin Ostler died. I think this be the most villainous house in all London Road for fleas: I am stung like a tench.'

The low standards of Shakespearean inns were improved in

1616 when Giles Mompesson, MP for the rotten borough of Great Bedwyn, Wiltshire, established a new monopoly on granting licences to inns. By 1621, there were 13,000 licensed premises in the country.

These new inns were vastly more comfortable than Shakespeare's dingy inn at Rochester. In 1617, Fynes Moryson wrote, in his *Itinerary; or Ten Years' Travels throughout Great Britain and other parts of Europe*:

> The world affords not such inns as England hath, for as soon as a passenger comes, the servants run to him: one takes his horse, and walks him till he be cold, then rubs him and gives him meat . . . another gives the traveller his private chamber, and kindles his fire, the third pulls off his boots and makes him clean.

Tolls, introduced by the first Turnpike Act of 1663, paid for improved roads, allowing fast coaches to supplant the old slow coaches and carriers' wagons.

The more sophisticated road network led to the first road atlas, published in 1675 by John Ogilby (1600–1676), a courtier, theatre owner, poet, dancing master, translator and compiler of atlases and geographical works. Ogilby's *Britannia . . . an Illustration of the Kingdom of England and Dominion of Wales: by a Geographical and Historical Description Thereof* consisted of a hundred strip maps with the road divided up into sections, each of twenty or so miles. This first atlas covered a total of 2,519 miles.

Through the eighteenth century, the road network stretched its tentacles across the country, paying for itself by those tolls. Many toll houses survive today – often set at an angle to the road, with a window facing the approaching traffic, where the toll could be collected. The improved turnpike roads often led to older, minor roads disappearing. Two out of the three Great North Roads in Huntingdonshire are now just bridleways.[9]

The new wave of coaches and post-chaises brought a tide of money for improvements to the inns. There was no set form to them, beyond the principle of having one yard surrounded by lodgings, and another for stabling and wagons. The traditional London coaching inn consisted of a house facing the street, equipped with sitting rooms and eating parlours; that facade was punctured by an entry and exit to the courtyards behind. A ground-floor passage connected the bar with the coffee room, with a drawing room on the first floor.

Dickens described the coaching inn complex of the White Hart in Southwark in *The Pickwick Papers* (1837):

> A double tier of bedroom galleries, with old clumsy balustrades, ran round two sides of the straggling area, and a double row of bells to correspond, sheltered from the weather by a little sloping roof, hung over the door leading to the bar and coffee-room. Two or three gigs and chaise-carts were wheeled up under different little sheds and penthouses.

As highway robbery increased with growing road traffic and a rise in jobless soldiers, some coaching inns, in cahoots with the highwaymen, had 'hides' added, where the likes of Dick Turpin – himself the son of the innkeeper at the Crown at Hempstead, Essex – could be concealed.

Highwaymen had been a problem since the thirteenth century. In 1285, a statute was passed, commanding that 60ft trenches be built between main roads and woodland, so travellers could spot highwaymen emerging from the trees. Traces of the trenches survive in Hatfield Forest, Essex, and Wychwood Forest, Oxfordshire.

The eighteenth-century traffic boom meant old Tudor inns – like the George Hotel in Stamford, Lincolnshire, originally built in 1568 – were given ornate makeovers. The stable yard at the back of the George still consists of three ranges of late-medieval buildings. The fourth range is the hotel, given an elaborate, three-storey, five-bay front by George Portwood in 1724.

By the late eighteenth century, coaching inns were the heart of Georgian life. Dinners, dances and public meetings brought in the gentry from the surrounding country, and elaborate extensions were built to house assembly rooms and ballrooms. These ballrooms were planned on a spectacular scale, their walls – so Evelyn Waugh described them – 'encrusted with plaster sphinxes, garlands, goats, Muses and urns'.[10]

Coaching inns sited at the terminus of a London route were particularly extravagant – like the Old Ship Hotel in Brighton, built facing the sea, between the two piers. A late-seventeenth-century inn, the Old Ship, was rebuilt in 1755, and soon drew in the local gratin. Fanny Burney dined there in 1779; a decade later, coaching inns were stamped with the royal seal of approval when the Prince of Wales visited a ball held in his honour at the Old Ship, taking in the Adamesque Assembly Room, with its shallow vaulted ceiling, and ballroom built in 1767 by Robert Golden.

Jane Austen was a regular, with her mother and sister, Cassandra, at the ballroom of the Dolphin Hotel in Southampton, then the fashionable town of Hampshire. She went as much as she could, she wrote, in order 'to have a good bargain'. The Dolphin was originally built in the fifteenth century; in 1760, it was given its robustly confident, red-brick, pedimented facade, with a stuccoed, rusticated ground floor, and its mammoth, swelling bow windows on the upper floors, either side of the arms of William IV and Queen Adelaide.

Coaching traffic mingled with high society and military and naval top brass at what was the finest eighteenth-century house in the city. The historian Edward Gibbon, a captain in the Hampshire militia, visited often. Thackeray wrote *Pendennis* there from 1848 to 1850; Queen Victoria stayed, too, stabling her horses at the Dolphin on the way to Osborne House on the Isle of Wight. Even as late as 1914, Field Marshal Haig used the coaching inn as his HQ for the embarkation of the British Expeditionary Force for France.

The golden age of the coaching inn was the early nineteenth century. In one of the biggest expansions of the road network, between 1803 and 1823, over 1,000 miles of roads, with new bridges, were laid across the country, at a regulation 60 feet wide.

By 1835, most main roads had been coated with the new type of tarmac, thanks to John McAdam's revolutionary 'macadamized' road surface. Previous roads built by the Scottish engineer Thomas Telford (1757–1834) were three-decker sandwiches of gravel, laid on small stones, laid on stone blocks – pretty much the same as the old Roman roads.

The system developed in 1816 by McAdam (1756–1836) worked without the expensive foundation, depending instead on a cambered layer of crushed stone on large stones, with a surface of ground stone bound with the macadamized material, set hard by rain and traffic.[11] Tarmac, a mixture of ironstone slag and bitumen, was first produced in 1902, and developed by the County Surveyor of Northampton.[12] By 1930, most English roads had been coated with tarmac; many smaller, rural roads remained with their flint surfaces intact into the 1950s.

For all these advances, the coaching inn was doomed by the advent of the railway. In 1829, Stephenson's Rocket made its maiden journey; the following year, the Liverpool and Manchester Railway opened. By 1845, the train's victory over the horse was complete. Once the sprawling coaching inns began losing custom to the new railway hotels, they became half-empty pubs or were converted into private houses.

Staffordshire – the Potteries viewed from Basford, 1850. Note the train in the middle distance, sounding the death knell of the coaching inn.

Still, coaching inns left a semantic legacy to the trains: the terms 'booking office' and 'waiting room' were handed on, and the guard of the coach became the guard of the train. For many years, the train guard wore the old coach guard's uniform, including the tall hat worn by the Fat Controller in *Thomas the Tank Engine*.

Memories of the coaching inn live on, too, in countless pubs called the Coach and Horses, like the Soho local of the late Jeffrey Bernard, the *Spectator*'s Low Life correspondent. *Private Eye*'s fortnightly lunches are still held there in the first-floor dining room. The former editor, Richard Ingrams, and current editor, Ian Hislop, preside over a merry table, with simple fare washed down with plenty of wine to get the gossip flowing.

The atmosphere is not far removed from the old coaching inns, caught in the old song bellowed in early-nineteenth-century stagecoaches:

> It is a cold and stormy night, I'm wetted to the skin,
> But I'll bear it with contentment until I reach the inn,
> And then I'll get a-drinking with the landlord and his kin.

Railways dominated the English transport system until the growth of the mass-market car in the middle of the last century. The first long English car journey ever made – by a 'petroleum motor carriage' in 1895, travelling fifty-six miles between Hampshire and Berkshire – took five hours and thirty-two minutes.[13] By the 1930s, cars could easily go at 70 mph, and were being allowed to go faster and faster: the 1930 Road Traffic Act abolished the 20 mph speed limit.

The volume of cars, too, was expanding, now they were affordable: the Morris Minor, introduced in 1931, and the Ford Model Y, built in Dagenham, Essex, from 1932, were Britain's first £100 cars. For all the advances in prewar car design, the roads they ran on lagged behind in sophistication. In 1939, the 276-mile-long Great North Road from London to Newcastle was still entirely single carriageway. These early roads were tremendously dangerous, too: the number of road deaths was higher in the 1930s than today.

That sophistication gap between car and road continued until the arrival of the motorway – the great landscape monument of the second half of the twentieth century. Even today, our motorways remain a pale imitation of German autobahns and Italian *autostrade*; let alone America's splendid freeways, with their expansive grassy central reservations, minimizing accidents (decreased, too, by lower speed limits) and allowing the use of smaller crash barriers.

Still, for all their international shortcomings, British roads have vanquished the railways, just as railways eclipsed horse-borne road traffic in the 1830s: 84 per cent of all journeys are now made by road.

And it's likely to stay that way. In March 2011, the Transport Secretary, Philip Hammond, admitted that the domination of road over rail is such that the rail infrastructure could no longer handle the volume of traffic on the roads: every 1 per cent fall in road traffic, he said, would lead to a 16 per cent rise in the passenger load of already overcrowded trains, if the traffic were transferred to the railways.

There is another powerful difference between our roads, and American and Continental ones. Of the five most popular Google questions about the English, 'Why do the English drive on the left?' is number one; followed by '. . . drink so much?; . . . have such bad teeth?; . . . dislike the French?; . . . make fun of the Welsh?'

The most popular – if apocryphal – reason is that, in the Middle Ages, you drove on the left to keep your right arm free to wield your sword or lance at approaching traffic. In 1300, Pope Bonifacio VIII formalized the practice by telling all his pilgrims to stick to the left. While we clung on to the habit, as did most of our colonies, the French moved to the right after the Revolution. The left side of the road had previously been hogged by the aristocracy, forcing the peasantry to the right – a habit formalized after the Revolution.

America increasingly drove on the right after the War of Independence. The custom gradually spread to Canada, but only slowly; Newfoundland, once a British protectorate, drove on the left until 1947.

In September 2009, Samoa, in the South Pacific, switched to the left. The Government said it was more convenient to import right-hand-drive cars from Australia and New Zealand than expensive American gas-guzzlers.

Our approach to road travel differs significantly from Continental Europeans, and not just because of the side of the road we drive on. For one thing, we haven't gone through the bicycling revolution that hit the Continent over a century ago. Even though bicycling is on the up – bike use on London's roads has more than doubled in the last decade – we are still not a natural bicycling country.

You don't see ranks of elderly men, shrink-wrapped in Lycra, racing along A-roads on skeletal racers, the way you do in France. The British like their children to learn how to ride a bike – a third of all UK households own a bicycle – but they think it's an activity best confined to childhood. Fewer than 5 per cent of all British journeys are made by bicycle, and only 3 per cent of British workers bicycle to work.

The idea that adults were too grown-up to bicycle was present from its Victorian beginnings. In 1888, a horse-rider complained to the police about being held up by racing bicyclists on the Great North Road. The National Cyclists' Union, terrified that anti-bike legislation would be introduced, declared that all mass-start road racing should be banned; it was forbidden until the 1950s.

Bicycling continued to be a second-class mode of transport into the twentieth century. The Cyclists' Touring Club, founded in Britain in 1878, even opposed bicycle paths in the 1930s; in their defensive paranoia, they thought bike paths might prevent bicyclists using the road.[14]

We have only recently imitated what countries like Holland did in the 1970s, i.e. make a conscious decision to turn from the car towards the bicycle; thus the woefully inadequate state, and limited amount, of our bike lanes. Two per cent of secondary school children bicycle to school in Britain, compared to 30 per cent in Holland.

For most of the twentieth century, the British Government

promoted cars over bicycles. Encouraged by the beginnings of a motorway network, the oil and car lobby, and the discovery of North Sea oil – and not least because car manufacture employs more people than bicycle frame-building, and oil people are richer than bike people – the car industry took precedence over bicycling interests.

Railways suffered, too, from the deferential attitude to the all-powerful car; the bulk of our freight now goes by road instead of by rail, unlike on the Continent.

This dismissive attitude towards bikes is also latently to do with snobbery – up until the 1960s, the bicycle was regarded as the poor man's transport in Britain, as it still is in India; while the car was seen as the symbol of the future, money and postwar progress.

For a century, we have worshipped the car over the bicycle. And that love of cars, combined with an inadequate road system, has led to a hatred of bicyclists. Bicycling is still seen as an odd way to get about; something you do as a child, or for pleasure, never a pragmatic way of getting around.

The same attitude exists in America; but not in Continental Europe. On a recent trip to Groningen in northern Holland, I took a taxi at rush hour and it was practically the only car on the streets. In 1972, the Groningen authorities made a conscious decision to make the bicycle the dominant mode of transport, closing off the city centre to all private vehicles, and allowing only buses, taxis and business vehicles. Sixty per cent of all journeys in the town are now made by bike.

Bikes were soon understood to be the best way of getting to work. No one turned up too sweaty at the office, because no one was bicycling particularly quickly – they all followed a steady universal pace. Bicycling was so completely incorporated into daily life that couples bike hand in hand, each leaving one hand on the handlebars.

If you did this in England, someone would throw something at you; in Holland, it is no different to walking hand in hand.

As Britain moved out of the years of rationed austerity after the war, and the new motorways appeared in the late 1950s, car ownership soared; and new street furniture was needed to accommodate the new arrivals on the road.

The man responsible for buying it was Ernest Marples, the Conservative Minister of Transport from 1959 to 1964. Marples introduced parking meters (designed by Kenneth Grange, the man who designed the Intercity 125 in 1968), seat belts, traffic wardens and double yellow lines.

Single yellow lines were first used by police in 1956, on the kerbs of the West End, to stop illegal parking outside Chinese restaurants. Double yellow lines were introduced by the Road Traffic Act of 1960; although a Yorkshire farmer, George Bamber, used them in the late nineteenth century as boundary markers around his farm, inspired by the markings on his sheep.[15]

Street furniture has been around for a while. Milestones came in under Charles II; the Romans used them, too, but none survives in situ. The London–Dover Road was equipped with mile marks in 1663. The earliest surviving milestone was set up at Trumpington, near Cambridge, in 1727. By 1773, an Act was passed, enforcing milestones on major roads.[16]

Street furniture proliferated with the spread of turnpike roads through the eighteenth and nineteenth centuries. Bollards – originally wooden posts erected to protect pedestrians from carriages – became popular after the end of the Napoleonic Wars in 1815. Swanage, Dorset, became the centre of bollard manufacture. Old military hardware, especially cannons, was used. Bollards were made in different materials in different counties, with granite used on Dartmoor and millstone grit in Bakewell, Derbyshire.[17]

Pedestrian crossings, with their Belisha Beacons (originally twice their current height), were introduced in 1934 by Leslie Hore-Belisha, the Transport Minister, after he was nearly run over by a sports car in Camden High Street, north London. But, still, before the war, there was barely any other street furniture needed to keep the sparse traffic in check.

Even as late as 1969, when the Beatles were photographed for their *Abbey Road* album – in Abbey Road, St John's Wood, north London – there wasn't much street furniture around. There are no yellow lines, no parking signs, no parking payment machines and, even with free parking, very few parked cars. A VW Beetle is breezily parked on the kerb to the left, and a cab further down on the right, but there are no other cars parked in the first fifty yards beyond the famous zebra crossing, which has no white zig-zags leading up to it. The road, too, is almost completely, blissfully empty – off in the distance, between the heads of Paul McCartney and Ringo Starr, you can just make out a solitary pair of cars about to pass each other.

These days, yellow lines, white zig-zags and even red lines are thickly painted over our streets, now jam-packed with parked cars.

Over the last two decades, the growth in street furniture has been exponential: according to the Campaign to Protect Rural England and the RAC Foundation, 70 per cent of rural road signs are now unnecessary. That street furniture has also grown increasingly minimalist and utilitarian in look – the old black iron flambeaux on top of traffic lights were gradually removed through the 1970s.

There are a few honourable exceptions to the street furniture invasion: in 2003, Kensington Council removed as many signs as possible from Kensington High Street, and accidents fell by 47 per cent. In 2011, European street-planning initiatives were introduced in nearby Exhibition Road. There are fewer road markings and no difference in height between kerb, pavement and road; an 80cm strip of ridged paving helps the blind work out when they're approaching the road. The idea is that drivers, previously mollycoddled by signage, then begin to take their own precautions against crashing.

Beneath all that street furniture, basic road construction hasn't changed much in recent years; as I saw recently, when my own street, Caversham Road, in Kentish Town, north London, was dug up. Workmen had dug a 5ft-deep trench in the road. A club sandwich of tarmac on concrete was revealed, over a layer of rubble from buildings blitzed in the Second World War. Underneath that was 50-million-year-old London clay from the Eocene period.

Towards the side of the road, by the Dartmoor granite (known as 'Big Granite') kerbstones, the workmen had exposed the old Victorian road, made up of sarsen silcrete setts. Placed together in a grid, like flat cobblestones, these small cubes of sandstone came from Cranborne Chase. A few original wooden cobbles – like those in Endell Street, Covent Garden – still survive in England, often near hospitals and in rich areas, where silence was at a premium.

The new road the workmen built in Caversham Road had a foundation of hardcore, or crushed stone. On top of that, they laid the classic ingredients of the modern road: two layers of bitumen mixed with tiny chunks of limestone.

Our tarmac roads remain peculiarly susceptible to potholes. In colder countries, like Sweden, the road stays frozen for months and then thaws once, at the end of winter. In England, it's freeze-thaw-freeze-thaw. In a bad winter, like those of 2009–10 and 2010–11, the freeze-thaw process happened over fifty times.

That cycle is appalling for road surfaces: potholes are formed when the water seeps into tarmac, freezes and then thaws, cracking and crumbling the road surface. When the ice melts, more water seeps inside the crack and the problem worsens during the next freeze. When the crack is wide enough, the surface collapses and a pothole develops. Recent cold snaps are thought to have taken the number of potholes up to 2 million, one hole for every 180 yards of the 200,000 miles of local roads in England and Wales.

And why does water get beneath the surface? Aside from old age, the most frequent cause is roadworks. However well a road is mended, there'll be spots where the old and new surfaces just don't meld together. By opening up a road once, you reduce its life by up to 60 per cent. Those cracks are usually caused by the 'utility openings' made to repair water and electricity lines, gas pipes and communications cables. Thirty-seven utilities have the right to dig up London's roads; 90 per cent of the work is done by BT, Virgin Media, Thames Water, EDF Energy, National Grid and Scotia Gas.

Pavements and kerbstones have a longer shelf-life than the potholed roads they flank. Yorkstone, originally quarried in Yorkshire but also quarried elsewhere, is the classic paving stone. The tight-grained sandstone – rich in iron oxides, feldspar, clay, mica and quartz – weathers so gracefully that it's often ripped off the streets by opportunist cowboys. There are other varieties of paving stone, too: in Shropshire, they used Dhustone, a basalt from the Clee Hills.

Kerbstones, which have to bear the brunt of bad parking, still tend to be made of granite, as they have been since the early nineteenth century. Granite kerbstones for much of England came from Cornwall and the Channel Islands in the nineteenth century, where they were carried as ballast for ships taking vegetables to the mainland.

Across the country you'll see granite kerbstones that have been 'chitted' – i.e. roughened and dimpled, to stop pedestrians slipping. Merged with the granite in the kerbstone, there are also pools of darker diorite – another igneous, volcanic and extremely hard stone. Diorite was used on the steps of St Paul's Cathedral to take the footfall of millions of visitors, whose shoes have buffed the dark, dull stone to a gleaming sheen.

Both diorite and granite were heavily quarried in Leicester-shire in the nineteenth century. The granite of Mountsorrel, Leicestershire, was first quarried for road stone in the late 1820s, when a group of Scotsmen, from the granite city of Aberdeen, came south to dig it out.

Pink-granite Leicestershire setts were used to pave roads all over England, and the M1 was largely built on a foundation of crushed Mountsorrel stone. A whole hill in Markfield, Leicestershire, once topped by a windmill, was quarried into oblivion for road-building.

Much of our British road-building stone has now been quarried out. When Exhibition Road was relaid in 2011, in line with those European street-planning initiatives, they had to use Chinese granite because the original quarry in northern England had run out of stone.

We now can't even provide enough domestic salt for gritting the streets in winter. Our pink rock salt comes in 6mm granules, from Winsford in Cheshire, Boulby in Cleveland, and County Antrim. Cheshire has been mined for rock salt since Roman times; many of the county's meres were formed by salt-mining subsidence, caused by hundreds of miles of subterranean tunnels.

But domestic salt supply is limited. When demand outpaced our 30,000-tonnes-a-week domestic capacity in January 2009, in the worst snow since 1981, 21,000 tonnes of salt were shipped from Egypt.

These days England's roads not only roll less merrily and less mazily than in Chesterton's time; they are also increasingly unlikely to be made out of English materials.

3. Ornamental chimneys and a
fetish for brick: at Tudor Hampton
Court, the corkscrewing, diamond-
patterned chimneys are topped
with mini-crenellations.

4. Nikolaus Pevsner thought the greenness of Durham distinguished
it from Continental cathedral-castle cities like Avignon and Prague.

5. Pleasure in al fresco dining, and indifference to weather: *The Garden
of Hampton House, with Mr and Mrs David Garrick Taking Tea* by Johan
Zoffany, 1762. The earliest painting of an English picnic shows the
actor at his villa by the Thames.

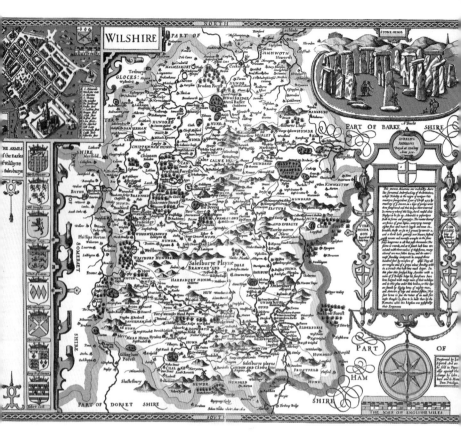

1. Wiltshire, from John Speed's 1611 map of England. The county has already been largely deforested, and the modern constellation of villages, towns, cities and historical sites, like Stonehenge, is in place.

2. *Mr and Mrs Andrews* by Thomas Gainsborough, 1750. Robert and Frances Andrews lived at Ballingdon House, Sudbury, Suffolk. Half portrait, half landscape, the picture shows, to the right, the long, straight rows of wheat sown with Jethro Tull's drill, invented in 1701.

In the Canterbury Cathedral archives lies the 1072 Winchester Accord, signed with the mark of the illiterate William the Conqueror in the chapel of Winchester Castle. William agreed in the document that the southern province of Canterbury should take precedence over York, which had once been the capital of the Roman province of Britannia. After his savage northern campaign in 1069–70 – the Harrying of the North – he appreciated that there was a real division between the rebellious north and the more easily pacified south.

You can still see the effects of William the Conqueror's campaign, and the divide between north and south, in medieval settlements in County Durham, planned by Norman hands in the eleventh and twelfth centuries.

Norman control was imposed from above by the dirigiste construction of new villages, built on one of three different plans: two rows of buildings, often farmhouses, facing each other across a green or street; four rows of buildings ranged around a square; or single farms. The four-row developments were set up by chartered boroughs; the two-row ones by medieval villeins. Bishop Auckland and Darlington have examples of both two-row and four-row settlements.[1]

This was settlement by invader's decree, as opposed to the usual, natural, organic growth of English villages. County Durham also faced border raids from Scotland; which might explain the number of villages with big greens protected by encircling settlements, like Easington, Trimdon, Hett, Hamsterley and Heighington.[2]

Even if it has been almost a thousand years since England was successfully invaded, war, and the fear of border invasion, has helped dictate England's look ever since, right up until the Second World War. In 1940, 18,000 pillboxes were built after Dunkirk, and many still survive: of the 300 built for the Taunton Stop Line,

10. North and South: The Great Divide

The coal miners built what we know as modern Britain – it was the coal-fired engines that fired the factories, fired the trains that took the goods around the country and to the ports, coal-fired ships that took our goods abroad, protected by coal-fired naval warships. So, if you object to coal-mining, you are really saying that we should have remained a little island off the north-west coast of Europe – a romantic idea. That's what would have happened.

Tony Benn, *Cornerstone* magazine, Summer 2010

Unusually for him, Tony Benn was spot on. Britain's great leaps forward were largely funded by two things: wool in the Middle Ages and the coal beneath our feet. Wool may not be so important these days, but coal is still the second-biggest source of energy in the country.

Coal is formed by long-compressed mud, jungles, dead ferns and mosses. And it just so happens that the Midlands and the north of England – like Wales – are particularly rich in that long-compressed vegetation. So the titanic industrial efforts used to extract coal from the ground – and the associated iron- and steel-making plants, and metal-bashing factories – were concentrated in the Midlands and the north.

The north–south divide – and all related ee bah gum, it's grim up north material – was born; or, to put it more accurately, was widened. A north–south divide existed long before the first great coal mines were dug.

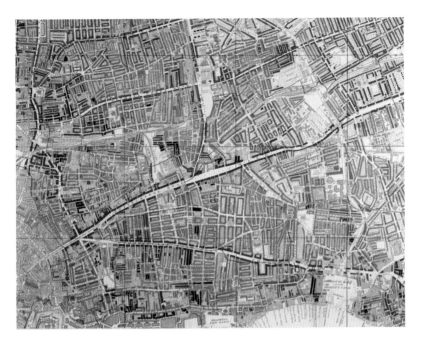

12. Thanks to the south-westerly wind, and the docks, east London was poorer than the west. Whitechapel in 'The Descriptive Map of London Poverty' by Charles Booth, 1889 – areas marked in black were inhabited by the 'lowest class. Vicious, semi-criminal'. Red areas were 'Middle-class. Well to do'.

13. *Train Landscape* by Eric Ravilious, 1939. Chalk downs produce gentle hollows and broad, spreading humps. The Westbury Horse, Wiltshire, was carved out of the escarpment on Salisbury Plain to reveal the white chalk beneath.

Shell guide to the roads of Britain - Ermine Street

GO WELL – GO SHELL SHELL *The Key to the Countryside*

HEALTH of the COUNTRY
COMFORTS of the TOWN

LETCHWORTH
The FIRST GARDEN CITY

14. Straight as a die: Roman Ermine Street, now the A15 between Scunthorpe and Lincoln, painted by David Gentleman in 1964. Planned, post-enclosure landscape lies on either side, with straight hedges and symmetrical fields.

15. 'Scudamore', a sixteenth-century farmhouse in Letchworth, Hertfordshire, was used by advertisers a century ago, to draw people to the first new garden city. The half-timbered building reflected the influences on the garden cities – Arts and Crafts, rural, English.

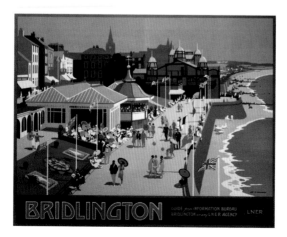

BRIDLINGTON GUIDE from INFORMATION BUREAU BRIDLINGTON or any L N E R AGENCY LNER

16. Playful seaside architecture: a 1930 London and North Eastern Railway poster. All the peculiar elements of the English seaside are there – the bandstand, beach huts, pavilion and floral clock.

17. A love of jokey historical references: Sir John Soane's 1815 monument to his wife, St Pancras Old Church, north London.

18. And its descendant, Sir Giles Gilbert Scott's K6 phone box, designed in 1935 – this one is in Market Harborough, Leicestershire.

The South Downs

your BRITAIN · *fight for it* now

ISSUED BY A·B·C·A

19. Chalk, the most English of stones. The connection between quintessential England and the chalk downland of the South Downs is made explicit in this 1942 wartime poster.

20. In *Withnail and I*, a drunk Withnail drives his Jaguar Mark 2 down the M6 from Cumbria to London in 1969. In fact, he's driving around the M25, near Rickmansworth, Hertfordshire, shortly before the motorway opened in 1986. Motorway signage hasn't changed since 1958.

21. *The Road Across the Wolds* by David Hockney, 1997. The Yorkshire Wolds – post-enclosure, planned countryside, dotted with isolated farms and criss-crossed with straight hedges, tree-lines and woodland edges.

a mini-Maginot line running from Seaton, Devon, to just north of Bridgwater, Somerset, two thirds remain. The Taunton Stop Line, designed to stop German armoured fighting vehicles invading from the west, was one of fifty Second World War defensive lines across the country.

Because the English are now on good terms with France, as well as Scotland and Wales, it's hard to think of England's northern and southern borders as either hostile or defensive. But that's what they were for centuries – like the India–Pakistan border is today – and border counties still bear the marks of those days.

Nikolaus Pevsner called Northumberland 'the castle county of England', with its 500 castles, buildings and defensive pele towers (also found in the borderland of Cumbria).[3] In a similar way, Kent's identity was forged by being the closest county to the Continent. As frontier territory, it needed a military presence early on; in the second century AD, the Romans' *Classis Britannica* – the British Fleet – was based at Lympne and Dover.

Kent's closeness to the Continent meant that, when Pope Gregory sent St Augustine to England in AD 597, Canterbury was his principal outpost; it remains the centre of English Christianity. There are still remains of ten seventh-century churches built by Augustine or his converts in Kent; with another in Bradwell, Essex. Kent benefited, too, from the waves of Norman and Gothic architecture that flooded in from France after the Conquest.

The county's nearness to France led to the import of French building materials – particularly the excellent Caen oolitic limestone from Normandy – by the Normans, through the Middle Ages, and on into the Victorian age. This expensive stone is often used as trimming on window frames, doorways, gargoyles, pinnacles and finials. Bell Harry tower, the central tower of Canterbury Cathedral, has a core of half a million bricks wrapped in Caen stone.

Today, there are more castles in Kent than any other southern county. Rochester Castle has the highest keep in England. In Essex, another international border county, the biggest keep in Europe is at Colchester Castle, built in the late eleventh century on the Roman foundations of the Emperor Claudius's first-century temple.

The Welsh border was also defensive for centuries. Herefordshire has a chain of castles running through the county, continuing into Monmouthshire to the south, and Shropshire to the north, where the medieval frontier architecture is similar to that of the northern borderlands. Church towers on the Welsh borders have such thick walls that they were probably also military refuges. The church at Ewyas Harold, Herefordshire, has 7ft-thick walls, and Monnington-on-Wye Church, also in Herefordshire, has battlements and cross-shaped arrow-slits.

For all the talk about England being full of castles, plenty of counties don't have many of them. Hampshire, a coastline border county like Kent, needed fewer castles, because it was naturally protected by its thick woods; and its chalk uplands were underpopulated and relatively poor.

Castles thrive where battles are threatened. Somewhere like Oxfordshire may be in the heart of England, but it was never the country's military cockpit; so the county is light on Norman castles. After the Conquest, the Thames was defended further east, on the banks at Windsor and Wallingford, in Berkshire, and, further afield, at Buckingham, Canterbury, Winchester and Cambridge.

Norfolk has no Norman castles, apart from Norwich, because the county had little tactical advantage, moored as it is on the north-eastern edge of East Anglia. Bedfordshire has no castles at all, except for Norman motte and baileys. These were the simple early-Norman castles – with a motte (a giant artificial earth mound with a wooden tower) next to a bailey (an enclosure formed by steep banks and ditches). It's a safe bet that any surviving motte dates to within a century of 1066.

Southern border counties were even more heavily fortified in the early nineteenth century, as fears of a Napoleonic invasion grew. In 1806, the Martello towers at Folkestone, Dymchurch, went up; Fort Clarence, Rochester, was built in 1812. The Western Heights at Dover – which could accommodate 4,000 soldiers, buried within the hillside – were built in 1814.

Another chain of southern forts – Palmerston forts – was thrown up around Portsmouth in 1859, with the renewed threat of French invasion. Further forts were built around the British coast through the 1860s, from the Bristol Channel to Chatham, from Plymouth to Sunderland.

Throughout the medieval period, the divide between north and south persisted. Fertile southern areas that were rich then remain rich today. In 1334, Berkshire and Oxfordshire, then worth £20 per square mile, were two of the richest counties in England, as they still are. In the 2001 census, a third of households in Oxfordshire had three cars or more; Oxford had the third-highest proportion of professionals in England and Wales, 23.4 per cent of the employed population.

Until the Industrial Revolution, the south was much more heavily populated than the north, and more generally in the swing of things – even in the late seventeenth century, only a quarter of the English population lived north-west of the line from Boston, Lincolnshire, to Gloucester.

Before the modern age, the north was considered remote, colder, on the way to the Arctic. To the south lay Europe – or pretty much the rest of the world, as we then knew it, until the discovery of America in the late fifteenth century and the expansion of trade links with the east in the sixteenth century.

A reverse pattern existed – and exists – in Italy, where the more temperate north looks down on the intense heat, supposed laziness and fecklessness of those in the Mezzogiorno, down in the barbarous south. Both England and Italy consider themselves more civilized the further they get from harsh weather.

It is in the south that the Cinque Ports were set up by Royal Charter in 1155, for trade and defence. Two of them, Sandwich and Hythe, have particularly grand churches as a result. Medieval prosperity is still apparent in Kent: there are more monumental brasses in Kent churches than in any other county; Cobham, with sixteen brasses, has more than any other English church.

The shape of England, with pretty much a linear outline heading north–south, leads neatly to north–south splits; as it does in Italy, also built along a rough north–south spine. Countries aligned along an east–west axis, like America, are more likely to define themselves by those compass points.

Admittedly, there are strong east–west splits, too, along the length of England. Rivers naturally flow to east or west from the country's central spine. In the Midlands, the Arrow, Alne and Avon rivers drain west into the Bristol Channel and the Atlantic; the Cole, Blythe and Anker rivers head east to the North Sea, via the Humber and the Trent.

Coal deposits aren't restricted to the Midlands and the north, either. Coal is found in Kent and the south-west, particularly in Somerset.

But it's that much harder to get the stuff out of the ground in the West Country. When south-west England was twisted and crushed 250 million years ago by the geological phenomenon known as the Hercynian orogeny, the Somerset coal seams were flipped on their head, at hard-to-get-at distorted angles; certainly much harder to get at than the seams in the Midlands and the north.

Rural Somerset might well look like the industrial north today if its coal had been easier to extract; County Durham was all high moors and rolling hills until coal was discovered and industry invaded the landscape.

And Devon and Cornwall might have looked like Sheffield if they'd found coal there, not tin. Disused West Country tin mines don't spoil the modern landscape; with their derelict chimneys and engine houses for hauling up water and waste rock, they even add a maudlin, faded grandeur to the scene.

The heaps of spoil left by early 'streaming' tin-miners, who picked ore from streams, were relatively small. Later tin-miners cut tunnels and sank shafts into hillsides, particularly in Cornwall and on Dartmoor. But time has softened these minor scars, and the landscape has if anything gained drama from this minor surgery.

Copper mining in Cornwall, which peaked between 1700 and 1870, didn't destroy the landscape, either, not least because the ore was shipped to Swansea for the messy process of smelting, and south Wales took the aesthetic hit instead.

Industrial effects on the landscape can occasionally be enormous outside the north. The china clay mines in Cornwall produced a new geological layer of mining spoil, moulded into streaky brown and white moonscapes. In St Austell, mining for kaolin, a type of aluminium silicate, formed its own set of mini-Alps from the spoil. Excavation also produced its own distinctive landscape: the Eden Project in Cornwall is built in a disused china-clay pit.

There are industrial remnants left, too, in the supposedly pampered urban south. The old workers' leisure club from the Huntley and Palmer biscuit factory still survives in Reading, once known as Biscuit Town (with Reading FC known as the Biscuit Men, and Reading Prison as the Biscuit Factory). The art deco Hoover Factory on Western Avenue, Perivale, Middlesex, built in 1935, is now a supermarket.

The large-scale effects of the Industrial Revolution may have dodged much of the south – there was never much heavy industry going on in, say, Thomas Hardy's Dorset. But that's not to say that southern, and western, counties didn't have their great industries, too. It's just that those industries were either cleaner, or belonged to an earlier age, when the effect on the landscape was on a smaller scale.

Or, indeed, to a later age, when technological advances restricted the effect on the landscape. When the first black-and-white, live satellite television pictures from America arrived here in 1962, there had to be a receiving dish to catch them. That relatively unobtrusive dish was at Goonhilly Downs Earth Station, on the Lizard, Cornwall; as close as possible to America. The Lizard – at Poldhu – was also where Marconi did his first radio experiments in 1901.

These modern innovations, carried through the air, or along cables on the seabed, don't disturb the landscape the way large-scale mining did.

Britain's modern oil industry, too, leaves barely a mark on the landscape. In January 2011, 6 million barrels of crude oil were discovered beneath the thatched cottages, rolling fields and ancient coppiced woodland of the West Sussex hills. Walking around the picture postcard hamlet of Forestside, on the edge of the South Downs, by the Hampshire border, there's not much to show that you're in the Klondike of south-east England.

Horses and sheep graze the fields round the drilling site in Markwells Wood. All you can hear is a birdscarer, the occasional pheasant flushed from the undergrowth, and the odd bang from a nearby shoot.

In a clearing in the hanging woods, fringed with bracken and silver birch and beech trees, invisible from all directions, is a flat, square patch of gravel.

About the size of three tennis courts, this gravel patch, bordered by a 6ft-high mesh fence, juts out over the edge of the hill. In the middle of that gravel is a 12 by 12 feet concrete platform, with a bright-red stopper at its centre, like a giant New York fire hydrant. Hundreds of millions of gallons of oil come gushing through this tiny little puncture in the earth's surface.

Pre-drilling surveys revealed that the oil was trapped in a fault in the Great Oolite stone stratum below; a fault running east–west across the county – the reason they've been striking oil in this corner of England since 1980.

There are ten oilfields in the Weald basin, with the oilfields running into East Sussex, in Storrington, and all the way to neighbouring Surrey, at Bletchingley, by the M25. Further north, in Berkshire, in 1994, the Queen gave permission for exploratory drilling in the grounds of Windsor Castle.

The offshore oilfields in the North Sea are well-known. Our onshore sites aren't so familiar but, in fact, prospectors have been finding oil under British soil since 1945. There's oil, too, in Nottinghamshire, Derbyshire, Lincolnshire and Yorkshire, although, admittedly, in small amounts: the only large onshore site in Britain is at Wytch Farm, Poole, Dorset, the biggest onshore oilfield in Western Europe.

Once the oil is drawn from over a mile beneath the earth's crust at Forestside, the well will be capped, and the patch of gravel returned to woodland. The only manmade structures on the horizon will again be the ancient houses of Forestside: with distinctly unindustrial names like Glebe View Cottage, the Willows and Virginia Cottage.

The sixteenth- and seventeenth-century iron industry in the neighbouring East Sussex Weald left a much deeper mark on the countryside than modern oil exploration ever will. The county is still scattered with old hammerponds, formed by dams that powered hammers for crushing iron ore. The surrounding forests supplied the timber, burnt for smelting the metal from the local ironstone.

If the modern oil industry leaves the land almost untouched, the non-mineral industries of the Industrial Revolution often enhance the look of a place. In genteel Bradford on Avon, Wiltshire, you can still see the fetching water- and steam-powered mills – there were thirty of them in the town – which became defunct in the late nineteenth century when the wool industry migrated to Yorkshire.

The Cotswolds were once an industrial heartland, also devoted to wool production. Cotswold is thought to mean 'sheep enclosure in the rolling hillsides'; sheep were so valuable there in the Middle Ages that they were known as the Cotswold Lion. Old mills survive in Wotton-under-Edge and Painswick. There are still signs of industry around the rivers, required for fulling (or washing) wool, particularly in the Little Avon, Ewelme and Frome valleys. These date from the days before steam power replaced water power, allowing cotton and wool mills to leave the river valleys. The local towns – Tetbury, Cirencester and Stroud – and their churches expanded on the back of the wool industry.

As late as 1801, the fabric towns of the Cotswolds – Witney, with its blankets; Chipping Campden, with its silk and wool – were some of the most heavily populated in England. Fewer people live in the Cotswolds now than in the Middle Ages.

The industry's effects on the landscape, though, are that much less than in the north because its source materials – sheep and grass – were agricultural, not mineral. You didn't need to gouge into the landscape and there was barely any spoil to deal with.

Leicestershire's industry also grew out of sheep-farming. In 1724, Daniel Defoe wrote, 'The whole county seems to be taken up in country business. The largest sheep and horses are found here, and hence it comes to pass, too, that they are in consequence a vast magasine of wool for the rest of the nation.'

Because of all that wool money, there are plenty of large fourteenth- and fifteenth-century churches in Leicestershire. The trade also led to the growth of wool-combing and spinning in the county in the fifteenth century; and in turn to the hosiery industry moving there from London in the seventeenth century.

Plenty of light was needed, and so extra windows were put into hosiery workers' cottages – you can still see the long, top-floor windows on the houses in the village of Shepshed. The textile industry expanded in Leicestershire well into the nine-teenth century, with large steam-powered mills built in Leicester, Loughborough and Hinckley.

Alongside Leicester's canal, heartland of the city's industry, the old dyeing factories survive, fitted with louvred roofs to let the fumes disperse. Industry was boosted by cheap coal trans-port along the River Soar, made navigable as far as Leicester in 1794, and Loughborough in 1777.

Fumes from those dyeing factories apart, Leicester's indus-tries were relatively clean and small-scale – meaning the city wasn't transformed to the degree that northern cities were by the Industrial Revolution.

The grim clichés of northern life are deepened by the wildness of northern landscapes.

Wuthering Heights can only wuther – the word means 'howl' or 'eddy' – if there are some moors for the wind to go wuther-ing through. Heathcliff's gritstone moors of Yorkshire are open, bare land with black hollows and crags, where the wind and rain can wuther away to their hearts' content.

Bleak, wuthering weather depends on being high on the hills. Dip down from the moors, head east of Knaresborough, and you hit the rolling, wooded farming country of the Vale of York, west of the Jurassic hills made of sandstone and limestone. The vale lies on a flat bed of Magnesian limestone – known also as Redlands limestone, it's responsible for the fertile, red soil of the area. It's also wonderful building stone – used to build Ripon and York Minsters. All around is rich agricultural land support-ing prosperous farmers, chocolate box villages and picturesque market towns.

The landscape is far from uniform in the industrial areas of the north. In the West Riding of Yorkshire, the steel and coal works in Sheffield and Rotherham may have scarred the land; but the wool and worsted mills around Bradford, Halifax and Huddersfield laid down a handsome, robust, architectural relief over the natural beauty of the country.

Whether for good or ill effect, the greater scale of the industries of the Midlands and the north altered the lie of the land that much more deeply than southern industries. The changes were so deep that echoes survive of the first industrial landscapes of the 1760s and 1770s – particularly in the ironworks at Coalbrookdale, Shropshire, Richard Arkwright's spinning mill in Nottingham, and Josiah Wedgwood's factory at Etruria in the Potteries.

Victorian social division can still be spotted today in the layout of industrial towns and cities. In these hilly northern areas, it was easier to build on the flat valley floor. But living in the depths of the valley, where water gathered and natural drainage was bad, wasn't healthy. Manufacturing tycoons gravitated to mansions on top of the hill; working-class housing was consigned to the valley floor. The word slum, first used at the height of the residential building boom in the 1820s, is derived from the Low German *slam*, meaning mire.

The population expansion brought by industry was staggering. London may have grown sixfold from 1800 to 1900, but that was nothing compared to the growth of the northern industrial cities. Birmingham, Manchester, Liverpool and Sheffield, once small medieval towns, became colossal cities on the back of unprecedented volumes of trade and manufacture.

There had been coal-mining and weaving in Lancashire since the thirteenth century; by 1375, Edward III had set up a colony of Flemish weavers in Manchester. Cotton was imported to Lancashire from Cyprus and Smyrna as early as 1600.

But the industrial identity of the north, and the deepening of the north–south divide, only really set in during the late eighteenth century, when the weaving of cloth from cotton began in Lancashire, helped by the 1774 reduction of tax on cotton goods from 6d to 3d a yard.

A quick succession of revolutionary inventions intensified the northern wool industry: John Kay's fly-shuttle in 1733, followed by Hargreaves's spinning jenny in 1765, Arkwright's water-frame and Crompton's mule in 1780, and Boulton and Watt's steam engine in 1787.

The effect on the look of the north was immediate, and on an unprecedented scale.

Before cotton-spinning arrived in Preston in 1777, it was a small Lancashire town of 6,000. By 1877, once industry had got a foothold, its population was 90,000.

In 1829, Middlesbrough was a hamlet of forty people, centred around a single farmhouse on the River Tees. The 1845 extension of the Stockton to Darlington railway to Middlesbrough singled it out for expansion (on a carefully planned grid, incidentally). The fastest-growing town in British history, Middlesbrough was nicknamed the 'Infant Hercules' by Gladstone. The first blast furnace was built in 1851; in 1875, the first steel plant opened. By 1901, once iron ore was discovered in the neighbouring Eston Hills, 90,000 workers lived in 'Ironopolis'.

Wordsworth described the effect:

> Meanwhile, at social industry's command,
> How quick, how vast an increase!
> From the germ
> Of some poor hamlet, rapidly produced
> Here a huge town, continuous and compact,
> Hiding the face of earth for leagues.
>
> The Excursion (1814)

The power of industry was so great that, while Middlesbrough grew at a lightning rate, non-industrial cities nearby were barely changed. Durham's population in 2001 (29,091) was barely bigger than in 1900 (20,000), and not much more than in 1840 (17,000).

Birmingham began life as an Anglo-Saxon hamlet, named after the Anglo-Saxon Beorma tribe who settled there. Built on poor soil at an awkward splitting point in the River Rea, it first expanded because it was a handy meeting point for farmers from nearby richer villages.

Between the sixteenth and the nineteenth centuries, Birmingham grew from a small Midlands town into one of the world's leading centres of manufacture, the 'city of a thousand trades'. Now, it's the second-biggest city in Britain, with a population of 977,087 in 2001. You can diagnose the late date of the city's development by its lack of medieval churches; particularly when compared to medieval metropolises such as York or the City of London.

Birmingham is neither on the sea nor on a navigable river, but it did have two minor advantages. It got its market charter in 1166, but was never incorporated as a borough. That meant it was open to outside labourers and craftsmen, but had none of the constraints on trade imposed by a traditional burgess system.

The city was also an early industrial centre, if a small one. In the Middle Ages, Birmingham was one of a handful of Black Country villages at the centre of iron and coal production. It helped, too, that the city was on the south-eastern edge of these villages – and so closer to London.

Early in its history, Birmingham had established itself as a place for metal manufacture, helped by plenty of streams and water mills. A Birmingham goldsmith is recorded in 1406. By

1643, Prince Rupert, Charles I's commander in the Civil War, sacked Birmingham because its gunmakers were supplying Parliament's armies.

You can see this process – of medieval, small-scale industry leading to exponential development and diversification – in Sheffield, where cutlery was made as early as 1540, when the antiquary John Leland wrote of 'many Smiths and Cuttelars in Hallamshire [the parishes of Bradfield, Ecclesfield and Sheffield]'.

The same went for Coventry – which made cutlery in the thirteenth century, cloth in the fourteenth century, gloves in the fifteenth century, buttons in the sixteenth century, clocks in the seventeenth century and ribbons in the eighteenth century. Weavers' houses still survive in the city, their close-set second-floor windows positioned in front of the looms.

Coventry's diversification didn't stop there. It moved from ribbons in the early nineteenth century, via watch-making and sewing machine manufacture, into bicycle-making in the 1870s, and then on to cars; William Morris's Oxford factory made the same jump from bicycles, via motorbikes, to cars in 1913, with the manufacture of the first Morris Oxford. Coventry's Daimler factory was built in 1896, laying the foundations for the city's long car-making history.

Back in Birmingham, the metal industry diversified from metal toys, trinkets and boxes, into electroplating – invented by Elkington's of Newhall Street – along with diamond trading and case-making in the Jewellery Quarter. Small-scale manufacture in Birmingham's houses-cum-workshops flourished from 1830 until 1880. In the early twentieth century, bigger T-plan factories were built, with long workshops stretching at right angles to the front office, casting as much light as possible on to the factory floor.

The expansion of Birmingham and the diversification of its industries were accelerated by the railways. The London and Birmingham Railway, opened in 1837, was the first main line in Britain. As a result, Birmingham's population grew from 86,000 in 1801 to 147,000 in 1831, and 233,000 in 1851.

As industry increased and diversified, those workers had to be housed. Birmingham's twentieth-century municipal housing programme – 50,000 houses built in 1939, mostly plain brick cottages in pairs and rows – was the biggest in England.

Looking at these vast population movements, it seems odd that our Industrial Revolution was smaller than that of many of our Continental neighbours, even if it was the first.

We were the first in so many ways – the first to develop the industrial architecture of the iron bridge, the first to pioneer dock warehouses on a grand scale, the first to use ornamental cast iron so widely. A lot of it is still visible in the iron railings in front of so many terraced houses; some of those railings have remained black ever since they were repainted in 1861 to mourn Prince Albert.

To begin with, Europeans were staggered by the size of British industry. The Prussian architect, Karl Friedrich Schinkel, said of Manchester in 1826, '400 large new factories for cotton-spinning have been built, several of them the size of the Royal Palace in Berlin, and thousands of smoking obelisks of the steam engines 80 to 180 feet high destroy all impression of church steeples.'[4]

Still, we never had the really enormous factories on the scale of those built in the later nineteenth century, and the twentieth century, in Germany and Russia; the factories that helped foster the mass labour movements which became fertile breeding grounds for Communism.

We were, though, extremely competitive when it came to the scale of the industrial recession that so deepened the north–

south divide in the late twentieth century. Cities, so quickly pumped up by the industrial boom, deflated just as dramatically when recession hit.

The 1980s recession is the one that sticks in our minds; the one that has had the most powerful psychological effect on the north–south divide.

But there were earlier recessions. In 1675, Bristol was the second city of Britain, having accelerated ahead of its medieval rivals, Norwich and York. Its maritime trade was hampered, though, by the River Severn's vast tidal range, which made it tricky for ships to reach Bristol's port. They sometimes waited for a month for a strong enough wind to carry them up the Avon.[5] When transatlantic steamships arrived in the mid-nineteenth century, Bristol was just too far from the ocean; and Liverpool increasingly took over its sea traffic.

Bristol Harbour in decline, 1890. A collier stranded at low tide. Bristol Cathedral is on the hill to the right.

Things got worse for Bristol with the end of the slave trade in 1807; a noble moment in British history, certainly, but it didn't do much good for the balance sheet of Bristol's port, largely built on slave-trading money. In 1809, Bristol had a floating harbour installed – eighty acres of tidal river were enclosed, at a cost of £600,000, allowing ships to remain constantly afloat – but it still wasn't enough to match Liverpool's growth. With the arrival of Liverpool's deepwater port, along with the Bridgewater Canal and subsequent north-western canals, Bristol lost even more Atlantic trade.

By the early nineteenth century, the trading fortunes of Birmingham and Manchester had eclipsed Bristol's. The collapse of Bristol's port trade was deepened by the 1908 expansion of the Avonmouth Docks at the mouth of the River Avon, which could accommodate much bigger ships. The city docks finally closed in 1973.

You can diagnose industrial rise and decline in the civic monuments of the various cities. Birmingham and Manchester are largely nineteenth-century metropolises, their town halls and civic buildings planned on a vast scale; in a mixture of Gothic Revival, like Manchester's Town Hall, built in 1877 by Alfred Waterhouse, and high classical, like Birmingham's 1834 Town Hall, a gigantic, delicate Greek temple.

Bristol's architectural treasures date from its eighteenth-century golden days – and preceding centuries, right back to the discovery of America – before it lost out to the north. Its golden years are reflected in the name of the streets: Washington Breach, Newfoundland Lane and Jamaica Street, recalling the profits made from shipping slaves to the West Indies, and bringing tobacco and sugar back to Bristol.

The best of Bristol's terraces, particularly in Clifton, are late eighteenth century, before the financial collapse of 1793 brought on by the Napoleonic Wars. Credit was withdrawn and Bristol, on the cusp of a building boom, suffered badly. More than sixty builders and developers went out of business. The recession lingered on as late as 1828, when a cash-strapped developer applied to the Merchant Venturers, the entrepreneurial society that ran much of Bristol, for a licence to build much smaller houses on Cornwallis Crescent, in Clifton.[6]

Bristol's industrial decline in the early nineteenth century came early enough for it to diversify. In 1934, despite the recent depression, J. B. Priestley described Bristol's recovery:

> [The city had achieved] a new prosperity, by selling us Gold Flake and Fry's chocolate and soap and clothes and a hundred other things. And the smoke from a million gold flakes solidifies into a new Gothic Tower for the university; and the chocolate melts away, only to leave behind it all the fine big shops down Park Street, the pleasant villas out at Clifton, and an occasional glass of Harvey's Bristol Milk for nearly everybody.[7]

When the modern industrial recession came in the second half of the last century, Bristol was better insulated than the colossal cities built on the back of the Victorian industrial boom. Because Bristol's docks began their steep decline much earlier, the city wasn't as badly affected as London and Liverpool by the British dock collapse of the 1960s and 1970s.

Since 1648, Liverpool had traded in slaves, cotton, tobacco and sugar. Through the seventeenth and eighteenth centuries, its trade with the West Indies and Virginia flourished. But Liverpool's really golden days were that much later, in the nineteenth and early twentieth centuries, when it became Britain's greatest Atlantic port: its docks received the bulk of American cotton for the Lancashire mills; in the 1840s, Liverpool began to develop its Atlantic liner business. The city's population was 118,972 in 1821; 286,487 by 1841.

The fortunes of British docks weren't helped by container

ships, which first arrived in 1963. Thanks to containerization, companies could pre-pack goods in identical containers, which were then rolled on and off ships at both ends by lorries.

Gone were the days of dockers loading, say, 200,000 individual items on to a single small ship; thousands of dockers were left with nothing to do. These days, 27 million tons of containerized trade, 40 per cent of all British seaborne imports, arrives through a single dock, Felixstowe, every year.

Recessions struck the Midlands and the north from the 1930s onwards. By 1933, half of Lancashire's prewar cotton trade had disappeared. Blackburn became known as Dole Town. In the late 1960s, British steel production began its decline, due to cheap foreign imports, with the national steel workforce collapsing to 16,000. By the time the Redcar furnace closed in February 2010, steel-making in Britain had shrunk to a small hub of works in Scunthorpe, Newport and Port Talbot.

In the 1980–82 recession, the West Midlands were hit much harder than anywhere else by the contraction in manufacture. Unemployment in Birmingham rose from 7 per cent in 1979 to 20 per cent in 1982.

This succession of body blows over half a century exacerbated the divide between north and south; one that survives today, even with the recovery of many northern cities.

New factories, in the genuine mass-production sense of the word, are rare but not unfindable. The JCB factory in Rocester, Staffordshire, and the Honda car factory in Swindon, Wiltshire, are both built on a grand scale. The 200 ceramics factories in the Potteries in the 1970s have now shrunk to thirty; but several of them, like the Emma Bridgewater factory, founded in 1985, are thriving.

In the old industrial heartland, the north's cityscapes have survived through diversification: the art deco Wills tobacco factory in Newcastle, derelict for a decade after its 1986 closure, is now a chic block of flats. The Wills tobacco factories in Bristol have also been converted into flats, clustered round the Tobacco Factory Theatre.

Post-industrial renaissance – Sir Titus Salt's textile mill on the banks of the River Aire, built near Shipley, West Yorkshire, in 1851. The mill now houses companies, shops, restaurants and a David Hockney gallery.

Small-scale workshops are more the order of the day now, even if they are sometimes housed in old factories, like those in the old Bryant and May match factory in Garston, Liverpool. The factory now has a thousand more people, employed in dozens of small businesses, than it did in the original, single-use factory.

Still, for all its recovery, the north remains more dependent on government money and jobs than the south; the state stepped in to fill the gap when the industrial jobs vanished.

Coalition cuts, of roughly 410,000 public-sector jobs and

£81bn of spending, will be felt that much more in the north, which has the highest levels of public-sector jobs in England. In the north-east, around 23 per cent of the workforce are on the public payroll; the figure is 21 per cent in the north-west.

The effects of the Industrial Revolution – and the Industrial Recession – still ripple through the housing sector, too. New housing developments in the north-west fell by 59.1 per cent in 2010, compared to pre-crunch levels. That figure fell by only 29.1 per cent in the south-east. Despite the national housing shortage, in Newcastle in 2011 there were still boarded-up terraces that once belonged to steel, coal and shipbuilding workers. In October 2011, the average house price in the south was more than double that in the north.[8]

Wherever house prices are higher, wherever private-sector employment is higher, and the closer you get to London, the more manicured the countryside is, after generations of cultivation and gentrification.

Political differences also shadow the north–south divide. The 2010 election divided rural Britain in two: largely Labour, SNP and Liberal Democrat north of north Yorkshire, largely Conservative anywhere further south, until you hit Wales and the West Country.[9]

That political division was even represented in the number of street parties held for Prince William's wedding in April 2011. The Local Government Association reported that there were just four party applications in Liverpool, eleven in Newcastle and thirteen in Manchester. In the small borough of Richmond, south-west London, there were forty-four.

The north–south divide is deepened by the London effect – the magnetic power the capital has not just over Britain, but over the world. Before William the Conqueror invaded, London was neither the formal nor informal capital of England. Canterbury was the religious capital, Winchester the secular one. It was only in the eleventh century that London became first the informal capital of England, as the country's biggest, richest city, and then the formal one. As late as 1338, London still had a population of less than 40,000; in the same year, Florence's population was 95,000.

In the last thousand years, London's supremacy over the rest of England – and Europe – has only intensified. London has become a vortex for the young and talented, sucking them away from other English cities; and for immigrants, too, who think of England as London and vice versa. London is now an international city, drawing in the super-rich: more than half the homes sold in London in 2010 worth £1m or more were sold to foreign buyers.[10]

London's economy moves independently of the rest of England. During recessions, London is always first in and first out of a housing downturn, with the regions usually lagging by a year or two. The richest 10 per cent in Britain are more than 100 times richer than the poorest 10 per cent; the richest 10 per cent in London are more than 250 times richer than the poorest 10 per cent. Without London – taking out the richest and the poorest in the country – you end up with a much smaller divide between north and south.

As someone born and brought up in London, I find it harder and harder to find born-and-bred Londoners living in the city – and people are increasingly surprised to hear that I am one of them. I found it just as unusual trying to meet a native New Yorker when I lived in the city five years ago.

But even New York doesn't dominate America, the way London does Britain. In 2011, there were almost as many annual daily trips on the Tube, 1.1 billion, as there are on the entire national overground rail network. Roughly half of all English bus journeys take place in London.

The north–south divide that has split England for a millennium has deepened dramatically over the last eighty years, with the decline of northern industry. Over the last twenty years, the divide has also shifted: these days, it isn't so much between north and south, as between London and Not-London.

11. How Railways Made the English Suburban

Some three or four mile out of town,
(An hour's ride will bring you down),
He fixes on his choice abode,
Not half a furlong from the road:
And so convenient does it lay,
The stages pass it every day:
And then so snug, so mightily pretty,
To have an house so near the city.

Robert Lloyd, *The Cit's Country Box* (1757)

In March 2011, Savills Estate Agency listed the ten most expensive villages in England. They were all in the suburbs of London or Manchester – particularly in the gilt-edged Alderley Edge/Wilmslow/Hale triangle in Cheshire.

The most expensive was East Horsley, Surrey, where 46 houses worth more than a million pounds were sold between 2007 and 2011. The next nine were Cookham, Windsor and Maidenhead (41 million-plus houses); Alderley Edge, Cheshire (36); Chalfont St Peter, Bucks (35); Prestbury, Cheshire (32); Penn, Bucks (24); West Clandon, Surrey (24); Stoke Poges, Bucks (23); Bramley, Surrey (22); and Wonersh, Surrey (21).

Some villages weren't included because they had become almost urban in character, but they had an even greater number of million pounds-plus houses. In Virginia Water, Surrey, there were 125 sales of more than £1m from 2007 to 2011; in Gerrards Cross, Buckinghamshire, 115. The international village – handy for Heathrow, the M4 and good schools – has arrived.

As for international towns, Oxshott, Surrey, won the prize for Britain's most expensive town. Oxshott's 6,000 residents are right at the heart of what Savills calls a wealth corridor – the area enclosed by the A3 and the M25, where large houses rarely go for less than £2m. The corridor is enriched by access to those main roads – meaning the centre of London is reachable in thirty-five minutes.

These gilded suburbs are increasingly geared to the demands of urban professional life. Before the Big Bang hit the City in 1986, reforming Britain's Stock Exchange, the first train of the morning left Haslemere, Surrey, at 7.15 a.m. After the Big Bang, British Rail laid on an extra train, at 6.44 a.m. It now leaves at 5.21 a.m, as laid-back British hours catch up with the merciless regimen of international business.[1]

Surrey and the other Home Counties were originally enriched, not by the roads, but by the arrival of the train in the nineteenth century, when the umbilical railway connection brought the country right into the town. As early as the middle of the nineteenth century, Dickens was calling south-western Essex 'London-over-the-Border', as rural villages like Walthamstow, West Ham and Stratford were drawn into the city by the train. The 1883 Cheap Trains Act made commuting that much more affordable, while the late-nineteenth-century agricultural depression meant suburban house-building became more profitable than farming.

In the Middle Ages, Surrey was so remote that it didn't have a single large medieval church. It was the poorest of the Home Counties; almost entirely rural, its heaths and woodland were nearly impenetrable. It is still England's most thickly wooded county, and a much more diverse county than its image suggests.

Because Surrey's geological strips run from west to east, a five-mile journey, heading south, takes in five different types of landscape. On the northern border with Berkshire and London, clays and sands run down to the Thames, with the Bagshot Sands producing heathy scrubland and the odd hillock. Next come the North Downs, sculpted out of chalk, rising as they march south, reaching 800 feet at their highest, giving distinctive views down to London from the heights of Epsom racecourse. Above the Mole Valley towers Box Hill, with its handsome, swelling concave slopes. Then a chalk ridge, running from London to Winchester, forms the Hog's Back, only 400 yards wide, for ten miles.

East of Dorking come the Upper Greensand layers, leading down to a Gault Clay valley, and ending in southern Surrey – once an industrial area, where the timber was harvested for shipbuilding and ironstone. You can still see the vestiges of industry in the names – Hammer Bottom and Furnace Farm, near Haslemere – in the iron tomb slabs at Crowhurst and in the old hammerponds.

Surrey was treated as the rural, varied county that it is, until around eighty years ago, when the snobbery directed at dreary, gin and Jag, comfortable suburbia got going.

The suburbanization of northern Surrey had begun as early as the end of the seventeenth century, when Daniel Defoe wrote about commuters riding to London every day from the country.

But Defoe also understood how very agricultural Surrey was – and still is – in character. At the same time as writing about early commuters, he could also call Farnham, Surrey, 'the greatest (corn market) in England'.

The first big suburban fortunes were made in the late seventeenth and early eighteenth centuries by financiers and merchants living in Carshalton and Tadworth, both in Surrey, and Mitcham, in Merton (also in Surrey until the creation of

Greater London in 1965). These speculators started a suburban building boom which ended in 1720 with the collapse of the South Sea Bubble.

But that building boom was tiny compared to the changes brought to Surrey by the train. Until 1885, Oxshott was a hamlet of humble pig farmers. Then the trains came, and Oxshott's fortunes – and its buildings – were transformed.

The tide of money coming up the line from Waterloo, and later up the A3, utterly changed the look of the place. There are no listed houses in Oxshott, and only a few Georgian and Victorian houses, reflecting its limited size before the late nineteenth century. For decade after decade, rising property prices brought repeated waves of demolition crews to Oxshott. Mock Tudor 1950s houses, and detached homes from the 1960s, '70s, '80s and '90s, were replaced by neo-Georgian mansions with electronic gates.

Pressure for building space meant Surrey's upmarket suburbs, like St George's Hill, Weybridge, or the Wentworth Estate in Virginia Water, were gradually surrounded by mass boxed housing. Weybridge, once a pretty eighteenth-century hamlet by the Thames, attracted new lower-middle-class residents, thanks to the arrival of the railways in 1850. Another wave of richer commuters came in the 1890s, engulfed in turn in the 1930s by the general sprawl of outer London, as council housing and private developments expanded into Surrey.

A fifth rich layer of development came to Surrey in the 1960s with the creation of small, private developments built in older gardens. These were designed in a modernist style by Eric Lyons of Span Developments; the developers built seventy-three modern estates across the south-east, notably New Ash Green in Kent.

Lyons had worked for Walter Gropius, the German founder of the Bauhaus School, and the Span developments reflect the sharp, angular, avant-garde lines of Bauhaus – set off with traditional English features like stock brick and hung tiles.

It wasn't just housing that migrated to the suburbs, but the whole apparatus of human life, shipped out by the arrival of the train. The migration was accelerated by refugees from the pea-souper fogs that shrouded London during the coal-burning days of the nineteenth and early twentieth centuries.

Schools and universities joined the exodus. Charterhouse School moved from its medieval home in Clerkenwell, in central London, to Godalming, Surrey, in 1872. Royal Holloway College, in Egham, Surrey, was founded as a women's college by the entrepreneur Thomas Holloway in 1879.

Surrey became the land of the mad. A dozen lunatic asylums were set up in Surrey in the nineteenth century. Five were built in Epsom alone, by the London County Council, on the site of the old Horton Estate in the 1890s, along with a colony for epileptics. By the 1900s, a fifth of the population of Epsom were mental patients. Thomas Holloway built the Holloway Sanatorium next door to Royal Holloway College in 1885. Nearby Egham Station was only forty minutes from Waterloo; an insane relation could be conveniently exiled from London, but easily visited in a day trip.

The suburbs became the land of the dead, too. In 1832, Parliament passed a bill allowing private commercial cemeteries to relieve crowding in parish church graveyards. A group of burial grounds, the so-called Magnificent Seven – Highgate, Kensal Green, Norwood, Abney Park, Brompton, Nunhead and Tower Hamlets – were built in a hoop around London in the 1830s and 1840s, to accommodate the dead produced by the biggest metropolis in the world. London's population grew from 1 million in 1800 to 2 million in 1850. Practically all of them were bound to end up underground; the first official cremation in Britain didn't take place until 1885. Even five years later, London still had no crematoria – the one in Woking, Surrey, was the closest to the capital.

To add to the spread of cemeteries, the first publicly funded cemeteries were built in Exeter in the 1850s; and the First and Second World Wars made their own bleakly impressive contributions to the numbers of dead and buried. Again, the railways helped: Brookwood Cemetery, Surrey, had its own railway and special station for mourners. Until recently, Chelsea Pensioners were buried or cremated there.

The suburbanization of the Englishman had begun, as railways hollowed out the population of the city centre and transferred it to the urban fringes. The City of London's population of 123,000 in 1841 shrank to 27,000 in 1901; meanwhile, the Greater London population grew from 959,000 in 1801 to 4,425,000 in 1901.

Across the Home Counties, railways had a revolutionary effect on buildings; not to mention the effect on people's accents, on the diversity of the people, from once-remote towns, they could now marry, and even on the time of day. Railway Time – standardized time across the country – was first applied in Britain by the Great Western Railway in November 1840.

Ever since Robert Stephenson built his Rocket in Newcastle in 1829, the railways had shaped England – not just by creating the suburbs and drawing distant rural areas into the orbit of the great cities; but also in the primary sense of laying thousands of miles of track across the country.

As well as criss-crossing the country with rails, cutting into it, being embanked above it, or carried over it in viaducts, the railways brought prosperity to the towns in their path. York, an ancient city of major importance, swelled with the trains. Gainsborough and Spalding in Lincolnshire and March and Peterborough in Cambridgeshire were all enriched by the railway.

Other towns were almost entirely created by their rail connection. Eastleigh and Crewe were both new railway towns. Surbiton was nicknamed Kingston-on-Railway after it materialized in the 1840s; Woking and Redhill, in neighbouring Surrey, were railway creations, too.

Swindon, Doncaster and Ashford were new rail engineering centres. Swindon's housing stock was massively expanded to accommodate railway navvies. Croydon grew rapidly with the early arrival of the trains in 1839. Wolverton and Bletchley mushroomed as industrial towns because of the railways.

Victorian railway engineers sliced into – and built on – the English countryside on a scale never seen before, unmatched until the motorways arrived a century later. With the Great Western Railway came Brunel's brick Maidenhead Bridge, built in 1839 – then the bridge with the widest arches in the world. In conjunction with steamships, trains also enabled the construction of docks on a vast scale, from the Royal Victoria Dock (1855) to the King George V Dock (1912–21), now the site of City Airport.

Even the steepest inclines of the new railways were so shallow that they led to extremely deep cuttings and high embankments. The engineer for the London–Southampton line, Joseph Locke, insisted on nothing steeper than a gradient of 1 in 250. Robert Stephenson accepted no more than 1 in 330 on his lines, apart from the initial steep rise from Euston to Camden coming out of London.

Brunel was a perfectionist – nothing more than 1 in 660 for him. His Great Western Railway viaducts and embankments not only changed the Bath cityscape but also scorched into the English mind the first view of that city from the railways: the Rome of the West Country, sprawling across the hill above the cathedral.

The new railways didn't just connect city with city; they also created whole new areas of Victorian cities, as the London and Birmingham Railway did when it carved through Camden Town in 1836.

> The old by-streets now swarmed with passengers and vehicles of every kind; the new streets that had stopped disheartened in the mud and wagon-ruts, formed towns within themselves, originating wholesome comforts and conveniences belonging to themselves, and never tried nor thought of until they sprung into existence. Bridges that had led to nothing, led to villas, gardens, churches, healthy public walks. The carcasses of houses, and beginnings of new thoroughfares, had started off upon the line at steam's own speed, and shot away into the country in a monster train.
>
> Charles Dickens, *Dombey and Son* (1848)

Large parts of London were reshaped around the new termini, with wide, straight approach roads laid towards them, and Tube lines dug in a rough circle to connect the stations.

While generally enriching any town they passed through, the railways also spread poverty around the termini. The pattern continues today. Look at the immediate environs of, say, King's Cross or Paddington – seedy, low-rent areas, rich in drug addicts and prostitutes, while, just beyond their purlieus, the super-rich have colonized mile upon mile of terrace, in Islington and Bloomsbury, in Notting Hill and Lancaster Gate.

This isn't an exclusively English phenomenon, as you'll see if you take the Eurostar to the run-down doughnut of land around the Gare du Nord, in Paris, or the windswept concrete apron around Rome's Termini station.

The pauperization is in stark contrast to the railway buildings themselves, often among the grandest, most expensive buildings in the city. St Pancras train shed, which shares its beggar and junkie population with King's Cross and Euston, was, along

with the adjoining Midland Grand Hotel, the greatest monument to the Victorian age when it was built in 1874 by Sir George
Gilbert Scott. The recently restored roof of W. H. Barlow's
train shed at St Pancras had the biggest span in the world when
it went up in 1868. The sky-blue roof colour was suggested by
Gilbert Scott – the first person to use the expression 'sky-blue',
incidentally.

But it doesn't matter how gold-plated your railway station is;
it's still a railway station. And a main railway station is the place
where poor immigrants arrive in a city; a place which they often
have no reason to move beyond.

Much of the large Irish population of Camden and Islington
is descended from the first immigrants who arrived on the boat
train to Euston from the Dublin–Holyhead line. Others are
descendants of the navvies who built that, and other railway
lines, in the nineteenth century. The same goes for the Gare du
Nord in Paris, its environs now taken over, in a minor exercise
in reverse colonization, by exiles from France's old North African colonies.

Throw in the fact that stations open late, are heated, and have
a wide selection of food shops and off-licences, and they become
a vagrant's paradise. Add in an ever-renewed supply of clueless
tourists with generous quantities of local currency strapped to
their waists, and it's no surprise that the poorest bees make their
way to the most easily raided honeypots.

The railways also changed England's industrial landscape by
killing off the canals, even if they took almost a century and a
half to do it. The last industrial canal contract – for a jam factory
on the outskirts of London – came to an end in 1971. It was the
final act in a long, slow decline. Canals began closing in the
1920s and '30s, with dozens more shutting down in the 1950s
and '60s.

It was a sad, ignominious end to the precursor to the train and the motorway, a form of commercial transport that had shaped England since the Romans. They dug the first English canals: the Itchen Dyke from Winchester to the Itchen, the Foss Dyke joining the River Witham to the River Trent, and Car Dyke from Peterborough to Lincoln.

In 1760, the Bridgewater Canal, excavated by the Duke of Bridgewater to carry coal from his Worsley mine to Manchester, was the first modern canal not to follow an existing watercourse in Britain – itself the first country to build a national canal network.

Canals thrived from the 1760s until the 1820s, with the trains beating them into submission from the 1830s onwards; although the Manchester Ship Canal, completed in 1894, allowed Manchester to become England's third port, after London and Liverpool.

Trade dictated their path – copper was transported along the canals in Tavistock, Devon; pottery on the Mersey and Trent canals; and coal in Manchester and Merseyside. In 1766, the Grand Trunk Canal was begun, connecting Stoke-on-Trent with the Mersey and the Trent, taking Josiah Wedgwood's porcelain from his Etruria works in Stoke to Liverpool and Hull and across the world.

Before the advent of canals, the price of these commodities – coal in particular – was largely due to the cost of transport; during heavy rains, when the roads were damaged, coal doubled in price. Canals slashed costs. A horse could drag 400 times more on a boat than in a wagon. Now, unless the canals froze, which rarely happened, the waterways remained constantly open.

Each canal had its own identity – the Grand Union was lined with pollarded willows and Lombardy poplars; classical lodges were built on the Gloucester and Sharpness Canal. They all shared a pleasing, winding aspect, necessary to avoid any hills that lay in their way.

Just like the railways, the canals enlarged the towns they passed through: Stourport, in Worcestershire, was created at the meeting between the Staffordshire and Worcestershire Canal and the River Severn; the town declined, too, with the eclipse of the canals.

Again like the railways, they left their engineering mark on the country – seventy canal aqueducts survive in Britain. The first significant aqueducts were built by the Duke of Bridgewater: one for his colliery at Worsley; with another, erected in 1761, to take the Bridgewater Canal over the River Irwell at Barton upon Irwell. A 1776 extension of the Bridgewater Canal meant raw cotton could be transported to Manchester by water. By the end of the century, cotton-weaving and trading had replaced wool as Manchester's staple business.

Canals moved building materials from their natural home – the Bath Stone used to build much of Devizes, Wiltshire, was floated up the Kennet and Avon Canal. Local tiles covered most British roofs until 1765, when canals allowed for the easy and cheap transport of lightweight Welsh slate from Lord Penrhyn's Caernarvonshire quarries; by 1800, he was sending 12,000 tons a year to London. Cornish and Cumbrian slates, too, were transported across the country to roof new houses.

Trains made the transport of building materials across England even easier. That golden-yellow Bath stone became increasingly popular in the mid-nineteenth century, much of it excavated in building the railway tunnel at Corsham, near Bath. The spread of this one big batch of stone across England put many Victorian limestone quarrymen out of work.[2]

When the trains arrived in Berkshire in 1840, they brought urban wealth and beauty right into the rural property market. An early commuter belt mansion, such as mock-Tudor Aldermaston

Court, Berkshire, was built in 1851 by Philip Hardwick, for the enormous sum of £20,000.

Gerrards Cross and the Chalfonts, in Buckinghamshire – although later preserved in virgin countryside by the Green Belt – became a sort of outer Outer London because of the railway, which reached Gerrards Cross in 1906. Harrods vans would travel from Kensington as far as Gerrards Cross and no further.

The suburbs were brought even closer to London by the Tube. The Metropolitan Line, from Paddington to Farringdon Street, was the first underground line in the world in 1863. When it was extended out into the suburbs, to Aylesbury via Amersham, in 1892, it coincided with the building of England's last main line, the Great Central. Cross-country travel had yielded to suburban and inner-city commuting.

Alongside these new rural stations, the Metropolitan Railway Company developed its own slice of suburbia. So-called Metroland was carved out of old family landholdings, like the Vache estate at Chalfont St Giles, and Amersham's Weller estate. Metroland houses tended towards a retro country cottage look, with tiled and gabled roofs, latticed windows, and plastered or half-timbered fronts.

Connection to the Metropolitan Line brought prosperity to the suburbs; as it still does. In March 2011, Chorleywood, Hertfordshire, was found to be the least deprived town in England. Large four-bedroom houses go for more than £1.2m. It helps that it has its own helipad and exit on the M25, at junction 18. Described by John Betjeman as 'essential Metroland', Chorleywood has been a commuter village – now with a population of 9,000 – ever since the Metropolitan Railway opened a station there in 1889.

The Tube was a crucial network for connecting the town centre with its outskirts, because the railway rarely penetrated into the heart of London. Overground trains were kept out of central London by an 1846 parliamentary commission, which ruled that surface railways shouldn't enter the city centre. (This was slightly modified in 1860, when railways started crossing the Thames from the south.) Because of that parliamentary ruling, the main termini are placed in a ring around the centre of London, all connected by the Circle Line.

A nearby Tube station became vital for mass-market commercial ventures. When Herbert Chapman took over as Arsenal manager in 1925, he was determined to change the name of the nearby Tube station, Gillespie Road, to that of the club. He realized how vital the Tube was to making Arsenal one of the biggest clubs in the world. He got his way and, in 1932, Gillespie Road changed its name to Arsenal. They went on to win the First Division title in 1933, 1934 and 1935.

The migration of London to the Home Counties through the nineteenth century led to worries that they would be completely swallowed up by London. In 1938, those worries produced the Green Belt, the buffer of country between city and suburb which survives today. Further green belts were imposed after the Town and Country Planning Act of 1947: there are now fourteen of them, covering 13 per cent of the country.

After 1951, varying densities of development were prescribed in concentric circles around central London. There were to be 200 people per acre in central areas, and 136 people per acre on the further-flung rings; with the Green Belt sealing the outer layer.

This careful calibration of distance from central London is logically reflected in decreasing house prices, which drop by 60 per cent, compared with city centre figures, if you live an hour's train journey from the capital.[3] The commuters' rush to the suburbs became a stampede with the Rent Act of 1957. The Conservative Government envisaged that removing statutory restrictions on the rent of privately let accommodation – in place since the First World War – would encourage landlords to maintain and invest in privately rented properties.

Housing supply duly increased, as the Government intended; but so did rents. Flats in South Kensington that had been rented out for £150 per annum rocketed to £500; the less well-off middle classes rushed to the suburbs, and the rich parts of London became even richer ghettos.

Proximity to London has always brought in money. Buckinghamshire has an exceptional collection of eighteenth- and nineteenth-century country houses, built for nouveaux and anciens riches alike: such as the eighteenth-century palaces of Stowe and Middle Claydon, and the necklace of Victorian houses strung across the Vale of Aylesbury by the Rothschilds.

Being close to London also meant few of those houses were ever knocked down for lack of commercial demand. If their owners sold up, in moved offices and training colleges, like Hedsor House and Denham Place, or hotels like Cliveden and Hartwell House, or schools like Wycombe Abbey (all in Buckinghamshire).

One reason why there are so many great Elizabethan and Jacobean houses in Hertfordshire is that they are only a day's ride from the city. Often, like Little Wymondley and Sopwell, they were built after the dissolution of the monasteries by civil servants and courtiers on the site of monastic abbeys.

For the same reason, closeness to London, Hertfordshire was home to the first two garden cities, Letchworth and Welwyn Garden City. They were founded in 1903 and 1920 respectively, pioneers in Sir Ebenezer Howard's campaign to build new developments in virgin countryside, rather than adding to the urban sprawl building up around long-standing cities, London in particular.

The garden city may not fit in with the clichéd analysis of Englishness – as the spiritual home of old rural buildings, of the ancient castle and the country house. But, in fact, we are now a largely urban and suburban race, and around 40 per cent of us live in houses built since 1965.

Between 1958 and 2011, 300,000 Barratt Homes were built – more than one in seventy of all homes in England and Wales. Richard Seifert's architectural practice, founded in 1947, and responsible for Centre Point and the NatWest Tower, put up more buildings in London than Christopher Wren ever did.[4]

English eyes tend to settle on the old and hallowed, on the rare gems built by architects like Wren, editing out the great waves of twentieth-century buildings across the country. They also censor the garden city, a revolutionary English urban movement that influenced new towns from Finland to Virginia, from Hong Kong to Germany.

Horrified by the squalor and chaos of Victorian city slums, Howard envisaged utopian cities where people would live in harmony with nature. He realized that cities were ideal for social opportunity, amusement and high wages. But he also could see no reason why those advantages shouldn't be combined with the joys of the country: the beauty of nature, fresh air, and an abundance of water, woods and meadows.

That was the thinking behind Letchworth, thirty-four miles outside London. He succeeded where Wren failed, in building a geometrically planned city. With the architects Barry Parker and Raymond Unwin, Howard turned 3,800 acres of agricultural land into a city strung along radial boulevards, with a high proportion of parks and open spaces. To maintain the greenness of the garden cities, Howard stipulated an extremely low population density of twenty-five houses per acre.

Garden cities should be of limited size, Howard said, wrapped in a green belt of countryside, with a careful combination of factories, shops and homes.

The idea was that the new cities shouldn't be commuter towns but would provide employment themselves, with workers walking to factories through gardens and parks threaded along the streets, enjoying the country right outside their front door. With the expansion of commuter life over the last century, and the growing domination of London, that part of Howard's vision has not been realized – Letchworth and Welwyn Garden City have largely become dormitory towns for the capital.

There was to be no government interference in the building of the garden cities, either. The land, owned by trustees, was leased to the citizens, who then managed the town themselves; within a decade, Letchworth was self-supporting.

Not everyone approved of the new cities. H. G. Wells said, 'A girdle of factories between house and country would not be so agreeable a prospect as it is to Mr Howard. Why help dot the countryside for sixty miles round London on every side with detestable little factory chimneys, each with its group of blighted homes about it?'

Wells was writing in the *Daily Mail*[5] – whose founder, Lord Northcliffe, provided £1,000 of seed capital for Letchworth, offering the garden cities company free advertising space in the *Mail*'s pages. The garden cities even became known as the Daily Mail Towns in the 1920s.

Wells's attack was typical of the sophisticated intellectual's horror at the popular English taste for old-fashioned-looking, comfortable, suburban homes. That didn't stop the new residents of the garden cities loving their supposedly blighted homes. They moved in their thousands from London, drawn by

Tube posters offering an urban-rural, sporting life less than an hour from Piccadilly.

The new houses were built on a larger scale than their tiny London homes, too, at the maximum size allowed under contemporary legislation. If anything, people liked the garden cities too much. Aimed in part at working-class residents, the developments were so sought after that they became predominantly middle-class enclaves.

Like Metroland houses, garden cities were built in an old-fashioned, ultra-English style. Letchworth Railway Station had mullioned and leaded windows, and a timber roof. The post office was housed in a handsome, Jacobean-style building; the bank was built according to traditional classical principles. Residents lived in neo-Georgian houses and mock-Tudor cottages with dormer windows and red-tiled roofs.

The gently curving streets were lined with trees, including cherry trees planted by Howard himself. His high-minded vision went a little too far only in the Skittles Inn in Letchworth. The pretty gabled pub with double verandahs had only one drawback for a quintessentially English group of home-owners – it served no alcohol. It lasted eighteen years before becoming an adult education centre.

For all the success of Letchworth and Welwyn, no more garden cities were built, but they had a major influence on the thirty New Towns built after the Second World War. Three out of the seven satellite postwar new towns are also in Hertfordshire – Stevenage, the first, built in 1946, followed by Hatfield New Town and Hemel Hempstead. The others near London were Crawley, Sussex, and Basildon and Harlow, both in Essex.

Milton Keynes, Buckinghamshire, founded in 1967, was not so much a new town as a new city, swallowing up three towns, sixteen villages and hundreds of acres of farmland. It was part of the third generation of new towns, including an expanded Swindon, Northampton and Peterborough, and Telford in the West Midlands.

The garden city idea took root across the world more successfully than it did over here – a rare example of England being a net exporter of an architectural style, rather than the importer it was, through the Gothic Middle Ages and the nineteenth century, and in the classical seventeenth and eighteenth centuries.

Germany created its first garden city, Hellerau, in 1909. Walt Disney acknowledged a debt to the movement in his EPCOT development – the Experimental Prototype Community of Tomorrow – in Orlando, Florida. There are descendants of the English garden city right across America: in Boston, Newport, Pittsburgh, New Jersey, Maryland, New Orleans, Tennessee, Los Angeles and Ohio.

The movement spread north into Canada and south into Argentina, too. Canberra, Adelaide and Melbourne all have garden city elements in their suburbs. India, Vietnam, Bhutan, Israel, Morocco, the Philippines . . . Sir Ebenezer Howard's tentacles extend around the globe.

Foreign planning students come to England to look chiefly at three eclectic urban developments: Bath, Regent's Park in London, and the garden cities.[6]

These developments are typically, and uniquely, English: varied, idiosyncratic, small-scale, urban domestications of grand prototypes.

The same adjectives apply to the greatest innovation of British architectural history – the terraced house, drawn from the grand sixteenth-century rural villas and urban palazzi of Palladio, stripped down to their bare essentials, and repeated on a mass scale across Britain. The Italian-inspired terraced house remains the most popular type of English home.[7] It isn't surprising that the two most popular soap operas on British television are set in terraces: a Victorian terraced square in *EastEnders*, an Edwardian terrace in *Coronation Street*.

Those same high-English characteristics apply to the eighteenth-century invention of the circus and the crescent in Bath, by the two John Woods, the architects who built much of the city. The accumulation of a series of terraced houses to produce a coherent single Palladian palace front – carried out particularly in London, Bath and Bristol from the early eighteenth century onwards – fits the pattern, too.

John Nash pulled off the effect repeatedly in his Regent's Park terraces. Throughout the scheme, apparent grandness disguised small-scale, domesticated usefulness. In 1824, on the edge of the park, in Park Village East, Nash built the first semi-detached houses in England – disguising two small houses within the unified skin of a single, grander, classical villa.

The triumphal arch of the Emperor Titus, built in the Roman Forum in AD 82, provided the inspiration for the entrance to Nash's Chester Terrace, also in Regent's Park. Again, a grand prototype was domesticated, and reduced to a usable, human scale. The central arch over the road was used by carriages, with the smaller side arches over the flanking pavements reserved for pedestrians.

Paris's Arc de Triomphe had the same Roman inspiration, but it was never meant for such humble, everyday use. Built from 1806 to 1836, the biggest triumphal arch in the world stayed in line with its ancient prototype as a hallowed military memorial, in this case to the dead of the Revolution and the Napoleonic Wars.

The English may be deft at refashioning grandness on an urban and suburban domestic scale; but, in our peculiar, self-loathing way, we're not too good at patting ourselves on the

English domestication of grand designs – John Nash's Chester Terrace, Regent's Park, London, built in 1825. The terrace is disguised to look like one grand palace. The Roman triumphal arch, on the far left, is adapted for pedestrians.

back for it. The new indeterminate land of suburbia – neither city nor country, but on the fringes of both – excited a virulent snobbery in those used to the old certainties, in the same way that H. G. Wells attacked the new garden cities.

G. K. Chesterton called Surrey 'the debatable land between London and England. It is not a county but a border; it is there that South London meets and makes war on Sussex.' The pretty Surrey hills, thick with bracken, covered with pines, were criticized by George Bernard Shaw for being 'pretty-pretty, playing at mountains', as if the cynical hills had conspired to pull off this confidence trick.

A constant thread ran through these criticisms – that these suburban developments not only looked miserable, but must make their residents' lives miserable, too. Even George Orwell, who praised the classlessness of the new suburbs, recoiled at the restless, cultureless life they apparently fostered.

The snobbery continues into the modern age, deepening the metaphorical connection between suburban values and a safe, twee, chintzy dullness. Jonathan Miller applied the equation to Margaret Thatcher, talking of her 'odious, suburban gentility and sentimental, saccharine patriotism, catering to the worst elements of commuter idiocy'.[8]

Elsewhere across Europe, the English suburban house was much admired. At the turn of the century, Hermann Muthesius, cultural attaché at the German Embassy in London, wrote an influential book, *Das englische Haus*, singing the praises of the suburban home.[9]

Muthesius was impressed that the English lived mostly in houses, not flats, unlike his compatriots. He was impressed, too, by the English use of the corridor, as opposed to the inter-connecting rooms of Continental homes. Rooms leading off a corridor provided more privacy than those strung in an enfilade, where each room became a passage to another. As a result, the English didn't suffer from *Schwellenangst* – the threshold anxiety that struck Germans on repeatedly moving through one room to get into another. (At the same time, though, it must be acknowledged that corridors and halls do take up an enormous amount of space, leading to even smaller rooms.)

Muthesius particularly praised the neo-vernacular taste of the English suburbs: the detached houses with their plain facades, sash windows and tidy front gardens, testament to the English desire for cosiness, home ownership and the ownership of your own plot of land.

'The Englishman,' Muthesius wrote, 'sees the whole of life embodied in his house. Here in the heart of his family, self-sufficient and feeling no great urge for sociability, pursuing his own interests in virtual isolation, he finds his happiness and his real spiritual comfort.'

Our own anti-suburban snobbery seems particularly odd, given that our packed island is now, for most of us, a suburban island – 84 per cent of us live in the suburbs. And that doesn't just mean in the suburbs of the big cities. In rural England, too, people cleave to the suburbs – over a quarter of the population of Norfolk live within eight miles of Norwich Castle.

Even the Queen thinks of herself as living in suburbia, if a touch ironically. In 1981, her cousin, the Hon. Margaret Rhodes, living in Devon, was looking after her husband, who had cancer and needed to be close to a London hospital.

'I was up at Balmoral and we were riding on the hill ponies,' said Mrs Rhodes. 'She turned round in the saddle and said, "How would you like to live in suburbia?"'[10]

The Rhodeses soon moved to the Garden House in Windsor Great Park, just down the road from one of suburbia's leading castles.

Contrary to what Jonathan Miller and George Orwell might think, we also happen to like living in the suburbs. In the last decade, people have begun to like living even more in the exurbs – small, safe towns separated from big towns by thin strips of countryside. People like shopping, too, in exurban shopping centres like Lakeside and Bluewater – self-contained malls, with cheap, convenient parking and easy motorway access, far from the overpriced, traffic-clogged streets of the Victorian city centres. The exurban office is conveniently close, too, as companies flee high city centre rents.

The suburb and exurb are immensely adaptable housing patterns, ranging from enormous working-class suburbs like Becontree, Essex, to grander ones like St George's Hill in Weybridge, Wentworth in Virginia Water, or Winchmore Hill in Enfield.

Those supposedly dreary, conformist, suburban Home Counties have often been the most surprisingly avant-garde parts of the country. At the turn of the twentieth century, Surrey led the world in grand modern living, with houses by distinguished architects such as M. H. Baillie Scott, Sir Robert Lorimer, Sir Edwin Lutyens and Sir Mervyn Macartney.

In 1936, Walter Gropius, the German architect who created Bauhaus and the International Modernist style in Germany in 1925, built a large, ultra-modernist lab for Alexander Korda's film studios at Denham, Buckinghamshire. Also in Buckinghamshire in 1936, his fellow modernist, Berthold Lubetkin, built himself a dacha at Dagnall.

The first welded steel-frame building in Britain was erected in 1935, in sleepy, supposedly conventional Bexhill-on-Sea, east Sussex. The De La Warr pavilion was designed by Serge Chermayeff and Erich Mendelsohn in International Modernist style, for the socialist peer Earl De La Warr, who wanted a 'People's Palace' for Bexhill residents.

Far from being the sterile, uniform places loathed by fashionable writers, the suburbs provided the freedom and individuality never before available to millions of Englishmen. That freedom came most powerfully through the right to buy council houses – introduced by 'odious, suburban' Margaret Thatcher in 1980, leading to a million council tenants buying their property in the first year alone.

Owning your house allows you to decorate it as you wish – as you can see in the biggest housing development in the world, the 1921–32 Becontree estate in Essex, a beacon 'Homes Fit for Heroes' post-First World War development by the London County Council, aimed at refugees from the East End slum clearances.

Becontree is home to 100,000 people, mostly Londoners and descendants of Londoners, who once depended for work on the

Ford factory at Dagenham, opened in October 1931. Nicknamed Fordsville, it was the biggest car-manufacturing plant in Europe, with its own coke ovens, gas plant, foundry, power station, dedicated railway and private wharf on the Thames. Eleven million cars were built there, most of them by workers from the Becontree estate.

The 24,000 houses on the estate, spread over 3,000 acres, were built, again, in that high-English vernacular style: with cottages in a mixture of brick, tile and weatherboards, with bow windows, pantiles, and a few Fred and Ginger Hollywood art deco touches. They had inside lavatories, too, and satisfied the English desire for a plot of land, with front and back gardens.

This vast estate, alongside the 300-acre Ford Motor Works, once made for the ideal combination of well-paid industrial work and decent social housing. Then came the sad, familiar story of industrial decline. Car production stopped in 2002, leaving Dagenham with a shell business producing gearboxes and diesel engines. A 50,000-strong workforce shrank to 2,000. With the collapse of the factory, Becontree had the stuffing knocked out of it.

Despite these heavy blows, half the terraced houses in Becontree have been bought from the council over the last three decades. And you can see where the Becontree council houses have been privately bought. As Aristotle said, that which no one owns, no one will care for; and the privately owned homes are in better condition. The new owners have customized them, too, with bright white pointing, leaded, diamond-paned windows and house name-plates fixed to the wall next to the front door.

For all the industrial decline of Becontree, people still like living there; they certainly like it enough to want to buy their council houses and stay there, rather than flee. It was just fashionable commentators, and fashionable architects, who didn't like the look of the new suburban houses. The architects were annoyed that they were barely involved in the construction of the suburbs, built to architect-free, boilerplate plans, with hints of Jacobethan, mock Tudor, and Arts and Crafts.

The architects wanted to build high-rise, modernist blocks, free of the supposed affectation of historic style – which happens to be extremely popular among the English public. And popular taste will out. As those high-rise blocks have fallen to the wrecking ball, the suburbs have survived intact because their inhabitants like living in them, whatever their critics might say.

Those critics particularly loathed the mock-Tudor style – a style which remains popular. It is still associated with English-ness across the world, and much imitated, too. From Beverly Hills to Shanghai, a mock-Tudor gable is shorthand for English-ness.

The popularity of mock Tudor was helped by several associations: with the sixteenth-century triumph of Protestantism; with Elizabeth I's military success; and with the supposed high Britishness of Tudor monarchs, as opposed to the French kings who came before and the Dutch and Germans who followed.

Tudor literary associations helped the architectural style, too. As early as 1769, David Garrick was promoting a Shakespeare festival in Stratford, glorifying his Tudor birthplace; a replica of Shakespeare's home was built for the 1851 Great Exhibition.

Many of these associations are fairly mythical. The name 'Tudor' wasn't even associated with the ruling dynasty until 1757, when David Hume wrote *The History of England under the House of Tudor*. Later architectural reincarnations of Tudor buildings were equally suspect. That familiar black and white look is almost certainly a nineteenth-century version of what the houses were really like.

Much-mocked Tudor, accompanied by crazy paving and Islamic keyhole doorways. Cartoon by Osbert Lancaster.

Surviving buildings suggest the walls were originally covered with daub, a sort of clay, leaving them looking like stuccoed masonry; while the oak was left au naturel, to weather to a silvery grey. The best true impression is given in the exposed beams and buff-coloured daub of Shakespeare's birthplace.

The falsifying and cheapening of original Tudor work intensified with each revival: from a craze in the 1830s and 1840s (with concrete often used for the mock-Tudor panels), through Rothschild Tudor in the family's nineteenth-century estate cottages in Buckinghamshire, and late-Victorian workers' cottages in Port Sunlight, Cheshire, to the style's inter-war boom in suburbia. This was what Osbert Lancaster mocked as Stockbrokers' Tudor – the grander version – and Roadhouse Tudor, strung along the

A-roads, with only a single gable and a few nailed-on panels to signify the style.

What the mockers failed to appreciate is that, not only were these homes roomier than Victorian housing, but that people liked a touch of historicism – particularly rural, homely historicism – however light that touch was.

The historicist thread runs strongly through English tastes. Even fashionable English rock stars succumb to the drug of nostalgia. George Harrison lived in an extraordinary Gothic Revival mansion, Friar Park, on the outskirts of Henley: an elaborate chunk of French Flamboyant Gothic, inspired by the châteaux of the Loire. Inside, it's all classical, based on Louis XV and Inigo Jones interiors.

Jimmy Page, of Led Zeppelin, used to live in one of the great ornate Victorian houses of London: the Tower House, Melbury Road, on the western borders of Kensington. Again, this has touches of the French Gothic château; it was designed by William Burges in 1878, the most dazzling, fantastical of nineteenth-century architects, much admired by Evelyn Waugh and John Betjeman.

In another historicist impulse, the English regularly name the bungalow as their favourite sort of home; never the tower block, to the fury of avant-garde sophisticates.[11] The small, single-storey house was adopted from colonial India. The Hindi 'bangla' means Bengali and, thus, a house in the Bengal style.

Bungalows satisfied the English desire for home ownership on a limited budget, combined with that touch of history, and an island taste for things with a seaside flavour: the first British bungalows were built at Westgate-on-Sea and Birchington, both on the Kent coast, in 1869. They soon became popular seaside architecture; not least because they're less likely to block the sea view of the bungalow behind you.

★

Between the wars, the growth of the suburbs, and the housing stock in general, changed the face of Britain. Four million houses were built, three quarters of them private sales. In 1914, only 10 per cent of the 7.75 million British house belonged to owner-occupiers; the rest were owned by private landlords. By 1938, there were 3.75 million owner-occupiers out of 11.75 million households.

Continuing the pattern begun half a century previously by the railways, central London was gradually depopulated while Greater London mushroomed: Sutton and Cheam's population expanded from 29,000 in 1921 to 81,000 in 1951.

Rent control in private houses – with rents regularly frozen at pre-First World War levels – meant private landlords sold 3 million houses to owner-occupiers between the wars.

An increase in easy mortgages – particularly after the 1929 stock market crash, when people transferred their savings into building societies – sparked a boom in private housing estates. Mortgages could be got on a £200 a year wage, with building societies asking for as little as 5 per cent deposits and extending their repayment periods from fifteen to thirty years. The boom was helped by cheap land, energetic developers and government incentives. On old farming land, in the London suburbs, private houses for half a million people were built between 1931 and 1938.

These houses were built on a generous scale: semi-detached or detached, with those much-loved historical touches of Arts and Crafts, neo-Georgian, mock Elizabethan and mock Tudor, set off with archetypal English features: bow windows, often with stained glass in them, pebbledash and strips of timber; dubbed By-Pass Variegated by the *Daily Express* cartoonist Osbert Lancaster. Bow windows were particularly prized for snobbish reasons; they were never fitted on the new council houses.

Council housing also started to spread across the country on a big scale between the wars. The 1890 Housing of the Working Classes Act introduced the first council houses, granting all councils the option to build housing for the inhabitants of the relevant borough. Britain's first council estate, the Boundary Estate, built by the London County Council in the Old Nichol slum in the East End, was opened by the Prince of Wales in 1900.

Not long before, a series of charitable housing trusts had also been set up, among them the General Society for Improving the Dwellings of the Working Classes (1852), the Peabody Trust (1862), Sydney Waterlow's Improved Industrial Dwellings Company (1863), the Octavia Hill housing scheme (1865) and the Guinness Trust (1890).

The First World War really accelerated the council house building programme. The Homes Fit for Heroes election of December 1918 led to the 1919 Housing and Town Planning Act, giving all local authorities the duty to build housing for the poor in their area.

A million council houses were built over the next two decades, mostly in a cheap, stripped-down Georgian style. The two-storey brick cottages, with sash windows and hipped roofs, were planned in groups of fours and sixes. The Second World War brought an even bigger transformation in public housing; with 450,000 houses destroyed by bombing, and another 3 million damaged, a million local authority houses – including 170,000 prefabs – were built by the postwar Attlee Government.

In the new suburbs, both private and council-owned, further variety was introduced by the shape of the streets, which were in fact rarely called streets. They were drives, crescents, avenues and closes, wrapped around shopping parades, packed with new private and public amenities – lidos, libraries, post offices, pubs and the art deco Lyons Corner Houses and Odeons.[12] The first purpose-built cinemas were constructed in 1909; the earliest surviving is the Electric (1910) in Portobello Road. By 1939, the height of their popularity, there were nearly 5,000 cinemas in the country, before the rise of television led to their decline.

That art deco look didn't last long, but it had a powerful effect on that part of England that had expanded so much in the 1930s – the suburbs. Evelyn Waugh described art deco as 'par excellence the style of the arterial high roads, the cinema studios, the face-cream factories, the Tube stations of the farthest suburbs, the radio-ridden villas of the Sussex coast'.[13]

You can hear the sneer in Waugh's voice even now; he sounds much like his alter ego, Gilbert Pinfold, who 'disliked plastics, Picasso, sunbathing, and jazz – everything in fact that had happened in his own lifetime'.

It's striking, though, that every type of art deco construction he chooses to attack was built to improve the convenience and pleasure of human existence. No wonder so many people rushed to live in the inter-war suburbs.

For all Waugh's hatred of modern invention, modern technological advance over the last century has often been remarkably undestructive. The intrusion of air travel into the English landscape remained necessarily unobtrusive, for obvious reasons – the planes don't do much flying on the ground.

All the same, the weird silence over England after the Icelandic volcano, Eyjafjallajökull, grounded air traffic for six days in April 2010 showed how planes dominate our skies. On the ground, 1,700 airfields have been built in Britain over the last century. They range from grass strips to the colossi of Heathrow – once the marshy land around the hamlets of Heath Row and Perry Oaks, bulldozed in 1944 to create the wartime airfield – and Gatwick, previously a Sussex racecourse.

Four hundred and fifty airfields were built during the Second World War – most of them in the south and east, to face the enemy, with a ring of seven RAF fighter stations around

London, including Northolt and Biggin Hill. Around 300 survive. You can still spot the decommissioned ones, reduced to unusually flat, hedgeless, treeless fields. A dilapidated control tower often survives.

Air travel has rocketed over the last half-century. In 1946, Heathrow's first year, 60,000 people passed through London Airport, as it was then called; in 2010, 66 million did.

Even though Heathrow now offers 180 different routes, the actual airport parts of the complex are relatively limited in size, particularly when compared to the shopping parts. When the British Airports Authority was privatized under the Airports Act of 1986, Heathrow became more like a huge shopping centre with 70,000 staff, and a pair of runways thrown in.[14] BAA had worked out a powerful new truth about the English that emerged in the late twentieth century: if forcibly trapped in a confined space for two hours, they are at their happiest when they are allowed to go shopping.

The English shop has changed dramatically over the last twenty years – leading to a revolution in the way England looks.

12. Why England Doesn't Look Like England

> For the first time I feel somehow
> That it isn't going to last,
> That before I snuff it, the whole
> Boiling will be bricked in
> Except for the tourist parts...
> And that will be England gone.

> Philip Larkin, 'Going, Going' (1972)

The man in the white gloves doesn't have his lunch in the King's Arms in Oxford any more. Nineteen years ago, he'd be in there every day – pristine gloves, bottle-green suit, cream waistcoat, watch chain, stick-thin, pencil moustache, blanched complexion, in his late forties, a bit like Dirk Bogarde in *Death in Venice*.

Without fail he'd have the same thing for lunch – the roast of the day, followed by an apple which he'd carefully slice into discs before eating, gloves still on. I never talked to him but I liked the reliability of his odd presence, and I missed him on my return there recently. But, then again, where would he go these days after lunch? He didn't look like a Starbucks man.

Oxford twenty years ago, like so many pretty, provincial towns – Cheltenham, Guildford, Bath – was a perfect setting for the odd, the eccentric and the bohemian. I didn't realize it during my student days, but in 1993 I'd caught the tail end of a process that had been going on for half a century: the genteel decline of Middle England that produced all the right conditions for the down-at-heel yet civilized bohemian.

Those provincial towns long remained much as they'd been since the war – slightly broken-down, a mixture of shabby pubs, second-hand bookshops and antique clothes shops, with a selection of cheap lodgings where your average bohemian could survive, within shambling distance of the town centre.

Architecturally handsome, their medieval and Georgian buildings provided enough amiable places to browse in. The harmless, the talented, the mildly alcoholic, the intelligent yet unemployable eccentrics: they all flocked to the elegantly decayed bits of those towns.

All in all, they were the perfect habitat for people like my friend in the white gloves.

Anthony Powell caught the type in the literary journalist X. Trapnel in *A Dance to the Music of Time*. Based on the writer Julian Maclaren-Ross (1912–64), Trapnel leads a life of unrelenting observance of the bohemian code – heavy drinking, high-minded squalor, debts, philandering, shuttling from boarding house to hotel. Dressed in a pale, ochre-coloured tropical suit and black RAF greatcoat, dark-blue sports shirt, an emerald green tie patterned with naked women, and grey suede brothel-keepers, Trapnel spends the day drifting from pub to pub in Fitzrovia.

He lives near the knuckle, as Powell puts it, surviving on the odd book review. His lodgings are always disgusting – 'peeling wallpaper, bare boards, a smell of damp, cigarette smoke, stale food'.[1]

Classic shabby chic, in other words; and not so heavy on the chic.

What's particularly striking now is where those lodgings were: Holland Park, Camden, a flat in Notting Hill, a bleak spot in Bloomsbury. Today, the list reads like a gazetteer of fashionable, expensive London.

Trapnel finally washes up in Little Venice, now impossibly grand, but then (the book is set just after the war) it 'had not yet

developed into something of a quartier chic. Before the war, the
indigenous population, full of time-honoured landladies, imme-
morial whores, long undisturbed in surrounding premises, had
already begun to give place to young married couples, but
buildings already tumbledown had now been further reduced
by bombing.'

Since X. Trapnel's day, soaring property prices have worked
their way across London, sweeping away the boho-intellectual
world with it. In March 2011, George Orwell's once run-down
house in Gloucester Road, South Kensington – a 1,903-square-
foot, Georgian semi-detached house – sold for £2.2m, way
beyond the pocket of the modern journalist or author.

The X. Trapnels have long since fled these bits of London, all
now pure banker/lawyer territory. Their old haunts, in the *haut*
bohemia of Soho, are also collapsing. The Colony Room Club,
second home to Dylan Thomas, Francis Bacon and Jeffrey Bernard, closed in 2008, shortly after celebrating its sixtieth
birthday. The Coach and Horses has lost much of its allure since
its rude, popular landlord, Norman Balon, saw out his licence in
May 2006; the French House is now packed with binge drinkers
and tourists.

And the X. Trapnels don't gather in provincial bohemia any
more, either. The very rich, who also like pretty buildings, have
taken their place. Hedge fund managers live in the sprawling
north Oxford houses once owned by penniless dons. Russian
oligarchs fly in by helicopter to their children's sports days at
nearby prep schools.

In the cold, clear light of the credit crunch, it's easier to take
stock of the vast tide of money that rushed through these places
over the past two decades. The invasion of the chain shops is
well documented. But what's remarkable is just how saturated
these once odd, quirky towns now are with them, and quite
how chi-chi these particular chain shops are.

There's a Farrow & Ball paint shop in what was the rough part of Bath. Seaside towns – which became artistic colonies and, by extension, bohemian boltholes because of their beauty and cheapness – have been cleaned up and turned into kitsch versions of themselves.

Even with depressed property prices, no penniless artist could now afford to live in Newlyn near Penzance, home to the Newlyn School of painters in the late nineteenth century, or St Ives, also in Cornwall, colonized from the 1920s onwards by the potter Bernard Leach and the painter Ben Nicholson. These towns are now the victims of their bohemian fame, the haunts of weekending professionals who like to take in those artists' works at Tate St Ives.

Jamie Oliver has opened up one of his Italian restaurants in dingy George Street in Oxford. The area hasn't been as grand as this since the mid-1920s, when the undergraduate John Betjeman frequented the ultra-chic restaurant named after the street. There he spent 'evenings dining with the Georgeoisie. Open, swing doors, upon the lighted "George" and whiff of vol-au-vent! Behold Harold Acton and the punkahs wave: "My dears, I want to rush into the fields and slap raw meat with lilies."'

Anything a little downmarket, dusty or cheap can't survive in the shade of the onslaught of the glossy, the new and expensive. The majestic, rambling second-hand Oxford bookshop opposite Balliol College didn't stand a chance against the tide of new money. A boutique hedge fund has set up shop on the premises instead.

The old bookshop lingers on, in much reduced circumstances, with smaller premises, in a less fashionable part of the town. The same goes for the book warehouses on the edge of town by the railway station – a once scrubby bit of land, now home to the Business School, a gleaming limestone ziggurat with a green and yellow glass spire, built with £23m from its billionaire benefactor, Wafic Said.

I don't have anything against Mr Saïd – in fact his ziggurat is attractive. It's just that the city has changed. In a recent evening spent at an Anglo-German conference in Lincoln College, I met several students from the Business School. One was at the university's Environmental Change Institute; another doing a doctorate on Vladimir Putin and the possibility that he was setting up a gas cartel along the lines of OPEC.

All this is very up to date and, perhaps, useful. But somewhere along the line, education for education's sake – a bit of theology, a bit of Greek, anything at all that's a little interesting and a little useless, a little bohemian, in fact – seems to have gone by the wayside, along with the dusty bookshops and their broken customers.

Even Oxford Prison, a tremendously gloomy nineteenth-century job straight out of *Porridge* – it was in fact the prison used to house Noël Coward's Mr Bridger in *The Italian Job* – has become a hotel.

English beauty was traditionally an under-designed, accidental beauty – like the beauty of the classic English field gate, which happens to have the same aspect ratio (the proportion of a rectangle's shorter dimension to its longer one) as 35mm film, old-fashioned televisions and human vision.[2]

That accidental beauty is increasingly being regulated out of existence. In 2010, Herefordshire Council issued a listed-building enforcement notice against Alison Hall and James Rogers, of Acton Beauchamp, near Bromyard, for painting their 400-year-old cottage pink; they ordered them to paint it white like their neighbours.

It's true that most rural cottages were originally lime-washed and so turned out to be white. But that colour was a combination of accident and pragmatism; it wasn't laid down by diktat. Now preserved in aspic for long enough, this happenstance beauty has been set in stone by unnecessarily prescriptive legislation.

The antiseptic spick-and-spanification of provincial England has destroyed the pleasing air of decay. Gone with it are the anaemic men in cream waistcoats, the plump red-faced men in tweed jackets, cords and jerseys in Turkish carpet patterns; often gay, usually clever, a bit prickly, working off their hangovers in those bookshops or prep schools up the Woodstock Road, still cursing that doctorate in Anglo-Saxon linguistics they never got round to finishing thirty years ago.

I imagine they still eke out a living somewhere in these pretty provincial towns. It's not as if the chain stores have had the bohemian class machine-gunned; just that the town centre no longer has anything of interest to draw the bohemians in. The pubs they used to stretch out the day in are still there – but loud music and the smoking ban have driven them out of the snug.

All this isn't necessarily for the worse. The grey and brown postwar dreariness of Oxford I saw in 1993 was more limited and grimmer in many ways than the spruced-up version of 2011.

In 1945, there was one French restaurant, the Elizabeth, in Oxford, on St Aldate's, and one curry house, the Taj Mahal, in the centre of town, on the Turl. In 1993, things had barely changed. The Elizabeth was still there, the number of curry houses in the centre of town had doubled to a grand total of two, and there was a new Pizza Express. Nowadays, Oxford is bulging with banks converted into restaurants, a transformation also undergone by Chelsea, once, long, long ago, the bohemian heart of London.

There will always be run-down boarding houses and new-build residential developments in both cities, but they are increasingly on the far-flung fringes of town. Oxford's last outpost of cheap living is the concrete suburban jungle of Blackbird Leys, and it's a long time since any self-respecting blackbird chose to roost there, let alone a bohemian aesthete. Bohemians, like blackbirds, cannot survive when their habitats are smothered, by either concrete or by retail outlets.

Will they start flocking back to their old roosts as those shops are wiped out by the credit crunch? I don't think so. It's too late. Bohemia has been outpriced, forced into exile, and faces extinction – thanks to that extreme rise in house prices.

That rise has massively affected upmarket rural England, too. Country houses bought for a pittance – four or five thousand pounds – in the 1940s and 1950s, are now selling for two or three million pounds. Fifty years ago, these gold-plated nest eggs were in an awful state, with jungly trees tapping at the leaded window panes, lethal Edwardian wiring and dry rot seeping through the walls. Some of the houses were still scarred by open fires lit by soldiers during wartime requisition.

After the war, people thought these white elephants were doomed to decay and demolition. Thousands of houses fell to the wrecking ball; but those that avoided it have never been in better shape, despite the recession.

A quiet renaissance of the English country house has taken place; owners of big houses have discovered that, if they hold on to their properties for decades, the roof over their heads is a far better investment than shares, bank accounts or premium bonds.

What happened to bring about this great boom? There are two main factors: the sheer amount of money created around Britain over the past decade, much of it arriving in the pockets of foreign plutocrats; and, secondly, the sheer lack of cash in Britain after the Second World War, which sent property prices plunging in the first place. We may have won the war, but we did so at great expense.

Britain was nearly broke after six years of fighting; and that applied to the rich, too, who were selling off and demolishing country houses in their thousands.

When Evelyn Waugh wrote *Brideshead Revisited* in 1945, he was convinced that 'The ancestral seats which were our chief national artistic achievement were doomed to decay and spoliation like the monasteries in the sixteenth century.'

Gradual decay set in through the 1950s and 1960s, accelerated by the decline in domestic staff. But, by the 1970s, central heating was getting cheaper, and easier to install; and labour-saving devices, like Hoovers, had made a huge difference. The prosperity of the late 1970s and the 1980s, and improvements in transport, increased the value of these houses exponentially.

The really big money, though, came in the last decade – a decade of enormous bankers' bonuses, a decade when London became the international capital of the world.

Ever since the crash of 2008, even more foreign investors have flooded into the property market, as British tycoons felt the pain of the recession. In 2010, only 26 per cent of central London properties were sold to the British; before 2008, it was 40 per cent.[3] The new buyers tended to be the international super-rich, the sort with a number of houses across the world. That's why, if you go through Belgravia at night, you won't see any lights on in many of the houses.

We might like playing Monopoly in Britain – and owning hotels in Mayfair – but, in reality, Mayfair and all the other trophy locations in London are on the whole owned by foreigners. Just look at one well-known property buyer – Saif Gaddafi, Colonel Gaddafi's son, who bought a twelve-bedroom house in Hampstead for £11m in 2009.

Property prices, and the number of homes built each year, are the key not just to the extinction of bohemia, but also to the modern look of English towns. In the last half-century, average British house prices have grown by 335 per cent.

House price growth has long outrun earnings growth. On top of that, the rate of building of new houses has fallen considerably. Thirteen million homes have been built in the last fifty years in Britain, but the rate of building has slowed to a trickle: there were 425,800 new houses in 1968 (the peak year for private and council house building); only 156,816 in 2009. House-building is now at its lowest level since 1946.

The type of new houses has changed enormously, too. The number of new bungalows and semi-detached houses has slumped over the past thirty years, while the number of detached houses has grown. And the amount of single-person households has soared. In 2009, 231,490 couples got married – the lowest total since 1895.[4]

With the size of the housing stock lagging behind the growth in population – combined with greater single occupancy and the long-standing English preference for houses over flats – not only are more people living in smaller houses, but also more and more cars are piling up on the street outside.

Those new houses and buildings that have been built in the last half-century have vastly changed the look of England, largely thanks to the widespread use of steel and concrete. These materials – which don't belong to a particular country, let alone a particular county, as stone, clay and timber do – lend international anonymity to the modern townscape.

Iron had been used extensively on English buildings since the late eighteenth century – the cast iron bridge at Ironbridge, Shropshire, went up in 1779. Corrugated iron was first developed in 1830 to make lightweight roofs. Rolled wrought-iron was then used at the Palm House of Kew Gardens in 1848.

Once steel could be mass-produced, thanks to the Bessemer process, the first steel-framed buildings went up – among the first in England was the Ritz Hotel, Piccadilly, built in 1906.

Concrete was first used in England on a major scale by Sir Robert Smirke in 1817 for the foundations of the Millbank Penitentiary in Pimlico, on the site of the Tate Gallery. The first concrete buildings are even prized these days: in September 2010, a derelict 1873 concrete house, in Lordship Lane, Dulwich, listed Grade II, was saved from demolition because of its early use of the material.

Steel-reinforced concrete was used by François Hennebique for the first time, in France in the 1880s. It appeared in England in 1899 in a railway warehouse at Brentford Dock. There's no reason why the material should necessarily produce ugliness. The Liver Building, in Liverpool, built in 1911 by Walter Aubrey Thomas, remains one of the city's finest buildings, best known for the pair of pale green copper Liver birds flapping their wings on the towering twin domes.

Clothed in high-Edwardian baroque detail – all Doric pilasters, chunky volutes and deep-shadowed cornices – the Liver Building is, underneath, a distinctly modern building, sophisticated enough to vie with anything built at the time in New York. Beneath the 14in-thick skin of decorative granite lies the steel-reinforced concrete frame. The concrete was mixed on the spot, in the basement, with a new floor completed every nineteen days, showing what a staggeringly efficient material concrete is.

The Liver Building was the tallest building in the city for the next half a century, a slice of Manhattan on the Mersey – the papers at the time certainly called it a skyscraper. But it has none of the bleakness of the tower blocks that followed in its wake.

In fact, England didn't come off too badly in the 1930s, compared with the Continent. The first white concrete box, New Ways, Northampton, was designed by Peter Behrens in 1925, but the boxes took some time to migrate across the country. Ours was a delayed adoption of modernism – another example of innate English conservatism when it comes to embracing revolutionary artistic and architectural styles.

To begin with, in the 1930s, we adapted those white concrete boxes with traditional, historicist, English accessories: brick and timber cladding. The real horrors only started to appear after the war.

Coventry's first postwar city architect was pleased to see that the bombs gave him the opportunity to put his brutal plans into action. Air raids on Birmingham and London also opened up yawning acres of building space for the new nihilism. Until 1978, a quarter of medieval Bristol, bombed during the war, was given over to car parks until 1978.

Some sensible postwar urban rebuilding was done, compatible with the surrounding housing stock. Several architects even did the old English thing, and looked to the past. Basil Spence was inspired by Norman murals in a Sussex church when he designed the new Coventry Cathedral after its medieval predecessor was wrecked in the war.

In 1954 came the first tower blocks – the Government's replacement housing for people made homeless by slum clearances. These were the optimistic days when tower blocks were envisaged as streets-in-the-sky; magical, amenity-crammed, modern alternatives to the old, run-down terraced houses.

The 1957 Park Hill estate in Sheffield set the pattern for the next decade of council house tower blocks across the country. Lifts took the blocks higher and higher; the taller the tower blocks got, the bigger the government subsidies.

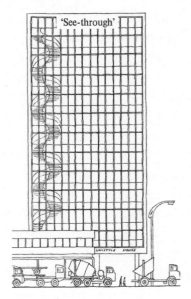

England stops looking like England. Historical references disappear, as Edwardian Queen Anne gives way to postwar concrete and glass. Extract from Peter Fleetwood-Hesketh's 'Street of Taste', in John Betjeman's *Ghastly Good Taste*, 1970.

As well as being plain ugly, the concrete, steel and glass of postwar tower blocks and office buildings don't vary much – relentlessly right-angled, relentlessly straight-lined. Ian Nairn (1930–83), the architectural critic, coined the term 'Subtopia' for this new generation of identikit buildings – 'Its symptom will be that the end of Southampton will look like the beginning of Carlisle; the parts in between will look like the end of Carlisle or the beginning of Southampton . . . Subtopia is the annihilation of the site, the steamrollering of all individuality of place to one uniform and mediocre pattern.'

That was part of the problem with the twentieth-century council estates: they did away with regional differences. The inter-war housing estates in the Bristol suburbs looked exactly like the ones in Birmingham and Nottingham.

The sheer size of these estates could be overwhelming, too. The 1919 Housing Act, requiring councils to build houses for the poor, was followed more assiduously in some counties than others. Norfolk built so many between the wars and after the Second World War that, by the late 1950s, 40 per cent of Norwich's population lived in council houses, the highest percentage in Britain.

A council building boom also meant fewer people lived in each house; 3.1 people per house in Norwich in 1957 was then the lowest rate in the country. All good news – if only the new wave of council houses had been built with more variety and beauty.

The earliest rural council houses, built just before the First World War, usually close to the middle of the town or village, often had a vegetable patch at the back and a decent front garden. Those high standards progressively declined. Massive demand, combined with misguided architects, led to cheap, concrete mass housing. The destructive views of those fashionable architects defeated the residents' natural desire for beauty and privacy – a desire much better accommodated in those inter-war suburban houses, so mocked by withering intellectuals.

In the 1960s, English town planners and city architects began to embrace, with plenty of zeal, if not much sophistication, the new minimalism of Le Corbusier's International Style, and Walter Gropius's Bauhaus School. Simple, stripped-down buildings that might just about work as small, stand-alone houses – like Le Corbusier's 1929 Villa Savoye in Poissy, France – did not work when inflated on to a vast tower-block scale, overpowering the low-rise terrace scale of England's Georgian and Victorian cities.

The damp northern climate had its effect, too, on our versions of modern architecture. The white walls that are so effective, and reflective, in southern heat, became stained and riddled with damp; the flat roofs leaked.

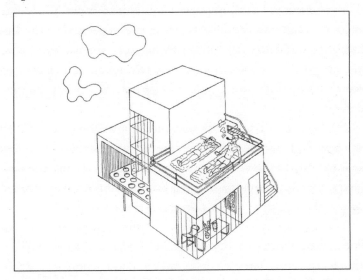

Not built for English weather: the flat roofs and white walls of Osbert Lancaster's Twentieth-Century Functional.

Planners weren't content with just erecting tower blocks. Alongside them, they lined up the other three horsemen of the apocalypse – the ring road, the urban highway and the shopping centre.

These didn't just hit the big cities – like poor Birmingham with its soul-destroying Bullring, a far cry from its medieval origins as an arena for bull-baiting; or London, deeply scarred by Westway, the continuation of the A40 that sliced through the city centre in 1970.

Regional towns got it in the neck too. In the early 1960s, High Wycombe got the full works – in 1960, a big chunk of the oldest part of town was demolished and replaced by a ring road and hideous shopping centre. Two years later, another part of the old town centre was hacked away, to house the horrible County Offices and another soul-sapping shopping centre.

Similar treatment was meted out to Norwich in the late 1950s and 1960s, through the savage dreams of H. C. Rowley, the City Engineer and Planning Officer from 1944 to 1966. Slough got hit, in 1968, by the architects, C. H. Elsom and Partners, who replaced the High Street – the old Bath Road – with shopping malls.

The soul of Leicester, an ancient Roman town, was all but extinguished by Vaughan Way, the urban motorway which in 1968 cut off the Saxon-Norman church of St Nicholas – and the Jewry Wall, the largest surviving fragment of Roman architecture in the country – from the rest of the town.

One of the wicked side-effects of the ring road – familiar, too, in American city developments – was the 'ring of blight' around the city. After the war, St Paul's and St Jude's in Bristol were both cut off from the rest of the city by an English version of the Boulevard Périphérique – the 1973 ring road around Paris that isolated the outer suburbs and so created marooned, heavily criminalized areas.

Slowly the tide turned. In 1967, government subsidies were removed from the tower-block council estates. The peak year for tower blocks was 1968, when 160 residential towers over 150 feet were built.

Then, in the same year, Ronan Point tower block in Newham, east London, collapsed, only two months after it was built. The golden days of the tower block had come to an end. The early 1970s saw a change from unadorned concrete council blocks to buildings with fewer storeys, and a more cottagey look, with brick walls and pitched roofs. In 1978, not a single tower block over 150 feet was constructed.[5]

Council houses also got bigger and more comfortable under

the Parker Morris standards, imposed from 1969. Under the standards, flushing toilets and central heating were obligatory, and a semi-detached or end-of-terrace house for four people had to have a floor area of at least 72 square metres. The legal requirement for Parker Morris standards was removed in 1980, by the Local Government, Planning and Land Act.

Gradually, many of the horrors of previous years have been demolished: in April 2011, demolition began on the Heygate Estate, the 1974 block for 3,000 residents in the Elephant and Castle, in south London. Hailed as a neo-brutalist masterpiece when it was built, it soon became crime-ridden and dilapidated. In its final days, it became a popular film set, used for the Michael Caine vigilante film, *Harry Brown*, and for episodes of *The Bill*.

The tower block had turned into an outdated yet iconic image of hellish urban living, as people returned to the English ideal, combining historicism and land ownership – the suburban semi-detached, with its own front door opening on to the street, and its own patch of garden at the back.

That stripped-down, modernist look was deeply unpopular on a mass, state-built, cheap model. But it has survived on the individual, privately built, expensive model; as applied to *grands projets* and small housing conversions alike.

Only recently, I met an enthusiastic, newly qualified architect, her eyes brimming with excitement at the prospect of turning ideas into buildings.

'What's your dream building, the one you'd build if you had all the money and all the time in the world?'

'A glass box.'

'Erm ... any particular glass box? Any features you might add to it? Anything you might want to put inside it?'

'No. Just the perfect glass box.'

The drive towards nothingness has been accelerated by the

end of the traditional teaching of architectural history in architecture degrees. The architect who was so keen on glass boxes
was shocked when I asked whether the classical orders of architecture were taught during her degree.

'Oh no – I'm not sure they'd be very useful these days,' she
said, in a tone which subtly implied this sort of knowledge was
not only an old-fashioned, fogeyish perversion, but also a posi-
tive impediment to free-thinking originality.

A few organizations are fighting a rearguard action against
this nihilist philosophy – Prince Charles's Foundation for the
Built Environment among them – but they are in a tiny minority. If you visit a rich, fashionable British household these days,
you'll see something that has never existed before in the civilized world – an active dislike of any objects that belong to a
human civilization previous to their own.

Nature may abhor a vacuum but, oh, how the modern rich
adore one. The stripping of the altars in the Reformation had
nothing on this.

Whether it's a sprawling Victorian hotel in Bournemouth,
converted into loft-style apartments for *Grand Designs*, a tumbledown Georgian rectory in the Cotswolds turned into a
boutique spa, or a byre-cum-bijou-bolthole in the Black Mountains, the answer's the same – strip out anything old and shabby,
and slop white paint all over it.

Richard Rogers, arch-nihilist of the age, has done it in
Chelsea, taking two lovely Georgian houses and knocking
them together into one big echoing void.

Take a look at a back garden in a fashionable bit of England,
and you will now see mini-versions of the Rogers approach.
Attached to the detailed, varied, jumbled-up silhouette and relief
of the Victorian terraced house, you'll find new, long, low, rectangular boxes of steel and glass: the minimalist side return.

This nihilism is now the style of the international rich – with its straight lines and abhorrence of wild nature, minimalism is essentially a foreign style, its roots formed in Bauhaus architecture in 1920s and 1930s Germany.

Kitchens become pristine laboratories; flat expanses of steel, glass and slate, with no food on show, or any sign that anything's ever been cooked or eaten there. There's great attention to cleanliness, too, with a bathroom per bedroom, each one a practical exposition of modern plumbing techniques, with free-standing baths and multiple sinks, all connected to gleaming copper pipes.

Back gardens have none of that horridly asymmetrical, unfashionably green grass or those ragged-edged, shambolic borders. The wild tradition of English gardening has come under attack on many fronts – from pared-down, symmetrical, minimalist fashion; from dictatorial makeover programmes. Planned grids of garden rooms and acres of decking and slate are interrupted by the odd square patch of flowers, planted in symmetrical matrices, grown to uniform height. English borders haven't been so geometrical since the Elizabethan knot garden.

The nihilist's desire for control, order and blankness, and his dislike of beauty and the past, mean there's nowhere calming or beautiful for the eye to rest; no magazine or book by the sofa; no way of putting your feet up on that sofa without compromising its snowy virginity. The house is on permanent standby for the estate agent's surprise visit. It is forever Year Zero. Old, pretty things have given way to new, ugly nothings.

A similar hollowing-out of the English High Street has taken place, too – not because of minimalism; but through a combination of the recession and the triumph of the chain shop. In 2010, Cambridge was declared King of the Clone High Streets. Of the fifty-seven shops on its main shopping street, all but one were chain shops. The most diverse high street was declared to be Whitstable's, in Kent.

Just as with the minimalist terraced house, the removal of detail from the High Street leads to the removal of variety. You end up with the repetition of street patterns across the country – and the arrival of the identikit High Street, with the same repeated units of chain shops and shopping malls.

The English taste for large-scale, enclosed shopping spaces can be traced back to the first Georgian, Victorian and Edwardian shopping arcades, themselves inspired by the glassed-in *gallerie* and *galeries* of Italy and Paris.

John Nash's Royal Opera Arcade, off Pall Mall, was England's first covered shopping arcade, built in 1818; emulated the following year by Burlington Arcade, a few paces north, off Piccadilly. Town-centre shopping malls and out-of-town megastores are their hulking great descendants.

The English High Street is a fairly recent creation; few modern High Streets, fully equipped with lines of shops, date from before the 1870s. Soon after, shopping arcades took off, reaching new heights in 1890s London, when the shopping parades of Muswell Hill, Acton, Crouch End and Streatham High Road, and the Palladian arcade in Bromley, all went up.

Their profits were improved by advances in lighting technology. Godalming, Surrey, was the first town with an electric light system in Britain, installed in 1881. Electric Avenue in Brixton, built in 1885, was one of the earliest shopping streets lit by electricity. (Pall Mall, central London, was the first street lit by gas, in 1807.)

At about the same time, the first shopping chains put down their roots: Marks and Spencer was founded in 1884, Sainsbury's in 1869. The thing about chain shops is that they tend to be extremely cheap shops, and the English have always been keen on a bargain. Unlike Continental Europeans, we prefer to spend money on housing rather than on High Street shopping – thanks to our long-standing obsession with home ownership. Seventeen per cent of our household income was spent on housing in 2011, much higher than Continental figures.

Because Britain has rarely been invaded or had revolutions, property ownership has always been pretty secure; safe as houses and all that (see Chapter 5). That leads to the great British pride in the home, our endless property-selling and home improvement programmes on TV, and our obsession with house prices and climbing on to the property ladder.

Throughout the twentieth century, while the percentage of British owner-occupier households soared, the English High Street grew more and more uniform as the chain stores began to dominate. In our time-poor society – with our relative indifference to fresh food – we have fallen more for the supermarket than our Continental neighbours have.

We spend a smaller proportion of our income on food than any other EU country; partly because of that preference for supermarkets over individual, family-owned, idiosyncratic shops. British supermarkets account for 97 per cent of food sales; and 76 per cent of the sales go to the big four supermarkets – Tesco, Sainsbury's, Morrisons and Asda.

As the big four battle for market share, their discount wars mean a basket of essential household items costs less in the UK than it does in, say, Carrefour in France or Edeka in Germany. But it also means our supermarkets are that much more dominant, and our High Streets that much more uniform.

Supermarkets have had a knock-on effect, too, on the look of English motorways. The M25 is ringed with vast depots, owned by pension funds, leased to the supermarkets, and run by logistics companies like Kuehne + Nagel. Internet shopping has accelerated the increase in depots – Amazon has built seven mega-warehouses near British transport hubs since 1998.

The supermarket's impact on the landscape is particularly extreme when you consider how tiny their landholdings are. In

2010, Waitrose was the biggest landowner, with 4,095 acres attached to its 231 shops, but that includes the Leckford country estate, in Hampshire. Next comes Tesco, with 2,545 shops spread over a mere 768 acres – about the size of a single, decent-sized, but by no means enormous, farm.

Thanks to better weather on much of the Continent – and a less powerful attachment to the home – Europeans also spend more time out of doors than the English; and that includes time spent on the High Street. Because they aren't spending all their money on their houses, they have higher disposable incomes, the current eurozone crisis notwithstanding. They've always tended to rent more, and to spend more on themselves and the *bella figura* – the sort of spending that the badly dressed, self-denying English have historically looked down on as self-indulgent.

And so England ends up as a world leader in chain retail shops; specializing in selling, among other things, cheap clothes – another reason we don't look as good as our Continental cousins.

English High Streets also end up with more low-budget shops than in Continental Europe: more charity shops (helped by tax breaks), cafés, fast food outlets, financial services shops, hairdressers, second-hand shops and pound shops. Poundland, 99p Stores and Greggs have all done extremely well during the recession: there are now more pound shops than bookshops in British town centres.

Our desire for cut-price pleasure is one of the few factors creating new life on the High Street. Between 1997 and 2010, Britain lost 3,460 pubs, 7,500 post offices and 1,310 public lavatories. Over the same period, it gained 1,270 bookies and 276 lap-dancing clubs.[6]

Chain coffee shops, too, have proliferated. The origins of our taste for coffee grew from different strands: the 1650s coffee houses of Oxford and London, the coffee taverns set up by the temperance movement in the 1880s, the Edwardian coffee houses of Soho run by Greeks, Italians, Turks and Arabs, and the milk bars of the 1940s. But the real boom came in the last twenty years, with the emergence of chains like Starbucks, Costa Coffee and Caffè Nero.

The carnage on the English High Street has been so brutal that even some chain shops have been destroyed. In April 2011, Oddbins went into administration, following in the footsteps of Victoria Wine, Unwins, Threshers and Bottoms Up – all wiped off the High Street by the big volume buyers of the supermarkets. In March 2011, one in seven shop units in Britain were empty; the figure rose to one in four in badly hit places like Stockton-on-Tees, Margate and Altrincham.

Even the great retail success of the late twentieth century, the Asian-owned corner shop – not normally on a corner, incidentally – has been in slow decline for twenty years. From 1992 to 2002, the number of Asian-owned small shops in Britain fell by 23 per cent, to around 11,500.[7]

Those corner shops that survive are also less likely to be run by Asians, as Turks in particular take over. Hindu men – once the cornerstone of the corner store – are the second most advantaged social group in the labour market after Jewish men. Social mobility has taken them out from behind the counter.[8]

Meanwhile, the French and Italians have managed to hold on to their local bakers, butchers and fishmongers. The French have a law that nothing can be sold for less than it cost the farmer to make it, meaning small shops can't be undercut by supermarkets running loss-leader products.

Some French supermarkets have even designed their aisles to be wide enough to accommodate the tractors that periodically roam up and down them, protesting against cuts in agricultural subsidies. Because of measures like this, you can find Continental charity shops – but they're usually on the outskirts of town in industrial estate sheds.

★

There is another major change to the English High Street over the last half-century – in the people who live and shop there.

In March 2011, Brian True-May, the producer of *Midsomer Murders*, got into trouble for saying that the programme worked because it had no ethnic minorities in it. However insensitive he may have been, he was certainly accurate about the make-up of the country: in 2011, 98.6 per cent of rural England was white.

The first black man in the English countryside was Olaudah Equiano, a Nigerian-born slave who moved to Soham, Cambridgeshire, in 1792, dying in 1797. Not too many of his compatriots have followed in his footsteps to the English countryside; even if hundreds of thousands of white Londoners have, migrating in particular to Essex and Kent – a classic example of so-called white flight.

Still, the ethnic make-up of England has undeniably changed over the last half-century. Between 1997 and 2009, 2.2 million more people came to live in Britain than left to live abroad – the largest influx Britain has ever seen. In 2011, almost one in eight people living in Britain – 7 million altogether – were born abroad. The biggest groups of foreign-born immigrants come from India, Pakistan and Ireland.

Immigration has had an effect on the look of England for centuries. The first curry house, the Hindostanee Coffee House in George Street, Mayfair, was founded in 1809 by Sake Dean Mahomed, from Bihar, India. It offered a place 'for the nobility and the gentry where they might enjoy the Hookha with real Chilm tobacco and Indian dishes of the highest perfection'. There are now 10,000 curry houses across the United Kingdom, with an annual turnover of £3.6bn.[9]

The Chinese, too, have had an enormous impact on our High Street, and our diet. In 1900, there were around 500 Chinese people in England; in 2000, there were 100,000 in London alone. A migration that began as a trickle in the seventeenth century increased in the eighteenth century, boosted by the trading activities of the East India Company and the nineteenth-century Opium Wars. The first Chinese settlements were in the docks, notably in Limehouse, east London. Wartime bombing and the decline of the docks shifted the Chinese population west to the cheap housing of Soho, now London's Chinatown.

Liverpool's Chinatown – the oldest Chinatown in the world – also grew out of a dockland settlement of the 1830s which migrated to the city centre as the docks declined. Newcastle – Britain's newest Chinatown, founded in 1982 – followed Manchester (whose first Chinese restaurant was set up in 1948) and Birmingham, with its first restaurant opening in 1959.

Waves of immigrants have continued to come ever since – from the Caribbean in the 1950s and 1960s, with the first Jamaicans arriving in large numbers on the *Empire Windrush* at Tilbury in 1948; and, in the last twenty years, from eastern Europe, particularly Poland.

In recent years, successful second- and third-generation immigrants have migrated to the suburbs, with their better schools and employment prospects, and lower crime rates. Sri Lankans have settled in the south of London, in New Malden and Mitcham; Greek Cypriots in the north, in Palmers Green and Southgate; Sikhs in the west, in Hounslow and Southall; and Hindu Indians in the north-west, in Harrow and Wembley. One in four people living in Harrow now have a Hindu surname.

The destination of one particular group is often sparked by one significant early migration. When the South Korean embassy moved to Wimbledon in the 1970s, the South Korean community followed: now 8,000 South Koreans live in nearby New Malden, the biggest South Korean population in Europe. There are twenty South Korean businesses in New Malden; the local Tesco's branch sells more fresh fruit and vegetables than any other outlet in Britain, because of the South Korean, and Sri Lankan, taste for healthy food.

Immigration has a self-evident effect on sociological history. There is, for example, more sectarianism in Scotland because of its immigration history. In Scotland, Catholics of Irish origin account for 12–15 per cent of the population; the figure is much higher in the west of Scotland. In England, the Irish population never got higher than 3.5 per cent, in the 1860s and 1870s.

Liverpool, whose port is so close to Ireland, was the most Catholic city in England, with its population reaching 25 per cent Irish or second-generation Irish in the late-Victorian period. Manchester's Irish population was less than half that, and Birmingham's even less. The Catholic population of Ulster in the early twentieth century, at around 35 per cent, was, of course, appreciably greater.[10]

Still, because immigrants tend to come from the poorer end of society, they have had relatively little effect on the architecture and landscape of England.

Yes, there are more Catholic churches in Liverpool than in Norwich. There are temples in Southall, known as Little India because two thirds of its 70,000 population are South Asian; Southall is home to London's largest Sikh population. The vast Shri Swaminarayan Mandir Hindu temple was erected in Neasden, north-west London, in 1995, to accommodate the large population of Hindus, many of whom arrived in the 1970s after being expelled from Uganda by Idi Amin. And there are newly built mosques in city suburbs across England, too.

But, because recent immigrants have usually made their way to ready-built English cities, they ended up living mostly in Victorian and Edwardian terraced houses. Their places of worship are often housed in places once held sacred by Georgian, Victorian and Edwardian – and Christian – residents. In Brick Lane, east London, there is a 1743 Huguenot church, later the Spitalfields Great

Synagogue, and now a mosque, the Brick Lane Jamme Masjid. It's no different to the widespread Renaissance practice of incorporating ancient Roman temples into Christian churches in Italy.

In Clitheroe, Lancashire, in 2007, there was an almighty row when local Muslims applied to convert the town's 1888 Mount Zion Methodist chapel into a mosque. The row was given added piquancy by a distinctive L. S. Lowry picture, *A Street in Clitheroe*, with the Gothic chapel on prominent display.

Clitheroe remains majority Christian by population, but the number of Muslim residents is growing. Still, their arrival isn't reflected much in the look of the place – hidebound, as much of modern England is, by planning restrictions. A condition for granting planning permission for any change in use of the old chapel was that there should be no domes, minarets or any call to prayer. So the look of the place will remain much as it was when Lowry painted it, even as the sociological make-up of the town changes.

Modern immigration, with its mass arrival of people, and minimal change in architecture, has the opposite effect to what you might call architectural immigration. The early seventeenth century brought Italian Renaissance architecture to England, but very few Italians. French neo-classicism brought plenty of French-inspired buildings to London in the eighteenth century, but not many French people.

The last time mass immigration coincided with mass architectural change was when the country was actually taken over by invaders. In 1066, the Normans brought Norman architecture with them across the Channel to Hastings. Gothic architecture, also a French import, followed a century later.

English architecture usually changes its look according to who's in charge, rather than who's just arrived – unless they're one and the same person.

Until the Reformation, the Church was the great builder of

England – 99 per cent of surviving pre-Reformation buildings
are churches, cathedrals or monasteries. Henry VIII changed all
that, with a religious revolution that had an extreme effect on
the look of certain counties.

Because Kent was so central to English Christianity, much of the
county, previously owned by religious foundations, was sold off or
given away after the Reformation. In places like Oxfordshire, never
rich in abbeys or monasteries, there were few opportunities for
these kinds of sales; thus the shortage of Elizabethan and Jacobean
palaces in the county. Other once-prominent religious cities went
into decline after the Reformation – Reading's flint monastery was
destroyed, and the city began its sad journey from medieval jewel to
run-down railway city.

Some historians have maintained that the Reformation provided a crucial underpinning to the modern English economy.
Private ownership of newly released land was more productive
than religious or state control. In France, a land ownership law,
vaine pâture, allowed free grazing on other people's land, meaning you could leave your cows to roam freely. But that also
meant that your next-door neighbour's cows could eat your
turnips – a bit of a blow to your farm profits.[11]

After the Reformation, noble families and the monarchy
became the principal patrons of England's greatest buildings,
with the odd exceptional religious building constructed by the
newly established Anglican church.

Giuseppe di Lampedusa, author of *The Leopard*, was horrified
at the change from Catholic England to Protestant England.

The Monster [Lampedusa's self-applied pseudonym], a Roman
Catholic and one of the pillars of the Church, weeps at the
thought that this country, in which the Christian centuries
erected such superlative monuments to its zeal, has escaped
from the paternal authority of St Peter's successor; it has besides
been punished artistically, because when it was outside the fold,

the wonders of Ely, Lincoln and York were superseded by their papier-mâché St Paul's.[12]

Lampedusa shouldn't have been so upset. Religion still dominates plenty of preserved, rural landscapes that haven't changed much since the Reformation.

The church, often built before the Reformation, usually remains the biggest building in the English village; its spire the village's tallest structure.

There are still 47,000 churches in Britain; four times the number of village halls or post offices. And there are 4,700 Church of England schools, too, attended by a million children; a quarter of all primary schools and 6 per cent of secondary schools are run by the Anglican Church. Churches still dominate the English horizon, despite the century-long decline of the religious fervour that built them.

Even in the nineteenth century – when a whole new layer of Victorian, mostly Gothic, churches was built across England – the support behind them was dying away.

'The common people are without definite religious belief, and have been so for centuries,' George Orwell wrote in 1941. 'The Anglican Church never had a real hold on them, it was simply a preserve of the landed gentry, and the Nonconformist sects only influenced minorities.'[13]

One inevitable result of over-zealous church-building and under-enthusiastic churchgoers is derelict and converted churches and chapels, a feature of the English landscape from as early as the First World War.

By the late nineteenth century, the state had begun to take over as Britain's main builder of non-domestic buildings. Schools are a good example. Until 1870, churches and charitable institutions were responsible for building schools, particularly after the Napoleonic Wars. National Schools were run by the Church of England; British Schools by the Nonconformists.

The Government provided grants for building schools after 1840, until the 1870 Act gave local School Boards the responsibility for building schools. They were usually built in handsome Queen Anne style, in red brick and white stone, with Dutch gables and enormous windows – their dimensions laid down by law, to produce as much light as possible for Victorian school-children to work by.

By 1876, elementary education was compulsory, and the Government gradually assumed responsibility for making bigger, uglier schools. The same went for health. Through the nineteenth and twentieth centuries, the Government took over the role of the local boards of the Poor Law Guardians, set up in 1834. Many hospitals today are on the site of old workhouses, such as Lambeth Hospital, Kennington, and St John's Hospital, Battersea.

Needing to economize – and dictated by pragmatism, rather than a desire to produce beauty, or the need to show off – the state has built progressively uglier, more stripped-down buildings. Minimalism by necessity, you might call it.

It is urban England that looks less and less like the bewitching England of legend these days, assaulted by the ugliness of state minimalism, boilerplate housing developments and the march of the chain shops and the supermarkets.

Meanwhile, out of town, rural planning restrictions – even tighter than urban ones – have kept intact the beauty of much of the English countryside. The strange survival of rural England goes right to the heart of the English character.

Conclusion: Town Mice and Country Mice

*I've known the area between Bridlington and Wetherby for 50 years
and it's hardly changed. I found out why in the end – it's grade one
agricultural land, so the villages aren't extended; there's nothing for
tourists, no tearooms, just these beautiful undulating hills.*

David Hockney, on returning to his native Yorkshire after half a
lifetime in Los Angeles. [1]

It's not just Yorkshire that has survived the modern age's assault
on the Englishness of England.

Across the country, big patches of rural land have fared much
better than in, say, Ireland, where lax planning bodies have
allowed all sorts of monstrosities through.

The Irish have rarely lived together in settlements along the
English village model that helped keep the surrounding country
untouched. Irish farmers' deep-rooted attachment to the land –
and the importance of land ownership in a place that was
politically and religiously divided for so long – has meant that
everyone wants a bungalow in its own field.

In Kerry, there's a so-called 'one-off house' for every kilometre of road, a sad distortion of Eamon de Valera's 1943 vision
of an Ireland 'bright with cosy homesteads'.[2]

The Wyndham Land Act of 1903 also allowed Irish tenants –
316,000 of them – to buy out their aristocratic landlords, leading
to many more, smaller farms, proportionally speaking.

In England, more privately owned big estates have survived –
leading to better preservation of the landscape, as well as larger

fields. Whatever you might think of an unfair land ownership structure, it often makes things look more beautiful.

To an astonishing degree, much of the countryside retains its prewar look, despite England being the most densely populated country in Europe. Something like three quarters of all the moorland that has ever existed in Britain is still there – and the British Isles encompass the biggest area of moorland in the world.

The survival of the countryside is largely due to a series of nineteenth- and early-twentieth-century rural preservation movements, begun when large-scale development was looming on the horizon.

London's woods were protected by the Commons, Open Spaces and Footpaths Preservation Society, founded in 1865. The Guild of St George, created by John Ruskin in 1870, helped preserve the Lake District. The Society for the Protection of Ancient Buildings, set up in 1877 by Philip Webb and William Morris, and the National Trust (1895) turned the preservation movement towards old buildings. The twentieth-century threat of urban sprawl was countered by Sir Ebenezer Howard's Garden City Association – later, in 1941, to become the Town and Country Planning Association – and the Campaign for the Protection of Rural England (1925).

The greatest preserver of all was a piece of legislation: the Town and Country Planning Act of 1947, which outlawed ribbon development, set up green belts and imposed the obligation of planning permission. The first national park, the Peak District National Park, was set up as late as 1951, driven by the same impulse: as post-war rural England fell prey to the bulldozer, and the first motorways were planned, the imminent threat to beauty sparked off its preservation.

Urban parks, too, grew out of a desire to preserve blocks of green land against the encroaching tide of slate and bricks.

Canterbury's public park, one of the first, was set up at Dane John as early as 1790. The institution of public parks accelerated through the nineteenth century, as a direct response to spreading urbanization. In 1833, the Parliament Select Committee on Public Walks was founded to promote public parks. Until then, all parks in London were royal parks: Hyde Park had been Henry VIII's hunting ground, expropriated from the monasteries.

You can chart the sprawling growth of London through the appearance of its parks, asymmetrical green gaps in the outwardly spreading lines of urban terrace: Regent's Park, another royal park, was landscaped by John Nash from 1811 onwards; Victoria Park was built in the East End in the 1840s; Kennington Park was carved out of Kennington Common in 1852; Battersea Park was set up in 1861, when the flat, low-lying Battersea Fields were dramatically landscaped; Wimbledon and Putney Commons were preserved by an 1871 Act.

In Birmingham – where Victorian industrial tycoons left their suburban estates to the city – there is more parkland than anywhere in Europe. Later in the nineteenth century, local authorities took up the practice: setting up Terrace Gardens in Richmond in 1887 and Brockwell Park, Herne Hill, in 1892.

When Lord Rosebery – then Foreign Secretary, later Prime Minister – opened Brockwell Park, he said, 'We have many parks, perhaps more parks than any capital in the world; but every day, gradually and by minute fractions, the process of building over small open spaces, the suburban gardens which are attached to the villas which are every day being pulled down, every day the process of destroying these is going on.'[3]

There was another burst of park-building after the war; in the 1940s came the idea of linked open spaces. This was realized in the 1970s in the Lee Valley Regional Park, stretching for twenty-six miles along the River Lee from Ware, in Hertfordshire, through Essex, before meeting the Thames at East India Dock Basin.

Victorian urban parks have survived well, while the handsome nineteenth-century buildings in the cities around them have often fallen to the wrecking ball – or the wrecking townplanner.

This division, between heavily knocked-about buildings and highly protected green space, is unusually English – and fits with a long-standing national rural obsession.

A preference for ancient rural Arcadia over urban modernism has been around for centuries. Most archetypal English views over the last millennium or so, in pictures, prose and poetry, have been rural. Most books about England are drenched, too, in rural sepia.

The Batsford guidebooks to Britain, which crystallized the typical view of the countryside in rich, travel-poster colour, from the 1930s to the 1950s, dipped into towns and villages; but only rarely, and then to examine medieval churches and inns, not cinemas, libraries or market halls.

This English obsession with the countryside is caught in Richard Ingrams's *England*, written in 1990. It's a witty, cynical compendium of all the things – run-down, urban and squalid, as well as rustic and wholesome – that are idiosyncratically English.

Ingrams said that he could easily have compiled a book called *Going to the Dogs*, reflecting the long-held English conviction that we are all irrevocably doomed. Just look at the index to the 1892, two-volume edition of Dr Johnson's letters.

ENGLAND, all trade dead II 120; poverty and degradation, 150; sinking, 264; fear of a civil war, 286; times dismal and gloomy, 370; see also INVASIONS.

Still, for all its gritty realness, Ingrams's book has a more-English-than-English cover – of evening light cast over a wooded valley, dappling the shaggy outline of an oak. The image of blissful, bucolic England triumphs again.

Our long-held obsession with the country helps explain why we produce so many good landscape painters, like Samuel Palmer, Paul Nash, John Constable, J. M. W. Turner and John Piper.

And it's why, studies show, our favourite pictures are landscapes, with water, open spaces, animals and low-branched trees. They are often in watercolour, too; much more frequently than on the Continent.

Perhaps this is self-evident, an example of the Kingsley Amis Principle of Aesthetic Preference: nice things are nicer than nasty ones.[4] But there's another phenomenon lurking behind the popularity of landscapes. The English idealize the country in a way seen nowhere else in the world; even though – or perhaps because – since around 1850 more of us have lived in the town than the country.

Our love of the country is not just visible on book jackets. It's there in the weekend sections of the newspapers, the countless articles on the joy of downsizing, on the nagging longing to chuck in city life and shift to a slower, more aesthetic, rural existence. When newspaper editors run a piece on quintessential England, it is invariably illustrated with a rural photograph.

This England, the quarterly illustrated magazine popular among expats – 'For all who love our green and pleasant land' – is an England of Palladian bridges in Wiltshire, island castles off Northumberland and cricket greens in Hampshire.

The images slip easily into the Big Book of English Clichés – an easy, fatal volume to draw from. The English have a devout faith in the existence of nice, but mythological, English characteristics, particularly the ones about us being eccentric, fair, polite, shy and decent. The idea of an unwrecked England fits neatly into the same anthology of national fairytales.

Terraced houses and Victorian town halls – things that are just as English as rectories and village greens – don't get into *This England* because they are urban. They belong to That England, where things aren't so picture postcard pretty.

We are the only nation – even in the English-speaking world – that refers to the rural part of our nation as 'the country'; as if England only consists of fields, rivers, mountains and moorland; as if the urban bits don't really count. We persist with the delusion, even while we secretly know it's the urban bits that really count financially: that's why we're prepared to pay so much for our houses the closer we get to the middle of a city.

This division between town and country has been around since England was absorbed into the Roman Empire – itself really an urban civilization, living off cheap corn grown in the country. Country life is only idealized in predominantly urban civilizations like ours – where we are detached from the backbreaking work in fields that were, until recently, little more than factories with the lid off.

Rural idealization doesn't happen in countries that remain essentially rural. The phenomenon doesn't exist in France, where they still regard the country as a place for working farms, not for leisure.[5]

There's a similar distinction in England between farmers who work the land and weekenders who use it for pleasure. Farmers, who view the land as a workplace, are unlikely to go for a walk – it's like visiting your office at the weekend. Only rural weekenders see a country walk as a treat.

Our rural fantasies extend to our national figure. John Bull is a stout, red-cheeked farmer straight out of the hallowed, mythical countryside; and, all the while, real farmers are becoming an endangered species – the number of British farmers has tumbled over the last two decades, from 477,000 to 353,000.

John Bull was himself an artificial creation, invented in 1712 by a Scot, John Arbuthnot, who described him as an 'honest, plain-dealing fellow, choleric, bold, and of a very inconstant temper'.[6]

Straight out of rural dreamland – a First World War postcard of John Bull.

This rural fixation is not always a fantasy, an artificial longing for a rural idyll that no longer exists. The country really does trump the town in the minds of real people, too, particularly among the upper classes.

From the early twentieth century onwards, the land-owning families of England demolished their London homes rather than sell their country houses. If Lord Sebastian Flyte's family had held on to their London house and sold their country one, Evelyn Waugh's novel would have been called *Marchmain Revisited*. But it is the city pile, Marchmain House, they sell when the current account begins to dwindle.

The Royal Family still choose Balmoral over the south of France for their summer holidays. In 1825, when George IV made Buckingham House his London palace, he plumped for an old country-house-style building, in a rural setting, rather than a new ordered urban palace, like Versailles or the Louvre. Buckingham Palace still has its distinctly Picturesque country house garden, with winding paths, a serpentine lake wrapped round an island, and a spreading lawn.

Country estates remained, and remain, the beating heart of the English aristocracy, while French nobles gathered round the court in Paris. With the monarch holding absolute power on much of the Continent, power accumulated around the urban court. In a parliamentary democracy like ours, power diffused into the regions, where landowners built their country houses and chose to be buried in the local parish church.

There's a charming theory that English horse-racing was born the day Charles I was beheaded. Royalists retreated to their country estates and devoted themselves to horse-breeding. Meanwhile, Oliver Cromwell improved the bloodline of English horses by importing purebreds from the Middle East and Italy.[7] When the revolution hit France 130 or so years later, the grander families, if they escaped the guillotine, sold the country château and hung on to the *hôtel particulier* in Paris.

Rural idealization was helped by country living standards, higher here than on the Continent. The rural life was a less bleak, more comfortable prospect in Britain at a much earlier stage than in other countries. By the end of the nineteenth century, most of the country was in reach of the new rash of railway lines, and so never far from London. The arrival of the car brought the metropolis even closer.

'Here today – in next week tomorrow!' booms Toad in *The Wind in the Willows*, as he dons his driving gloves and careers through Edwardian Berkshire.

Throw in several daily postal deliveries in Victorian England, and you need never feel very far from the action, however remote your house. Because the whole country had been so heavily settled, the chances of complete isolation, unless you went in active search of it, were low.

And, because England had been settled for so many centuries, there was usually a sophisticated social structure in place. Even in the furthest corners of the country, the ever-present infrastructure of big house, church, parsonage and market town produced a mix of classes and fortunes, providing a secure berth for people of any background. Practically all 1,600 market towns in Britain had this infrastructure established by the eighteenth century.

This complex, ancient social structure, combined with England's smallness and hospitable weather, mean the English tend to stay close to where they were born; despite the ease of movement that comes with a small country and extensive transport links.

At a New York talk in 2006, Tom Wolfe was asked what he thought the biggest technological innovation of the last century had been.

'I know I should be saying the internet or the computer or something,' he said, 'but, actually, for me, it's still the car. Until the middle of the twentieth century, my ancestors had lived in the Shenandoah Valley in Virginia, ever since the late eighteenth century.'

'Because of the car, and the social acceptance of moving, my family now all live in far-flung parts of the United States. Something like 20 per cent of Americans live within fifty miles of where they were born.'

In an increasingly mobile society, the English, too, are beginning to move further from their birthplaces; but, still, not to the same degree as in America.

We have largely stayed in the same place for generations: in 1997, scientists discovered that Adrian Targett, a 42-year-old history teacher, living near Cheddar, Somerset, was a direct descendant of Cheddar Man – Britain's oldest complete skele-ton, who'd lived in Cheddar in around 7150 BC.[8]

Part of the reason is that family roots were planted that much earlier here. In the American Midwest and beyond, those states were only substantially settled in the last century and a half. Few of today's Midwesterners are likely to have lived there even as long as that. Even on the East Coast, settled for 400 or so years, not many Americans have lived in the same state for more than a century.

When, in 1985, Route 66 – the 1926 road running across America from Chicago to LA – was superseded by a number of interstate highways, towns that had only recently been built to service the road died. Empire, Nevada, a company town built by the United States Gypsum Corporation in 1923, was completely shut down in 2011, when the gypsum business collapsed in the construction recession.

But when the Cornish tin mine industry disappeared in the last century, the towns that had flourished on the back of it clung on. Their medieval roots had been put down before the tin industry boomed; they survived long after the mining had gone.

This lack of mobility explains why English regional accents survive, and differ over such short distances. Reading is only forty miles from London along the M4 corridor, and yet a dis-tinctive rustic burr still survives in the old Berkshire market town. In America, you have to drive 225 miles south of New York before you hit Washington DC and encounter the sem-blance of a southern accent. In England, 100 years is nothing, and 100 miles is enormous; in America, it's the other way round.

This cultural and aesthetic worship of the country meant rural England became more than an agricultural factory for pro-ducing food. It was necessary that it should be beautiful, too. In other countries, food production and scenic beauty are different things. When Americans talk about the countryside, they mean the Rockies or the Great Lakes, not the wheat-growing prairies. On the Continent, landscape means the mountains or the lakes, not the agricultural areas. Here, beauty and agricultural productivity are combined.

The urban–rural split determines which towns are thought right for day trips, too – Oxford, Cambridge and York, say, untouched by the Industrial Revolution, with the Cowley car works nicely tucked away on the outer fringes of Oxford.

Who goes on a day trip to marvellous industrial and trading cities, like Manchester, Leeds or Cardiff, kept off the tourist schedules because they are too modern and urban, and not medieval, rural and undeveloped enough?

As part of the reaction against the Industrial Revolution, not only did we fetishize the country, but we also tried to ruralize the city, with our cult of the back garden, and our invention of the first garden cities.

The three most popular house names in Britain are The Cottage, Rose Cottage and The Bungalow. Even just having a name – any name, but particularly a rural name – makes your property 40 per cent more likely to be viewed by prospective buyers. There is still a rarity value attached to addresses without a number in them: only 1.4 million of the 26 million houses in Britain are named.[9]

A similar rural dream dictates the English lifetime structure of working in the city in your prime, before retiring to the promised land – the country – in old age. At the heart of the daily commute, too, there lies a deep-seated desire for the country, along with the availability of cheaper house prices. It's worth a daily three-hour return trip, so the thinking goes, to glimpse the sun set over the neighbouring field, before you go to bed at nine to prepare for the dawn commute.

Still, despite the cherished place of the country in English hearts, very few of us ever do end up downshifting. Town mice may dream of being country mice, but it remains a dream.

The overwhelming feature of modern England, ever since the Industrial Revolution, has been rampant migration from country to town, the explosion of the suburbs, and the emptying of the countryside. Eighty-six per cent of England is rural, and less than 8 per cent of the country is under concrete. But only 20 per cent of the population live in the countryside.

That urbanization process is intensifying across the planet, as Third World countries industrialize, and their populations begin to appreciate the greater riches and opportunities offered by cities. Cities reduce poverty and cut population growth, with people swapping big agrarian families for the smaller families found in the urban West.

The urban migration phenomenon applies not just to people in Third World rural areas moving to Third World cities; it also applies to Third World farmers moving to Western cities. There's a story of a teenage girl in Tower Hamlets, east London, who tells her sister how she longs to go back to the family farm in Bangladesh.

'You're welcome to it,' says her sister. 'By the time you get there, everyone else in the village will have left to come here.'[10]

The population shift from country to town is starkly clear on any rural train ride. After taking a five-hour train journey from Pembroke to a party in Dorset recently, I asked the Polish lawyer next to me at dinner what made the fields so English-looking.

'The huge difference between rural Poland and rural England is how empty the English countryside is,' she said. 'Go through fields in a train in Poland and they're still being worked on by the people who own them. Take a train through rural

England and you might not see a single person in a field for several hours.'

She was right. I remembered only one person in a field on my train journey from Wales: a man with his dog, out for a walk, using the country for pleasure, not a farmer working his land.

Britain industrialized – and was heavily urbanized – that much earlier than Poland. Its individual landholdings are much bigger, too, with major landowners farming as much as 100,000 acres, and cutting down on manpower as a result. In Poland, peasants might still live off a third of an acre, and cultivation is much more labour intensive and much less mechanized.

Still, this one-way traffic to the city doesn't stop us mythologizing the countryside, and equating it with the nation as a whole.

'It was a sweet view, sweet to the eye and the mind,' Jane Austen wrote in *Emma*, 'English verdure, English culture, English comfort, seen under a sun bright without being oppressive.'

'English' here means 'rural English'. That was understandable in 1815; the Industrial Revolution may have been in full swing, but towns and cities were yet to dominate England. But, even in the modern age, the equation between England and rural England has continued, an equation that hasn't been accurate for at least 250 years. It doesn't stop us believing in it.

The English attachment to the countryside and its ancient buildings is manifested in the vast membership of the National Trust. With 4 million members, it is the biggest heritage membership society in the country; much bigger, proportionally, than any other national conservation group in the world. It has overseas arms, too, like the Royal Oak Foundation, which gives Americans membership of the Trust – and a shared delusion in England as a predominantly rural country.

1,800 English country houses may have been demolished

since 1800 but, still, 50 million people visit one of the surviving stately homes every year; even if most of those visitors, after a day in the country, return to an urban home. Our national parks are just as adored. The Peak District in north Derbyshire is the second most visited national park in the world, after Mount Fuji in Japan.

'The British Character. Keen interest in historic houses', by Pont in *Punch*, 8 July 1936.

We may not be the best country at producing artistic or musical geniuses. No Beethovens or Mozarts have sprung from '*Das Land ohne Musik*' – the land without music – as England was called in a 1904 book by a German writer, Oskar Adolf Hermann Schmitz. But no country has as many individual rural preservation and conservation societies.

One art we are exceptional at is preserving rural beauty. Our poets and writers are still concerned with the pastoral, as they have been for centuries. No other European country publishes as many bird and plant books; no other similar-sized country has a million-strong bird appreciation society; no other country has an allotment system on such a vast scale; no other country is as obsessed with gardening.

While we have ring-fenced the beauties of the country, much of the best of urban England has gone – particularly its once untouched market towns and cathedral cities. But, then again, it's debatable whether the best of England ever really existed in the first place. In England, the good has always driven out the best. We never hit the heights of urban beauty seen in, say, Renaissance Florence. The English mind is too cautious – and sometimes too philistine – for that sort of grand-scale beauty.

Because of our make-do-and-mend, hodgepodge approach to urban planning, the idea of recasting a whole city in Renaissance style is anathema. But, so, too is the Ceauşescu School of Architecture – razing most of Bucharest to inflict a new brutalist landscape on the Romanian people; even if England's own Ceauşescu, John Prescott, had a pretty good go at it, paving Kent with building developments, tearing up decent Victorian terraced housing in the north-west with his grotesque Pathfinder project.

We are just too used to muddling through, incapable of seeing the *grand projet* through to the end. Just look at the results of the biggest national architectural project of the last half-century – the Dome. Weep by all means, but be grateful that we don't try large-scale architectural projects too often.

It's the same reason why Nazism never took off here – the bloody-minded, lazy, don't-tell-me-what-to-do, obsessive privacy of the English, combined with the tendency to mock anyone who does tell us what to do.

The English are tolerant, unconfrontational and, on occasion, unpleasant enough to let an Oswald Mosley, or a Nick Griffin, come to prominence. But they'll only let them get so far before they take against being shouted at.

And the same goes for the ugly changes to our urban landscape. Most cities and provincial towns have been scarred in some way, but the decline has only gone so far. Eventually, slowly, we come to our senses; and that widespread English love of the old, the picturesque and the asymmetrical ends up eclipsing the fashionable, small but powerful lobby behind the new, right-angled, ahistorical ugliness.

England is now a sort of halfway house – between modern uglification and ancient beauty; between shabbiness and neutered cleanliness; between Ye Olde Preserved Rural England and a rather less dazzling urban truth.

Halfway houses are difficult to describe. It's not so much 'How long is a piece of English string?' as 'Which piece of the string are you looking at?' The manicured section of country house life laid on for the benefit of Japanese tourists and members of the National Trust? Or the steel, concrete and glass, light-industrial estates that flank the railway line from Liverpool Street to Cambridge?

When I asked Norman Stone, a former Professor of Modern History at Oxford, about the relationship between the English and the look of England, he paused for a moment and then said, 'Well, I was struck by the quality of the flowers when I first came down from Glasgow on holiday in Lincolnshire, with some cousins in 1954, when I was thirteen. But then I can't really answer that question without getting very boring about medieval landholding laws.'

That, perhaps, is as good an answer as any. England has got some very good flowers and some very old laws.

On the surface, the two things have little in common; but they both grow out of a shared soil, climate, geology and geography; an unusually beneficial combination for the stable, long-term survival of *Homo Britannicus*, his legal system and his national flora.

A variety of flowers and a long-standing legal infrastructure. It's hardly as poetic as a 'precious stone set in the silver sea'. But it's a rather more down-to-earth, more accurate description of a place where people still just about rub along together; a place that still looks pretty unusual and – still, sometimes – unusually pretty.

Notes

Introduction

1. Office for National Statistics, 2011 Report.
2. Sarah Ruden, *Standpoint* magazine, June 2009.
3. Nikolaus Pevsner, *The Englishness of English Art* (Architectural Press, 1956).
4. George Orwell, *The Lion and the Unicorn* (Secker & Warburg, 1941).
5. Oliver Rackham, *The History of the Countryside* (J. M. Dent, 1986).

1. Weather Report

1. H. L. Mencken, *The American Language* (Knopf, 1948).
2. Nikolaus Pevsner, *The Englishness of English Art* (Architectural Press, 1956).
3. Robert Southey, *Letters From England* (1808).
4. Norman Stone, Introduction to Adrian Sykes, *Made in Britain* (Adelphi, 2011).
5. World Health Organization figures, 2011.
6. Southey, *Letters*.
7. Terry Jennings, *Atmosphere and Weather* (Evans Brothers, 2005).
8. Charles Booth, *Life and Labour of the People* (Macmillan, 1889).
9. *Daily Telegraph*, 17 August 2011.
10. Martin Gayford, interview with David Hockney, *Daily Telegraph*, 20 October 2010.
11. MigrationWatch research, 19 November 2011.
12. Southey, *Letters*.

13. Ian Fleming, *Dr No* (Jonathan Cape, 1958).
14. Pevsner, *Englishness of English Art*.
15. Environment Agency figures, 2010.

2. The Lie of the Land

1. Bill Bryson, *Notes from a Small Island* (Doubleday, 1995).
2. Oliver Rackham, *The History of the Countryside* (J. M. Dent, 1986).
3. Ronald Blythe, *Aftermath: Selected Writings 1960–2010* (Black Dog Books, 2010).
4. Halford Mackinder, *Britain and the British Seas* (William Heinemann, 1902).
5. Alec Clifton-Taylor, *The Pattern of English Building* (Faber, 1972).
6. Philip Macleod, Lecture at Eton College, Eton, Berkshire, 11 May 2004.
7. Rackham, *History of the Countryside*.

3. England's Feet of Clay

1. Oliver Rackham, *The History of the Countryside* (J. M. Dent, 1986).
2. James Owen, *Danger UXB: The Heroic Story of the WWII Bomb Disposal Teams* (Little, Brown, 2010).
3. Simon Jenkins, *England's Thousand Best Churches* (Allen Lane, 1999).
4. Niall Ferguson, *Civilization: The West and the Rest* (Allen Lane, 2011).
5. Mark Griffiths, *Country Life*, 5 January 2011.
6. Rackham, *History of the Countryside*.
7. Ibid.
8. Ibid.
9. Oliver Rackham, *Woodlands* (HarperCollins, 2006).
10. Rackham, *History of the Countryside*.
11. The Centre for Ecology and Hydrology figures, *Daily Telegraph*, July 2011.

4. *A River Runs through It*

1. Penelope Lively, *The Presence of the Past* (Collins, 1976).
2. Ralph Waldo Emerson, *English Traits* (1856).
3. H. L. Mencken, *The American Language* (Knopf, 1948).
4. *Daily Telegraph* obituary of Margaret Gelling, 8 May 2009.

5. *Why English Towns Look English*

1. Nikolaus Pevsner, *The Englishness of English Art* (Architectural Press, 1956).
2. John Goodall, *The English Castle* (Yale University Press, 2011).
3. Nikolaus Pevsner, Introduction to A. Savidge, *The Parsonage in England* (SPCK, 1964).
4. F. R. Banks, *English Villages* (B. T. Batsford, 1963).
5. Ibid.
6. Robin Dunbar, *How Many Friends Does One Person Need? Dunbar's Number and Other Evolutionary Quirks* (Faber, 2010).
7. Oliver Rackham, *The History of the Countryside* (J. M. Dent, 1986).
8. Norman Stone, Introduction to Adrian Sykes, *Made in Britain*, (Adelphi, 2011).
9. Christopher Howse, *Daily Telegraph*, personal communication to author, 18 November 2009.
10. Stone, Introduction to Adrian Sykes, *Made in Britain* (Adelphi, 2011).
11. Giuseppe Tomasi di Lampedusa, *Letters from London and Europe* (Alma Books, 2010).
12. Clive Aslet on the Scottish village, *Country Life*, 11 August 2010.
13. Candida Lycett Green, *The Oldie Magazine*, January 2010.
14. Zaha Hadid, interview with author, *Evening Standard*, 14 October 2010.
15. David Chipperfield, *Evening Standard*, 2 February 2011.

6. Georgian Hedge Funds

1. Oliver Rackham, *The History of the Countryside* (J. M. Dent, 1986).
2. Ibid.
3. Michael Wright, *C'est la Folie* (Bantam Press, 2006).
4. Max Hooper, *Hedges* (Collins, 1974).
5. Sue Clifford and Angela King, *England in Particular: A Celebration of the Commonplace, the Local, the Vernacular and the Distinctive* (Hodder & Stoughton, 2006).
6. Rackham, *History of the Countryside*.
7. F. R. Banks, *English Villages* (B. T. Batsford, 1963).
8. Rackham, *History of the Countryside*.
9. Penelope Lively, *The Presence of the Past* (Collins, 1976).
10. Rackham, *History of the Countryside*.
11. Ibid.
12. Clifford and King, *England in Particular*.
13. Ibid.
14. Ibid.
15. W. G. Hoskins, *The Making of the English Landscape* (Penguin, 1955).
16. Ibid.
17. Ibid.
18. Rackham, *History of the Countryside*.
19. George Orwell, *Coming Up for Air* (Victor Gollancz, 1939).
20. Rackham, *History of the Countryside*.
21. Guy Adams, 'A throwback to feudalism: David Cameron and the father-in-law from hell', *Independent*, 5 June 2007
22. Ralph Waldo Emerson, *English Traits* (1856).
23. Adam Nicolson, *The Gentry: Stories of the English* (HarperPress, 2011).
24. Peter Ackroyd, *Foundation: The History of England*, Volume I (Macmillan, 2011).
25. Philip Yorke, *The Royal Tribes of Wales* (1799).

7. A Love of the Picturesque

1. Google Street View Competition, March 2010.
2. Alexander Pope, 'Epistle to Richard Boyle, Earl of Burlington, of the Use of Riches' (1731).
3. William Hogarth, *The Analysis of Beauty* (1753).
4. Norman Stone, Introduction to Adrian Sykes, *Made in Britain* (Adelphi 2011).
5. World Health Organization figures, 2011.
6. Oliver Rackham, *The History of the Countryside* (J. M. Dent, 1986).
7. Lloyds TSB Research, 3 March 2012.
8. John Goodall, *The English Castle* (Yale University Press, 2011).

8. A Nation of Gardeners

1. Hugo Williams, *Times Literary Supplement*, 17 June 2011.
2. James Ravilious, *A Corner of England: North Devon Landscapes and People* (Devon Books, 1995).
3. Nikolaus Pevsner, *County Durham* (Penguin, 1953).
4. Friedrich Engels, *The Condition of the Working Class in England* (1845).
5. Noel Kingsbury, *Daily Telegraph*, 8 January 2011.
6. Adam Nicolson, *Daily Telegraph*, 26 May 2010.
7. Clive Aslet, *Daily Telegraph*, 1 June 2010.
8. *Sunday Telegraph*, 20 March 2011.
9. Winifred Holtby, *South Riding: An English Landscape* (Collins, 1936).
10. Charles Moore, *Daily Telegraph*, 24 February 2009.
11. Philip Toynbee, *End of a Journey: An Autobiographical Journey, 1979–81* (Bloomsbury, 1988).
12. P. G. Wodehouse, 'Lord Emsworth and the Girl Friend', from *Blandings Castle and Elsewhere* (Herbert Jenkins, 1935).

9. The Rolling English Road

1. *Daily Telegraph*, 15 December 2011.
2. *Evening Standard*, 16 November 2011.
3. Sue Clifford and Angela King, *England in Particular: A Celebration of the Commonplace, the Local, the Vernacular and the Distinctive* (Hodder & Stoughton, 2006).
4. *Motorcycle News*, March 2010.
5. Oliver Rackham, *The History of the Countryside* (J. M. Dent, 1986).
6. Ibid.
7. W. G. Hoskins, *The Making of the English Landscape* (Penguin, 1955).
8. Rackham, *History of the Countryside*.
9. Ibid.
10. Evelyn Waugh, 'A call to the orders', *Country Life*, 26 February 1938.
11. Penelope Lively, *The Presence of the Past* (Collins, 1976).
12. Trevor Rowley, *The English Landscape in the 20th Century* (Hambledon Continuum, 2006).
13. Juliet Gardiner, *The Thirties: An Intimate History* (HarperPress, 2010).
14. Bella Bathurst, *The Bicycle Book* (HarperPress, 2011).
15. *Evening Standard*, 3 November 2011.
16. Clifford and King, *England in Particular*.
17. Ibid.

10. North and South

1. Peter Clack, 'Early Settlement in the County', in Nikolaus Pevsner and Elizabeth Williamson, *County Durham* (Penguin, 1983).
2. Penelope Lively, *The Presence of the Past* (Collins, 1976).
3. Nikolaus Pevsner, *Northumberland* (Penguin, 1957).
4. Nikolaus Pevsner, *Lancashire: The Industrial and Commercial South* (Penguin, 1969).

5. Andrew Foyle, *Bristol* (Pevsner Architectural Guides, 2004).
6. Ibid.
7. J. B. Priestley, *English Journey* (Victor Gollancz, 1934).
8. *Daily Telegraph*, 29 December 2010.
9. Ian Jack, *Guardian*, 8 May 2010.
10. Savills, *World in London Report*, 2011.

11. *How Railways Made the English Suburban*

1. Philip Augar, *Financial Times*, 26 October 2011.
2. Ferdinand Mount, *Times Literary Supplement*, 1 January 2010.
3. *Halifax Report*, September 2011.
4. Trevor Rowley, *The English Landscape in the 20th Century* (Hambledon Continuum, 2006).
5. *Daily Mail*, 18 March 1905.
6. Christopher Woodward, Director of the Garden Museum, personal conversation, 26 September 2011.
7. *Halifax Report*, September 2011.
8. Ferdinand Mount, *Cold Cream* (Bloomsbury, 2008).
9. Hermann Muthesius, *Das englische Haus* (Wasmuth, 1905).
10. *Daily Telegraph*, 13 April 2011.
11. Mount, *TLS*, 1 January 2010.
12. Juliet Gardiner, *The Thirties: An Intimate History* (HarperPress, 2010).
13. Evelyn Waugh, 'A call to the orders', *Country Life*, 26 February 1938.
14. Chris Beanland, *Independent*, 1 March 2011.

12. *Why England Doesn't Look Like England*

1. Anthony Powell, *Books Do Furnish a Room* (Heinemann, 1971).
2. Antony Woodward, *The Garden in the Clouds* (HarperPress, 2010).
3. Office for National Statistics.

4. Ibid.

5. *Spectator*, 26 November 2011.

6. Valuation Office Agency, 2010 figures.

7. Sathnam Sanghera, *The Times*, 2 April 2011.

8. Ibid.

9. *Financial Times*, 3 December 2011.

10. Ed West, *Daily Telegraph*, 21 April 2011.

11. Norman Stone, Introduction to Adrian Sykes, *Made in Britain* (Adelphi, 2011).

12. Giuseppe Tomasi di Lampedusa, writing from York in 1927, *Letters from London and Europe* (Alma Books, 2010).

13. George Orwell, *The Lion and the Unicorn* (Victor Gollancz, 1941).

Conclusion: Town Mice and Country Mice

1. Martin Gayford interview with David Hockney, *Daily Telegraph*, 20 October 2010.

2. Frank McDonald, *Daily Telegraph*, 13 September 2011.

3. 'The History of Brockwell Park', www.brockwellpark.com.

4. Roger Kimball, *Times Literary Supplement*, 20 March 2009.

5. Jonathan Meades, *Guardian*, 17 March 2010.

6. Clive Aslet, 'A peculiarly British love affair?', *Country Life*, 10 June 2009.

7. John McEwen, *Country Life*, 30 November 2011.

8. Adrian Sykes, *Made in Britain* (Adelphi, 2011).

9. The Land Registry, 2011 figures.

10. Douglas Sanders, *Arrival City* (Heinemann, 2010).

Bibliography

Peter Ackroyd, *Albion: The Origins of the English Imagination* (Chatto, 2002)

—, *Foundation: The History of England*, Volume I (Macmillan, 2011)

Kingsley Amis, *The Amis Collection: Selected Non-Fiction, 1954–90* (Hutchinson, 1990)

Clive Aslet, 'A peculiarly British love affair?', *Country Life*, 10 June 2009

Jane Austen, *Emma* (1815)

Andrew Ballantyne and Andrew Law, *Tudoresque: In Pursuit of the Ideal Home* (Reaktion Books, 2011)

F. R. Banks, *English Towns* (B. T. Batsford, 1964)

—, *English Villages* (B. T. Batsford, 1963)

Jules-Amédée Barbey d'Aurevilly, *Du Dandysme et de Georges Brummel* (Lemerre, 1879)

Paul Barker, *The Freedoms of Suburbia* (Frances Lincoln, 2009)

Bella Bathurst, *The Bicycle Book* (HarperPress, 2011)

Hilaire Belloc, *The Historic Thames* (IB Tauris, 2008)

Alan Bennett, *An Englishman Abroad* (BBC TV series, 1983)

John Betjeman, *English Cities and Small Towns* (Collins, 1943)

—, *First and Last Loves* (John Murray, 1952)

Ronald Blythe, *Aftermath: Selected Writings 1960–2010* (Black Dog Books, 2010)

—, *Akenfield: Portrait of an English Village* (Allen Lane, 1969)

—, *Outsiders: A Book of Garden Friends* (Black Dog Books, 2008)

Charles Booth, *Life and Labour of the People* (Macmillan, 1889)

William Boyd, *Any Human Heart: The Intimate Journals of Logan Mountstuart* (Hamish Hamilton, 2002)

William Boyd, *Ordinary Thunderstorms* (Bloomsbury, 2009)

Jane Brown, *The Omnipotent Magician: Lancelot Capability Brown (1716 to 1783)* (Chatto & Windus, 2011)

—, *The Pursuit of Paradise* (HarperCollins, 1999)

Bill Bryson, *Notes from a Small Island* (Doubleday, 1995)

Kevin Cahill, *Who Owns Britain?* (Canongate, 2001)

Winston Churchill, *The Island Race* (Cassell, 1964)

John Clare, *Major Works* (OUP, 1984)

Sue Clifford and Angela King, *England in Particular: A Celebration of the Commonplace, the Local, the Vernacular and the Distinctive* (Hodder & Stoughton, 2006)

Alec Clifton-Taylor, *The Pattern of English Building* (Faber, 1972)

Emily Cockayne, *Cheek by Jowl* (Bodley Head, 2012)

Cyril Connolly, *The Unquiet Grave* (Hamish Hamilton, 1944)

Brian Cook, *The Britain of Brian Cook: A Batsford Heritage* (B. T. Batsford, 1987)

R. H. Cox, *The Green Roads of England* (Collins, 1914)

Charles Dickens, *Dombey and Son* (Bradbury and Evans, 1848)

—, *The Pickwick Papers* (Chapman and Hall, 1837)

Margaret Drabble, *A Writer's Britain* (Thames and Hudson, 1979)

Robin Dunbar, *How Many Friends Does One Person Need? Dunbar's Number and Other Evolutionary Quirks* (Faber, 2010)

Ralph Waldo Emerson, *English Traits* (Harvard University Press, 1966)

Friedrich Engels, *The Condition of the Working Class in England* (Penguin, 2009)

John Evelyn, *The Diary of John Evelyn* (OUP, 1959)

Niall Ferguson, *Civilization: The West and the Rest* (Allen Lane, 2011)

Ian Fleming, *Dr No* (Jonathan Cape, 1958)

Kate Fox, *Watching the English* (Hodder & Stoughton, 2004)

Juliet Gardiner, *The Thirties: An Intimate History* (HarperPress, 2010)

Simon Garfield, *Just My Type: A Book about Fonts* (Profile, 2010)

David Garrick and George Colman, *The Clandestine Marriage* (1766)

Margaret Gelling and Ann Cole, *The Landscape of Place Names* (Shaun Tyas, 2000)

William Gilpin, *Observations on the River Wye, and Several Parts of South Wales, etc. Relative Chiefly to Picturesque Beauty; made in the Summer of the Year 1770* (1782)

John Gloag, *2,000 Years of England* (Cassell, 1952)

John Goodall, *The English Castle* (Yale University Press, 2011)

Kenneth Grahame, *The Wind in the Willows* (Methuen, 1909)

Thomas Hardy, *The Complete Poems*, ed. James Gibson (Palgrave Macmillan, 2002)

—, *The Return of the Native* (Osgood, McIlvaine, 1895)

Susie Harries, *Nikolaus Pevsner: The Life* (Chatto & Windus, 2011)

Jacquetta Hawkes, *A Land* (The Cresset Press, 1951)

Gwyn Headley and Wim Meulenkamp, *Follies, Grottoes and Garden Buildings* (Aurum Press, 1999)

William Hogarth, *The Analysis of Beauty* (Yale University Press, 1997)

Winifred Holtby, *South Riding: An English Landscape* (Collins, 1936)

W. G. Hoskins, *The Making of the English Landscape* (Penguin, 1955)

A. E. Housman, *A Shropshire Lad* (Grant Richards, 1922)

Richard Ingrams, *England: An Anthology* (Fontana, 1990)

Kazuo Ishiguro, *The Remains of the Day* (Faber, 1989)

Jane Jacobs, *The Death and Life of Great American Cities* (Cape, 1962)

—, *The Economy of Cities* (Cape, 1970)

Henry James, *A London Life* (Macmillan, 1889)

Simon Jenkins, *England's Thousand Best Churches* (Allen Lane, 1999)

—, *England's Thousand Best Houses* (Allen Lane, 2003)

Anthony Jennings, *The Old Rectory: The Story of the English Parsonage* (Continuum, 2009)

Terry Jennings, *Atmosphere and Weather* (Evans Brothers, 2005)

Lucinda Lambton, *Palaces for Pigs* (English Heritage, 2011)

Giuseppe Tomasi di Lampedusa, *Letters from London and Europe* (Alma Books, 2010)

Philip Larkin, *Collected Poems* (Faber, 1988)

Penelope Lively, *The Presence of the Past* (Collins, 1976)

The Lonely Planet Guide to Great Britain, 8th edn (Lonely Planet, 2009)

Robert Lowell, *The Dolphin* (Faber, 1973)

Sarah Lyall, *The Anglo Files* (W. W. Norton, 2008)

Charles Lyell, *Principles of Geology* (John Murray, 1847)

Richard Mabey, *Flora Britannica* (Sinclair Stevenson, 1996)

—, *Nature Cure* (Chatto & Windus, 2005)

Robert Macfarlane, *The Wild Places* (Granta Books, 2007)

Halford Mackinder, *Britain and the British Seas* (William Heinemann, 1902)

Mary McCarthy, *Birds of America* (Weidenfeld & Nicolson, 1971)

H. L. Mencken, *The American Language* (Knopf, 1948)

Thomas More, *Utopia* (1516)

Fynes Moryson, *Itinerary; or Ten Years Travels throughout Great Britain and other parts of Europe* (1617)

Ferdinand Mount, *Cold Cream* (Bloomsbury, 2008)

Richard and Nina Muir, *Fields* (Macmillan, 1989)

Christopher Nicholson, *Rock Lighthouses of Britain* (Patrick Stephens, 1983)

Adam Nicolson, *The Gentry: Stories of the English* (HarperPress, 2011)

Robert O'Byrne, *Style City: How London Became a Fashion Capital* (Frances Lincoln, 2009)

John Ogilby, *Britannia . . . an Illustration of the Kingdom of England and Dominion of Wales: by a Geographical and Historical Description Thereof* (1675)

George Orwell, *Coming Up for Air* (Secker & Warburg, 1939)

—, *Homage to Catalonia* (Secker & Warburg, 1938)

—, *The Lion and the Unicorn: Socialism and the English Genius* (Secker & Warburg, 1941)

James Owen, *Danger UXB: The Heroic Story of the WWII Bomb Disposal Teams* (Little, Brown, 2010)

Jennifer Owen, *Wildlife of a Garden: A Thirty-Year Study* (Royal Horticultural Society, 2010)

Richard Payne Knight, *An Analytical Inquiry into the Principles of Taste* (1805)

Nikolaus Pevsner, *The County Guides to England* (Penguin, Yale University Press)

—, *The Englishness of English Art* (Architectural Press, 1956).

E. Pollard, M. Hooper, N. W. Moore, *Hedges* (Collins, 1974)

Alexander Pope, 'Epistle to Richard Boyle, Earl of Burlington, of the Use of Riches' (1731)

Anthony Powell, *Books Do Furnish a Room* (Heinemann, 1971)

Uvedale Price, *An Essay on the Picturesque, as Compared with the Sublime and the Beautiful; and on the Use of Studying Pictures, for the Purpose of Improving Real Landscape* (1796)

J. B. Priestley, *English Journey* (Mandarin, 1994)

Francis Pryor, *The Birth of Modern Britain – A Journey into Britain's Archaeological Past: 1550 to the Present* (HarperPress, 2011)

—, *The Making of the British Landscape: How We Have Transformed the Land, from Prehistory to Today* (2010)

Guido Puccio, *Customs on the Other Side of the Channel* (V. Bonacci, 1961)

Oliver Rackham, *The History of the Countryside* (J. M. Dent, 1986)

—, *Woodlands* (HarperCollins, 2006)

Ayn Rand, *The Fountainhead* (Scribner, 1986)

James Ravilious, *A Corner of England: North Devon Landscapes and People* (Devon Books, 1995)

Joshua Reynolds, *Thirteenth Discourse* (1786)

Tim Richardson, *The Arcadian Friends: Inventing the English Garden* (Bantam Press, 2007)

E. S. Rohde, *The Story of the Garden* (Medici Society, 1932)

Douglas Rose, *Tiles of the Unexpected Underground* (Capital Transport Publishing, 2007)

Trevor Rowley, *The English Landscape in the 20th Century* (Hambledon Continuum, 2006)

Vita Sackville-West, *Knole and the Sackvilles* (Heinemann, 1922)

Douglas Sanders, *Arrival City* (Heinemann 2010)

Adam Smith, *The Wealth of Nations* (1776)

Martin Sonnabend, Jon Whiteley and Christian Rumelin, *Claude Lorrain: The Enchanted Landscape* (Ashmolean Museum, 2011)

Robert Southey (under the pseudonym Don Manuel Alvarez Espriella), *Letters From England* (Cresset Press, 1951)

Gavin Stamp, *Britain's Lost Cities* (Aurum Press, 2007)

—, *Lost Victorian Britain: How the Twentieth Century Destroyed the Nineteenth Century's Architectural Masterpieces* (Aurum Press, 2010)

Laurence Dudley Stamp, *Britain's Structure and Scenery* (Fontana, 1962)

Bram Stoker, *Dracula* (Archibald Constable, 1904)

Norman Stone, Introduction to Adrian Sykes, *Made in Britain* (Adelphi, 2011)

Tom Stoppard, *Arcadia* (Faber and Faber, 1993)

Christopher Taylor, *The Archaeology of Gardens* (Shire Archaeology Series, 1983)

Emma Tennant, *More Good Work by Anon* (Heywood Hill, 2010)

Gillian Tindall, *The Fields Beneath* (Weidenfeld & Nicolson, 1977)

Philip Toynbee, *End of a Journey: An Autobiographical Journey, 1979–81* (Bloomsbury, 1988)

Evelyn Waugh, *Brideshead Revisited* (Chapman & Hall, 1945)

—, 'A call to the orders', *Country Life*, 26 February 1938, reprinted in *The Essays, Articles and Reviews of Evelyn Waugh*, ed. Donat Gallagher (Methuen, 1983)

David Wilson, *Moated Sites* (Shire Publications, 1985)

Simon Winchester, *The Map That Changed the World* (Viking, 2001)

P. G. Wodehouse, *The Code of the Woosters* (Herbert Jenkins, 1938)

—, 'Lord Emsworth and the Girl Friend', from *Blandings Castle and Elsewhere* (Herbert Jenkins, 1935)

May Woods and Arete Swartz Warren, *Glass Houses: A History of Greenhouses, Orangeries and Conservatories* (Aurum Press, 1988)

Antony Woodward, *The Garden in the Clouds* (HarperPress, 2010)

Christopher Woodward, *In Ruins* (Chatto & Windus, 2001)

Michael Wright, *C'est la Folie* (Bantam Press, 2006)

Philip Yorke, *The Royal Tribes of Wales* (1799)

Acknowledgements

With love and thanks to Ferdinand Mount, Julia Mount, William Mount, Mary Mount, Francie Mount, Tristram and Virginia Powell.

With deepest thanks to my long-suffering editor, Eleo Gordon, for her wise, patient guidance, to Gesche Ipsen, for superhuman powers of discovery, and to Emma Brown, Ben Brusey, Joe Pickering, and all at Viking and Penguin.

I am extremely grateful for the help of my agent, Peter Straus.

I am grateful to the editors of *Country Life*, the *Daily Mail*, the *Daily Telegraph*, the *Field*, the *New Statesman*, the *Spectator*, the *Sunday Telegraph* and the *Times Literary Supplement*, for allowing me to adapt articles that first appeared there.

My thanks to all those, listed below, who have provided invaluable help, particularly with journalistic commissions.

The staff of the London Library. John Goodall of *Country Life*. Tobyn Andreae, Paul Dacre, Henry Deedes, Laura Freeman, Leaf Kalfayan, Peter McKay, Sophia Money-Coutts, Andrew Morrod, Rachel Shields, Suzy Walker and Andrew Yates of the *Daily Mail*. Andrew M. Brown, Claire Cohen, Robert Colvile, Chris Deerin, Christopher Howse, Lucy Jones, Richard Preston and Damian Thompson of the *Daily Telegraph*. The students and staff of the City and Guilds of London Art School. Sarah Sands of the *Evening Standard*. All the staff at *Reader's Digest* magazine. Tony Ring, President, the Wodehouse Association. Mark Amory, Liz Anderson, Freddy Gray, Fraser Nelson and Mary Wakefield of the *Spectator*. Rose Aidin, Lola Armstrong, Philip Astor, Bella Bathurst, Hannah Betts, Ronald

Blythe, Allison Botero, Ian Browne, Julia Bueno, Nathan Burton, Sholto Byrnes, Peter Carson, Janine Catalano, Lopo Champalimaud, Toby Clements, Charles Clover, David Codling, Ned Cranborne, Dan Cruickshank, Marcel Dietsch, Ruth Dudley Edwards, Lindy Dufferin, Paige Dugdale, Ophelia Field, James Fletcher, Antonia Fraser, Nick Garland, Kate Gatacre, Tanya Gold, Grey Gowrie, Mark Handsley, Dan Hannan, Aimée Heuzenroeder, David Horspool, Richard Ingrams, Patrick James, Melik Kaylan, Paul Keegan, Ben and Sacha King, Tom Kremer, Lucinda Lambton, Michael Lacey-Solymar, Joshua Levine, Philip Macleod, Olivia Mann, Joan Marshall, Col McDonnell, the late Angus Macintyre, Douglas Matthews, Andrew McKie, Bill Montgomery, Charles Moore, Jeremy Musson, Robert Norton, Robert O'Byrne, James Owen, Thomas Pakenham, Barnaby and Nicole Phillips, Gary Phillips, Henrietta Phipps, Matt Pritchett, Michael Prodger, Stuart and Mary Reid, Tiggy Salt, Albert Scardino, Simon and Elizabeth Scott Plummer, Sasha Slater, Anthony Smith, Tim Sowula, Norman Stone, Sam Swire, Alex Travelli, Aldo Urbinati, Hubert Vandenbergh, Magnus von Wistinghausen, Jack Wakefield, Stephanie Warshaw, Molly Watson, Peter Watson, Alannah Weston, Hywel Williams, A. N. Wilson, Frances Wilson, Antony Woodward, Christopher Woodward, Peregrine Worsthorne.

Above all, deepest thanks and love to Sacha Bonsor, by far the best thing in England, or anywhere.

Index